DARK L

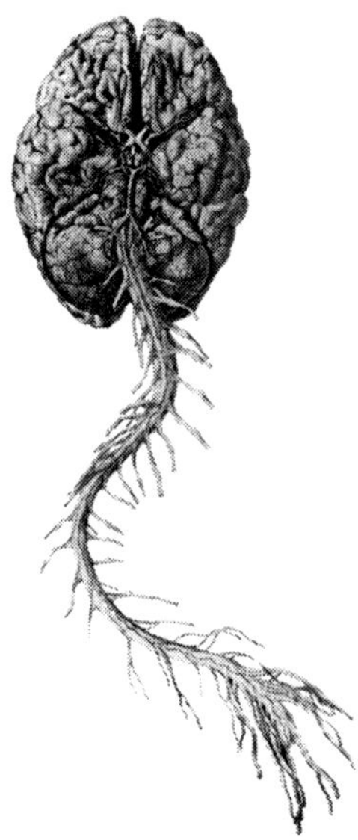

DAILY GRAIL PUBLISHING

Darklore Volume 6

ISBN: 978-0-9807111-8-9

Daily Grail Publishing
Brisbane, Australia
userhelp@dailygrail.com
www.dailygrail.com

Contents

"The cosmos is also within us. We're made of star-stuff. We are a way for the cosmos to know itself."

- *Carl Sagan*

If you would like to be notified of future releases of *Darklore*, please send an email to darklore@dailygrail.com. Please be assured your contact details will not be used for any other purpose.

Editor's Introduction

I am not, as they say, a good Christian. Long ago, my in-depth readings of both historical and religious texts dissuaded me from a belief in the divinity of Jesus Christ. With my intellectual ego primed, I spent the next few years getting in the face of any 'believer' I came across, pointing out the inconsistencies and moral obscenities in their 'Holy' text that they seemed happy to ignore. Until one day I had my own, private, revelation: these people had a framework for living their lives; it (hopefully) made them happy, and helped them wake up each day with a genuine optimism. Who was I to try and impose my framework upon them? It seemed as distasteful as Christian missionaries trying to 'save' the indigenous peoples they came across in Colonial times. I could, after all, be wrong myself...

Since that time, I have tried to remain mindful of the dangers of imposing my own conclusions upon other people. Certainly, there are exceptions – if you try to ram your belief down my throat, you will find yourself in a healthy debate. Also, beliefs can sometimes be dangerous, so we should always be testing them in some way, if at the very least on the basis of a 'net balance' of harmful impact upon both our own, and others, lives. But over time, I have become more and more convinced that stories, narratives, and even outright fictions are sometimes a necessity for staying sane in a sometimes crazy world.

Objective facts are of prime importance in evidence-based decision-making, particularly in matters of health, but for a rich and happy life we also embed ourselves within social narratives, enfolding ourselves in (sometimes dangerous) mythic structures. In this issue of *Darklore* you'll find explorations and examinations of this area, from Martin Shough's deconstruction of apocalyptic 'double sun' myths through to Cat Vincent's investigation of the construction of the modern monster meme of 'The Slenderman'. I hope you enjoy them all!

Image courtesy Cachét Whitman: http://pirate-cashoo.deviantart.com

The Slenderman

Tracing the birth and evolution of a modern monster

by *Ian 'Cat' Vincent*

We don't often get to see the birth of a monster. Just over two years ago, a new monster was born. Because it was born on the internet, we can see the exact moment of its conception. We can follow its growth from a pair of photographs into a full-fledged mythology. We can see the point where it crossed over from a merely imaginal creature into something that haunts the minds of many. And we can see exactly when it became a creature of true occult significance. Its path is clear and distinct. Its legacy is undeniable.

The monster's name is Slenderman. And its influence continues to grow.

Something Awful

Slenderman's birth-date is June 10th, 2009. Its father is a Photoshop artist who goes by the name Victor Surge. Its birth-place was a forum thread of the popular site somethingawful.com, noted for its many Photoshop competitions. The remit for this particular competition was, simply: "Create Paranormal Images". The resulting forum thread ran for two days before Surge posted his pair of pictures – at which point, the thread pretty much became solely about Surge's creation.

Both of Victor Surge's original Slenderman pictures are simple, evocative black and white images of children. In the first, a group of kids are walking away from, or possibly fleeing...something. In the second (see opposite page), other children are playing in a park, where a similar figure lurks nearly invisibly behind the slide and trees.

The monster in their midst appears to be an unusually tall, possibly bald, pale man in a black suit and tie, whose face cannot be discerned. In the second picture, there is a hint that the figure's bizarrely long arms are transforming into tentacles. In both images, the figure is barely visible, almost blurring into the background.

Under each image is a quote from the alleged original archivist. The first reads:

> "...we didn't want to go, we didn't want to kill them, but it's persistent silence and outstretched arms horrified and comforted us at the same time..."
>
> – 1983, photographer unknown, presumed dead.

The second quote gives the monster its name:

> "One of two recovered photographs from the Stirling City Library blaze. Notable for being taken the day which fourteen children vanished and for what is referred to as "The Slender

The Slenderman makes his appearance (Photoshopped image posted by Victor Surge to SA)

> Man". Deformities cited as film defects by officials. Fire at library occurred one week later. Actual photograph confiscated as evidence."
>
> – 1986, photographer: Mary Thomas, missing since June 13th, 1986.

The very next user comment, from 'slidebite', is prescient: "You just know a couple of the good ones are going to eventually make it to paranormal websites and be used as genuine." Even at this early juncture, there appears a tendency to blur the line between fact and fantasy. Surge's next comment, in response to a post hoping for more Slenderman pictures, reads: "Maybe I'll do some more research. I've heard there may be a couple more legit 'Slender Man' photographs out there. I'll post them if I find them."

Over the next five days, Surge posted several more pictures of the creature, whose name shifted from "Slender Man" to "Slenderman". Several other users were thoroughly hooked by the idea, contributing a variety of additions to the burgeoning mythology – from other 'Photoshopped' pictures to short prose pieces. Some contributors expanded on the background history – a tendency which soon became a popular past-time among aficionados. The earliest of these, from user 'Thoreau-Up' (15 June 2009, 0103hrs), tied Slenderman into German medieval folk tales:

> I've been following the signs for quite some time. There are woodcuts dated back to the 16th century in Germany featuring a tall, disfigured man with only white spheres where his eyes should be. They called him "Der Großmann"[Sic], the tall man. He was a fairy who lived in the Black Forest. Bad children who crept into the woods at night would be chased by the slender man, and he wouldn't leave them alone until he caught them, or the child told the parents what he or she had done.

'Thoreau-Up' then goes on to provide the following "chilling account from an old journal, dating around 1702 (translated from German, some words may be inaccurate)":

> My child, my Lars... He is gone. Taken, from his bed. The only thing that we found was a scrap of black clothing. It feels like cotton, but it is softer...thicker. Lars came into my bedroom yesterday, screaming at the top of his lungs that "The angel is outside!", I asked him what he was talking about, and he told me some nonsense fairy story about *Der Großmann*. He said he went into the groves by our village and found one of my cows dead, hanging from a tree. I thought nothing of it at first... But now, he is gone. We must find Lars, and my family must leave before we are killed. I am sorry my son... I should have listened. May God forgive me.

He finishes by remarking that there is "more evidence of the slender man, but this is one of the oldest translatable accounts. Anyone else in the thread found anything like this?"

A couple of hours after this post came the earliest hint that Slenderman's nature was moving beyond merely a collaborative fiction into an altogether more sinister realm. From a user simply named 'I' came this chilling post:

> The Slender Man. He exists because you thought of him. Now try and not think of him.

By the end of June 15, there was a notable growth spurt – several stories of Slenderman, set in time periods from 5000BCE to the Middle Ages to the 1950s to the present, appeared within a few hours. And, ominously, several members of the forum posted that they were having nightmares about Slenderman...

The next day, user 'LeechCode5' made a post which would perhaps go on to inspire the next stage of Slenderman's development:

> I'm suddenly imagining a Slender Man "documentary," done in a style similar to *The Last Broadcast* or that old Alien Abduction tv special. Interviews with witnesses of various encounters through the years, investigation into the different events brought up in this thread, and specialists analyzing photographs, intercut around home video footage taken by a missing family, showing them being picked off by the Slender Man. As we get further into the film, we also start to see behind the scenes footage of the making of the documentary, with crew members not showing for work and not answering calls, various production problems...then finally ending with a note that the director disappeared immediately after completion of the film.

The first of many such videos – *Marble Hornets* – appeared within days and became an enormous success on YouTube, inspiring a huge expansion of Slenderman's fan-base. But more of that later...

Although there were still some postings of new Photoshop art around the original "Create Paranormal Photo" theme, the majority of the somethingawful.com (SA) thread now revolved around Slenderman. Many of the fiction contributions took the form of transcripts from interviews with victims of Slenderman, often set in either police or psychiatric interrogation contexts. Some of these were rapidly adapted into short sound pieces, as a kind of minimalist modern radio play.

The outpouring of creativity around those initial pair of images was remarkable, even for a high-traffic site noted for its intensely creative and enthusiastic members. Debate ranged widely about the nature of Slenderman – trying to establish whether or not there was a single entity or several Slendermen, and what precisely its background and nature were. An apt comment from 'JossiRossi', (16 June 2009, 1927hrs) : "I think it should be said that the closer you think you are to understanding the Slender Man, the more incorrect you really are."

The metafictional aspect of Slenderman dominated from the start. One contribution from 'BooDoug187' (same day, 2228hrs) told the tale of Go Waita, a Japanese manga writer whose work had been directly influenced by Slenderman's entry into his personal life:

Koga: Well, I guess my first question is about your most famed creation, Suited Demon...
Waita: I didn't create him.
Koga: Oh... well who did? A friend?
Waita: He's real.
Koga: Real? A creature like that is real? Rapeing (sic) school girls...
Waita: The sex and surprise sex in my stories aren't my idea. That's something the editors and others wanted...the demon is real.
Koga: How do you know this?
Waita: I've seen it...it killed my sister.
Koga: You seen it kill?

Waita just looks at me. He then stands up, walks to his bookcase and pulls out a large, old sketch book. He opens it and shows me drawings of the Suited Demon carrying a young child into the woods. As I flip through the pages the story that plays out is like one that plays out in many of Waita's books, except no graphic sex.

Waita: The girl in those pictures is my sister. She was seven years old when the demon took her.
Koga: How did you see this happen?
Waita: I followed her and the demon into the woods. I was eleven at the time. I thought that the demon was a man...a child molester trying to harm my sister. I followed them into the woods...that's when I watch it happen.
Koga: You didn't try to help?
Waita: I couldn't I was stunned in terror when I saw it's true form... when I saw it tear into her... It didn't see me...or if it did it didn't

> care. I must have sat there for several hours because my father was the one who found me the next morning. I tried to tell the police what I saw but they said that I must have been in shock. That I must have been forced to watch some killer murder my sister.
> Koga: I see… I'm sorry to bring it up…but if this haunts you… why base so many of your stories on it? Almost all your books are on this demon.
> Waita: You don't get it…it's all I can draw…

This level of intense, terrified obsession as expressed by the fictional Go Waita underlies the entire thread. For several more days, the stories grew – as did the reports of nightmares. This example, from user 'LemoOHnade' (17 June 2009, 0720hrs), is pretty typical: "The Slender Man came to me in a dream and told me that he existed between 'everything' and 'nothing' and that time and matter are like toys(???), then he broke into tiny 'jellyfish' like things that swam away into my radiator."

One story offshoot of the original mythology involved a Black Ops branch of US intelligence known as 'Optic Nerve', who have had knowledge of Slenderman for decades, possibly centuries. Within this part of the story comes the first time one of Slenderman's key characteristics is expressed – that it is unkillable…

> I have read the notes, looked through the files. There is no way on God's green Earth we will be able to do anything to stop this thing. In all my years with working cases for Optic Nerve I have seen things and proven many times before that supposed "Gods" can be killed.
>
> But this…Slender Man… There is nothing in any records of anything thing even remotely hurting it. Reports ranging from small arms fire, artillery fire (the report from that Nazi Artillery team… that's what made me think about this) even full scale forest fires doesn't do anything!

> This is a complete and total waste of time and man power. There is nothing you can say to me, or anyone in this branch that will make us change our minds. In a sick sad way the only thing we can do is keep a record of this thing.
>
> We can't kill it No way in hell we can capture it.
> (user 'BooDoug187', 17 June 2009, 0819hrs)

A day later, the previously briefly-suggested idea of Slenderman becoming the basis of an Alternate Reality Game (or ARG, of which more below) is proposed in detail. By now, the SA thread had received wider publicity, notably from that infamous source of many an internet meme, 4-Chan. A Wikipedia page had appeared. It was suggested in the SA forum that a series of fake websites be set up to subtly introduce the Slenderman mythos into the internet datastream, leaving its fictional origins aside and seeing who would end up believing it – for, as they say on 4-Chan, "the lulz". It was pretty much too late for this to be completely successful – anyone could track their way back to the original thread and find its origins. Instead, the narrative takes on a blurry, liminal quality – truth and fancy overlapping almost indistinguishably.

Not long after this point, the Slenderman story acquired two major developments. The first was the initial appearance of *Marble Hornets*. The second development, one which moved the Slenderman mythos even further from the realm of pure fiction into that of the truly paranormal, was the first use of a particular word to describe Slenderman: tulpa.

Marble Hornets, Alternate Reality

The first mention of *Marble Hornets* comes on June 18th, 2009. User 'ce gars' posted to the SA thread regarding a student film he had collaborated on with a film school friend named Alex two years previously:

> It was called Marble Hornets and I think it was about a twenty something returning to his childhood home and recalling events that happened there. It was pretty pretentious film student fare, but I helped out for a few days before my summer classes started, and a few rare occasions after that. Everyone on the set seemed pretty excited to be making it, especially Alex. The set itself was about half a mile away from Alex's house, roughly a thirty minute drive away from where I lived at the time. It was a pretty heavily wooded area, I guess to give it a sparsely populated small town feel. Most of the movie took place outside.
>
> After about two months of off and on shooting, Alex dropped his pet project completely. It was really sudden when he let me know about it. When I asked him why, he told me it was because of the "unworkable conditions" of where he had picked to shoot. Which struck me as very odd since he had been living around that area since he was eight, and never seemed to have a problem with it. What's even stranger is that he acted incredibly distant when telling me this news. Soon after, he started avoiding me and from what I hear, everyone else. All he did was sit around his house.

User 'ce gars' (aka Jay) contacted Alex to see how he was:

> Something about him was worse than I'd originally thought. He had lost a good bit of weight, and looked pretty sickly. I pretended like I didn't notice and we just hung out for awhile. Right before I left, I asked him about Marble Hornets and what he was planning on doing with all of his tapes of raw footage. With almost no hesitation, he simply said "burn them".

> This caught me off guard. When I asked why he didn't just archive them for B-roll in future projects, he just said he never wanted to work with the footage again. He was completely serious about this. I couldn't understand why he'd just want to get rid of it completely. Surely it wasn't all that useless. So I asked if I could take a look at them.
>
> He agreed, but only under the circumstance that I never bring them back to him, and never discuss what was on them with him. He also highly discouraged me from showing any if it to anyone else. I laughed at this, and said that he must have accidentally made *The Ring* or something with the way he was talking. He didn't acknowledge this and brought me up to his attic, where he was storing the pile of tapes.
>
> There were tons of them...

Alex gave Jay the bag of tapes and unceremoniously threw him out of the house, saying, "I'm not kidding, don't ever bring this up around me again." Jay filed the tapes, and was only drawn to take another look at them when the Slenderman thread at SA nudged his memory.

> I've decided to begin going through the tapes later tonight. If I don't do it now, I probably never will. I'm hoping all I find is an unfinished student film and nothing else. That would sure put me at ease now that I'm thinking about it again. If there's interest, I'll post anything that I find on here.

The first clip was posted to YouTube on June 20th, 2009, and linked to on the SA thread. Further postings followed, continuing to this day.

Marble Hornets is, if nothing else, an exemplary example of the found-footage horror genre. The breakthrough film of this type – *The Blair Witch Project* – sums up the basic idea nicely; footage from a lost or vanished film crew is reconstructed and edited so as to tell the story of their disappearance. The lifelike *Cinéma vérité* elements, combined with the ability to make such films very cheaply indeed, have contributed to their popularity – even resulting in relatively high-budgeted Hollywood assays into the field, such as *Paranormal Activity*, *The Last Exorcist* and *Apollo 18*.

Even for such a fruitful genre, *Marble Hornets* is an exceptional piece of work. Made for an initial budget of around $300 by student film-makers Troy Wagner and Joseph DeLage, each episode slowly builds dramatic tension to a series of genuinely shocking moments. Certain scenes, frankly, scared the shit out of me – and I'm a lifelong horror fan who's done more than my fair share of intensely spooky field paranormal work.

Marble Hornets (hereafter referred to as *MH*) brings a series of disturbing new aspects to the mythos, which have been carried over into later works. Principle among these are:

- Slenderman is shown to have a powerful physical effect on those who he has chosen (or, perhaps, who have chosen to pursue him) – victims are prone to violent coughing fits, often accompanied with blood. They black out, losing periods of time from a few hours to three months. During these periods of lost time, they often perform activities very different from their conscious behaviour – including murder.
- Some victims take on sinister new personalities during these episodes; donning masks, scrawling bizarre messages. A key image in these scribblings is the so-called Operator Symbol – a circle with a cross through it, written in text as (x). This clearly relates to Slenderman in some way (the film-makers have referred to their version of Slenderman as 'The Operator' several times) but whether the Operator Symbol is used to represent, summon or protect one from Slenderman is unknown.

- The presence of Slenderman is shown to have an effect on audio-visual recording equipment – strange noises creep into the soundtrack when Slenderman (or those he is influencing) move into shot. The image itself distorts, flares, sometimes breaks down into static or apparently-random geometric figures.
- Slenderman seems to have an affinity with, and possibly control of, doorways and other passageways. He is seen to creep from the doorways of rooms previously shown to be empty, or to lure people through doors into places which by all rights should not be accessible through that door. In many ways, Slenderman is an avatar of liminality itself.

The *MH* story builds on this continually. 'Jay' (played by Wagner), the original uploader of the YouTube clips, soon finds himself haunted by Slenderman in the precise way that 'Alex' (the director of the original footage, played by DeLage) is shown to be within those clips. And then (some nine episodes into *MH's* initial run) somebody else, using the name 'totheark', began posting clips in response/commentary to Jay's posts – some of which show footage of Jay himself. Sometimes, postings by 'totheark' came from Jay's own YouTube account…

The 'totheark' postings are, of course, also part of the story Wagner and DeLage are telling. The clips attributed to 'totheark' not only counterpoint the initial Jay posts, but contain hidden clues to the nature of Slenderman concealed within them, using various forms of visual and auditory steganography (encoding messages within the content of another message). This aspect of the storytelling puts *Marble Hornets* firmly within another powerful internet-born motif, the Alternate Reality Game, or ARG. ARGs have been around since 1996, although there are many precursors and influences to the concept in fiction, such as the deeply odd British 1990s TV show *The One Game* and the David Fincher film *The Game*. A FAQ on the subject defines them as an experience "that encourages players (you!) to interact with a fictional world using the real world to do it."

Players of an ARG are asked to look for clues to further the game's storyline in a variety of media – websites, film clips, even co-opted advertising – and often take part in exchanges of email and other communication with those running the game. The ARG acts as a kind of filter through which the 'real' world can be seen, usually exposing a complex conspiracy within the context of the game. The more you participate, the more you learn. Players usually communicate on a variety of message boards set up either by the game creators or the players themselves (a very good, slightly fictionalized take on how ARGs work can be found in Walter Jon Williams' novel *This Is Not A Game*).

Often ARGs are a secondary form of advertising for a media product – one of the first ARGs was used to publicise the Spielberg film *AI*, and one of the most popular, "I Love Bees", was part of the ad campaign for the game *Halo 2.* Sometimes though, an ARG happens simply because a large and enthusiastic enough group of internet users decide to create one.

The first mention of ARGs in relation to Slenderman can be found in the Something Awful thread on 15th June 2009, 0223 – user 'MooseyFate' posted:

Example of image modification to incorporate Slenderman mythos – modified version by SA poster 'GyverMac' on the left, original on right.

> I LOVE this type of thing. Something just feels satisfying about causing mass hysteria. I think we could roll with this slender man thing. Maybe if we make enough images and maybe if some talents can make fake videos, it could grow to ARG proportions (minus the advertising).

Most, if not all, of the subsequent Slenderman material could be seen as facets of a single, massive ARG. The premiere website for followers and participants of ARGs is unfiction.com – and unsurprisingly, there is a great amount of material about Slenderman, and *MH* in particular, there. And by a great amount, I mean: the original *MH* thread alone was locked after 323 pages...and there are dozens of other *MH*-related threads.

Although *MH* was the first, it was far from the only video-based work to feature Slenderman. There are now dozens of such series, most of them posted in instalments to YouTube in the same manner as *MH*. They vary in quality – and degree of viewer involvement expected – greatly. One of the strongest contenders for the most popular Slenderman video series, EverymanHYBRID, takes the commonly-used elements of steganography much further: viewers are encouraged to join in with the storyline in various email-and-Twitter-based competitions, including trying to find the locations of a series of geo-cached boxes containing further clues to the story's deeper background.

All of these different but parallel stories feed into each other, with ideas from one moving to others almost as if by osmosis. This recently culminated in a series of crossover videos where characters from *Marble Hornets*, *EverymanHYBRID* and another popular series, *DarkHarvest00*, appeared in the same YouTube releases.

All of the various series, however, occupy the same mythological space, whether or not each story is considered canon within another series. For example, EverymanHYBRID actually refers to Slenderman as an internet meme within the episodes – the videos begin as a supposed DIY keep-fit show, where the creators had inserted a Slenderman background appearance as a joke... only for this to backfire drastically when their actions attract the unwanted attention of the 'real' Slenderman. As I mentioned earlier, metatextural elements are an integral part of the Slenderman mythos.

That mythos, as it has grown, has taken on more and more aspects which bring its fictional status across into a form of occult potentiality. Much of this revolves around a particular concept of the previously-fictional manifesting across into quotidian reality. This concept is best put in a single word of Tibetan - *Tulpa*.

'Thought-form'

The concept of Tulpas, the word itself, derives from ancient Tibetan magical and mystical praxis. The usual translation of the word is 'thought-form'.

The Tibetan mystical system is a complex patchwork – a syncretic mix of aspects of Buddhism, Taoism and the native pre-Buddhist Bön shamanic tradition. This mix is uneven at best – some areas of the Himalayan region spurned the majority of the Bön practices, while others barely paid lip service to the formal Buddhist arrangements which overlay their culture – not unlike a Voudon practitioner making a point of showing up to their local Catholic church every Sunday while maintaining a shrine to the Loas in their Christian disguises. As a result, some practices were more commonly available in particular areas. Most Buddhists would reject the tulpa idea as base superstition...but the idea remained entrenched in the native folklore.

The earliest report of the tulpa concept in the West came from a book written in the 1940s by the explorer and early Buddhist convert, Alexandra David-Neel. David-Neel was a remarkable woman. A determined explorer of both land and culture, she travelled extensively in the Far East (often with her son in tow!), eventually living in the Nepal-Tibet area, training formally in the Tibetan form of Buddhism and attaining the rank of Lama – one of the few women, certainly the only Western woman, ever to do so. In her book *Magic and Mystery in Tibet*, she describes her own experience with the tulpa concept – and her successful attempt to construct one:

> However interested we may feel in the other strange accomplishments with which Tibetan adepts of the secret lore are credited, the creation of thought forms seems by far the most puzzling.
>
> As I have said, some apparitions are created on purpose either by a lengthy process . . . or, in the case of proficient adepts, instantaneously or almost instantaneously. In other cases, apparently the author of the phenomenon generates it unconsciously, and is not even in the least aware of the apparition being seen by others.
>
> However, the practice is considered as fraught with danger for every one who has not reached a high mental and spiritual degree of enlightenment and is not fully aware of the nature of the psychic forces at work in the process.
>
> Once the tulpa is endowed with enough vitality to be capable of playing the part of a real being, it tends to free itself from its maker's control. This, say Tibetan occultists, happens nearly mechanically, just as the child, when his body is completed and able to live apart, leaves its mother's womb. Sometimes the phantom becomes a rebellious son and one hears of uncanny struggles that have taken place between magicians and their creatures, the former being severely hurt or even killed by the latter.
>
> Tibetan magicians also relate cases in which the tulpa is sent to fulfil a mission, but does not come back and pursues its peregrinations as a half-conscious, dangerously mischievous puppet. The same thing, it

> is said, may happen when the maker of the tulpa dies before having dissolved it. Yet as a rule the phantom either disappears suddenly at the death of the magician or gradually vanishes like a body that perishes for want of food. On the other hand, some tulpas are expressly intended to survive their creator and are specially formed for that purpose.

Fascinated by this concept, David-Neel decided to experiment with creating a tulpa herself. To avoid the Lamaist influence (as, I suspect, a form of control on the experiment) she decided to base her tulpa on quite another set of imagery – a plump, jolly Christian monk, not unlike Friar Tuck of the Robin Hood legends:

> I shut myself in tsams (meditative seclusion) and proceeded to perform the prescribed concentration of thought and other rites. After a few months the phantom Monk was formed. His form grew gradually fixed and lifelike looking. He became a kind of guest, living in my apartment. I then broke my seclusion and started for a tour, with my servants and tents.
>
> The Monk included himself in the party. Though I lived in the open, riding on horseback for miles each day, the illusion persisted. I saw the fat tulpa; now and then it was not necessary for me to think of him to make him appear. The phantom performed various actions of the kind that are natural to travellers and that I had not commanded. For instance, he walked, stopped, looked around him. The illusion was mostly visual, but sometimes I felt as if a robe was lightly rubbing against me, and once a hand seemed to touch my shoulder.
>
> The features which I had imagined, when building my phantom, gradually underwent a change. The fat, chubby-cheeked fellow grew leaner, his face assumed a vaguely mocking, sly, malignant look. He became more troublesome and bold. In brief, he escaped my control. Once, a herdsman who brought me a present of butter saw the tulpa in my tent and took it for a living lama.

> I ought to have let the phenomenon follow its course, but the presence of that unwanted companion began to prove trying to my nerves; it turned into a "day-nightmare". Moreover, I was beginning to plan my journey to Lhasa and needed a quiet brain devoid of other preoccupations, so I decided to dissolve the phantom. I succeeded, but only after six months of hard struggle. *My mind-creature was tenacious of life.* (Emphasis mine.)
>
> There is nothing strange in the fact that I may have created my own hallucination. The interesting point is that in these cases of materialization, others see the thought-forms that have been created.

The tulpa has been absorbed into modern magical theory via the Chaos Magic school – the inveterate pack-rat nature of Chaos practitioners means that few if any of the world's occult and mystical concepts have gone untapped…and the possibility of making imagination manifest in such a direct form meshes nicely with their concepts of Servitor and Egregore, and with the memetic transmission of occult ideas and powers. So, the possibility of constructing a tulpa is relatively well-known in modern magical praxis – which may or may not have influenced its appearance as an integral part of the Slenderman mythos.

The first hint within Slenderman canon that 'Slendy' was perhaps a form of tulpa appeared early on in the original somethingawful.com thread. As noted above, it was in the post from 'I' saying "He exists because you thought of him. Now try and not think of him."

The first direct reference to Tulpas, however, came on 20th July 2009 – the day after the first *Marble Hornets* video and only ten days from Victor Surge's initial post. Here is how user 'Soakie' put it:

> Has anyone thought about the possibility that we are creating a tulpa? It's a thought form that is realized through the efforts of a group of people. We might be creating the Slender Man, making him real. The Toronto Society for Psychical Research did this with an entity called

> "Philip" in the mid-1970s. There was a book written about it, called *Conjuring Up Philip*. "He" was a fictional person, knowingly created by the group. It was all fun and games until "Philip" started to take on a mind of his own. "Philip" became real, as far as any paranormal thing could be said to be real. So take all this with a big grain of salt.
>
> How long until there is agreement about what the Slender Man looks like? When will he have a specific MO? Can the hidden superstitious heart of the SA Goons give Slenderman an independent existence? Think about it, a few hundred or maybe even a thousand Goons, all looking at the pictures and creating the stories. I find myself looking at the shadows, imagining how they might fall together to show a lurking Slenderman. 'Slendy' pulls so many primal strings: his wrongness to our eyes, the hair on the back of the neck rising, the subconscious "Nonononono" that bursts across the imagination. He drags the monsters out of the back of our modern minds. He is a satisfactory boogie-man, pressing all the right buttons. Even if we don't really believe in the supernatural, even if our rational minds laugh at such an absurdity...we are cutting him out and sewing him together. We're stuffing him with nightmares and unspoken fears.And what happens when the pictures are no longer Photoshop creations...?

From this point on, Slenderman-as-tulpa became effectively canon. This raises an interesting, perhaps worrying, possibility: Even if Slenderman started out purely as an invented creature, has it stayed that way? Has naming it as a tulpa, in effect, given it the power to be created as one?

The problem with answering this decisively is an essential part of the nature of the beast. Although those involved in ARGs are (indeed, have to be) scrupulous in their discussions of what is and is not OOG (Out-Of-Game – i.e. actual comments regarding the creation and playing of the game rather than the story elements themselves), there is some inevitable bleed-through between the two. So, when (for example) the popular Fortean radio talk show 'Coast

To Coast' gets several callers describing their Slenderman encounters, can we – should we – take those stories to be true? Does it matter?

The Slenderman meme is spreading rapidly across the internet. At this point there are dozens of video series, dozens more first-person blogs telling serialized stories within the mythos. Hundreds, maybe thousands of enthusiastic creators, yet more following the phenomenon avidly. News articles about the phenomenon are starting to appear. Other media are beginning to pay attention to the Slenderman story. (The popular game Minecraft, for instance, added a character called Enderman – explicitly based on Slenderman – in a recent game update.) Popular bloggers and Twitter users often refer to Slenderman in their posts. Slenderman is going, as they say, viral. And as the virus spreads, so do the symptoms...

On the internet, nobody knows if you're a dog. Or a tulpa. And if enough people describe something as a thought-form...could this collective imagining actually make that form manifest?

And, if that form does manifest – this powerful, terrifying, unkillable thing called Slenderman – how can we fight it?

Ian 'Cat' Vincent was born on Imbolc-Groundhog Day in Gravesend, England, 1964. He is a lifelong student of the occult, and a former professional combat magician, curse-breaker and exorcist. In recent years, he has focused on exploring the utility of the 'hyper-real' (fiction-inspired) belief systems. His writing on Forteana and magic, especially on the personal magical style he terms 'Guttershaman', can be found at http://catvincent.com. He is also a staff writer at http://weaponizer.co.uk and http://modernmythology.net and co-curates the consciousness news/discussion group http://fuckyeahconsciousness.tumblr.com. He lives in England with his partner, the artist/writer Kirsty Hall. He is often found on Twitter as @catvincent.

He knows how to kill a Slenderman. Honest.

A Message in Stone

Are the so-called 'Trial Passages' at Giza the key to a greater mystery?

by *Mark Foster*

Just a stone's throw from the Great Pyramid lies a set of very odd passages that are rarely discussed, yet which have puzzled the greatest minds ever to have explored the Giza plateau. These passages lie roughly eighty-seven metres east of the Great Pyramid and are hewn into the desert rock of the Giza Plateau (see Figure 1). When they were first examined by Vyse and Perring in the 1840s they were thought to be passages from an abandoned pyramid or tomb, possibly even a fourth subsidiary pyramid of the Great Pyramid. However, later on, W. M. Flinders Petrie noticed that the passages seemed to be a very precise copy of the passages inside the Great Pyramid, under the shadow of which they were cut. Petrie believed that they had been built before work on the Great Pyramid commenced, as an attempt to mock-up the layout of the internal passages in the pyramid. Therefore they were named the Trial Passages.

Was this really their purpose? Why have we not uncovered trial passages for any of the other 4th Dynasty pyramids – or for a pyramid of any dynasty for that matter? Egyptologists tell us that Khufu's father, Snefru, built both of the giant pyramids at Dashur before Khufu started work on the Great Pyramid. Both the Red Pyramid and Bent Pyramid contain complex internal chambers and passages yet there are no trial passages related to these buildings. Why have we also found no trial passages connected with the Second and Third Pyramids at Giza? What if the Trial Passages had some other purpose that has been overlooked?

Before we head down this route let's study the Passages in a bit more detail. Take a look at Figures 2 and 3 and you will see the comparison. Figure 2 shows the passages inside the Great Pyramid

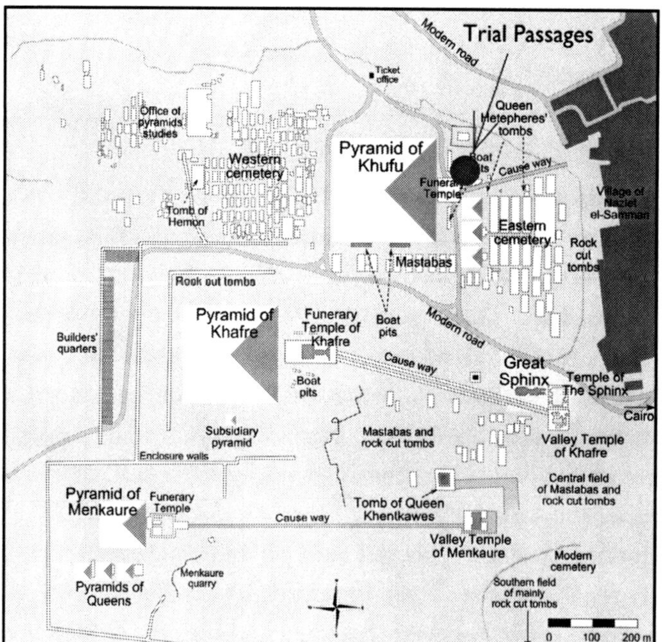

Fig. 1: Location of the Trial Passages (original image Messer Woland, CCASA 3.0 Licence)

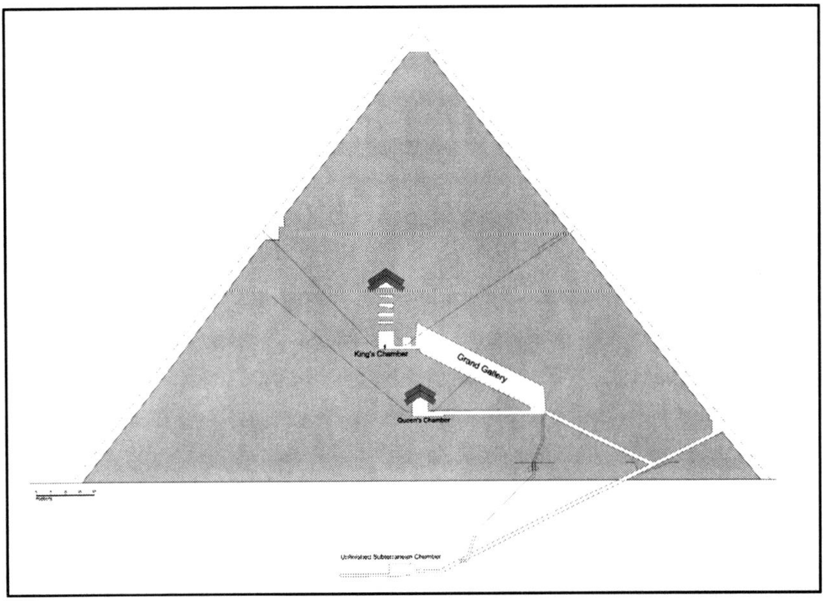

Fig. 2: Internal passages of the Great Pyramid (original image Messer Woland, CCASA 3.0 Licence)

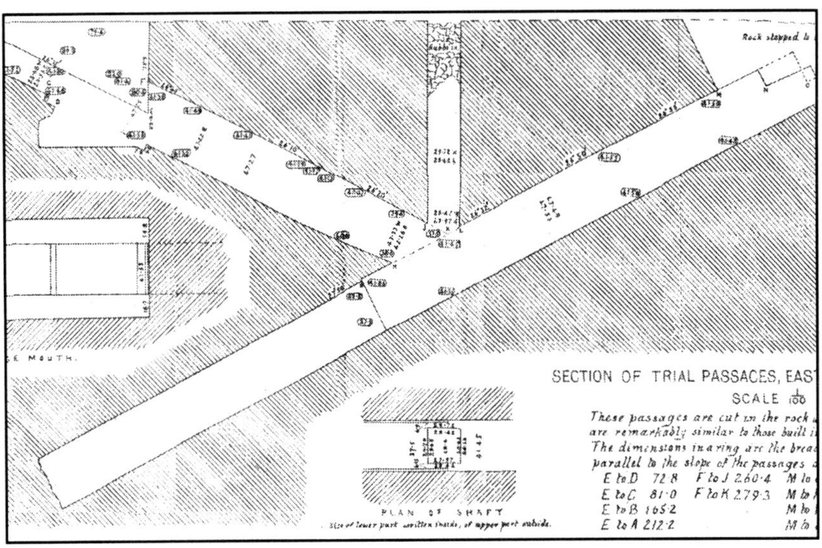

Fig. 3: Layout of the Trial Passages (from *The Pyramids and Temples of Gizeh*)

whereas Figure 3 shows the Trial Passages. Giza expert Mark Lehner, in *The Pyramid Tomb of Hetep-heres and the Satellite Pyramid of Khufu,* also agrees with the striking similarity and comments:

> As Petrie recognized, these passages clearly are a kind of foreshortened copy of the passages in the Great Pyramid.

Passage widths, heights, and angles all mirror the system of passages found inside the Great Pyramid. We have a Descending passage, an Ascending passage, the start of the Grand Gallery and the beginning of the Queen's Chamber passage. To further add weight to the idea that we are dealing with a replica of the inside of the Great Pyramid, the Ascending passage of the Trial Passages – where it meets the Descending passage – contracts just as it does in the Great Pyramid as if it were ready to accept plug-blocks. No plug-blocks have been found in the Trial Passages yet the builders went to the trouble of adding this feature.

Furthermore, Petrie in his work *The Pyramids and Temples of Gizeh* adds that there is also a passage that corresponds to the top of the well shaft found in the Grand Gallery in the Great Pyramid, however, in this case, the location is not in anyway identical to the position of this feature in the Great Pyramid. We shall return to look at this passage in more detail later on.

Leaving the matter of the well shaft to one side for the moment, the remaining passages bear such a close relationship to those in the Great Pyramid that Petrie concluded:

> The resemblance in all other respects is striking, even around the beginning of the Queen's Chamber Passage, and at the contraction to hold the plug-blocks in the Ascending passage of the Pyramid... The whole of these passages are very smoothly and truly cut, the mean differences in the dimensions being but little more than in the finely finished Pyramid masonry.

From this we can ascertain that a great deal of effort was expended to duplicate the internal passages of the Great Pyramid out on the desert floor, just a short distance from the pyramid itself. Furthermore, the fact that the mean differences in the cut passages are little more than in the Great Pyramid itself (the passages of which are highly praised by Petrie for their accuracy) raises the likelihood that the two constructions were carried out by the same builders and that a high degree of accuracy was a requisite for both sets of passages.

For What Purpose?

Having looked at the layout and features of the Trial Passages let's turn now to their purpose. I am going to put forward the hypothesis in this paper that these passages were never intended as a trial for the internal passages of the Great Pyramid, rather that they had some other, hitherto unknown, purpose.

Firstly, I mentioned above that they seem to be unique in that we have not found a single scrap of evidence for trial passages connected with any other pyramid constructed in Egypt. If this was a standard practice in Ancient Egypt I would at least expect to find trial passages connected with the 4th Dynasty Dashur Pyramids or the Second Pyramid at Giza. Unless new evidence presents itself in the near future we will have to assume that the Trial Passages as we know them are unique and an anomaly that has nothing in common with any other Pyramid. Furthermore, I fail to see what context there is for Ancient Egyptians having used trial passages to construct their monuments. There is simply no evidence to suggest that this was the case. If the Great Pyramid was the first pyramid constructed by the Ancient Egyptian builders then I could be persuaded that they may have needed such a set of trial passages for their first construction. However, Egyptology tells us this is not so and that prior to the Great Pyramid several other impressive pyramids were constructed, all with complex internal passages and chambers and all without trial passages built first to mock-up their internal layout.

Secondly, I could accept the possibility that they might be trial passages if they had been constructed out of masonry. The fact is they were not, they were instead carved out of the bedrock of the Giza Plateau whereas the majority of the corresponding passages inside the Great Pyramid were formed from masonry. I fail to see the benefits of carving these passages into solid rock when you are going to build using a completely different method when work commences on the Great Pyramid itself. Surely any experience gained would be negligible once the real construction began? I accept that a large part of the Great Pyramid's Descending passage was carved into the bedrock beneath the pyramid but if the architect was attempting to practice this art alone why did he then proceed to also carve passages into the bedrock that would be constructed from masonry in the Great Pyramid? The contraction of the Ascending Passage in the Trial Passages alone should make us sit up and realise that something is not right here. Carving such a feature out of the bedrock would have required great effort and the experience gained would surely be virtually useless when repeating this feature with cut stones later inside the Great Pyramid?

Therefore, I surmise that these passages could never have functioned as trial passages. Is it more likely that they have only been labelled as such merely because their true function has never properly been understood? If this is true, then what other possible function could they have had?

I certainly agree that the Trial Passages (I will continue to call them this for convenience, despite my belief that they do not assume this role) were meant to represent the internal layout of the Great Pyramid. We have also seen that the builders went to great lengths to convince us that we are in fact looking at a representation of the Great Pyramid so that we would be left with no doubt in our minds. Think for a moment about a map or the key to a puzzle. With a key

Fig. 4: Great Pyramid of Giza (photo courtesy Mark Foster)

we are able to solve a puzzle precisely. What if the Trial Passages were such a key left for someone to solve the "puzzle" of the Great Pyramid at a later date? For such a key to work we would have to be left in no doubt as to what the key was pointing us to and this seems to fit what we have seen inside the Trial Passages. Somebody went to a lot of trouble to construct the Trial Passages, all for apparently no practical reason – unless they were leaving us a very big clue carved in stone.

The First Part of the Riddle

History teaches us that it was the great Caliph Ma'mun who first discovered the granite plug-blocks stopping up the lower end of the Ascending Passage inside the Great Pyramid. Recent work by Ralph Ellis has shown that it is very likely that the tunnel Ma'mun carved into the Great Pyramid was carved outwards and not inwards as had previously been the case. I will not recount all the evidence here, but in short, it makes absolutely no sense that Ma'mum should tunnel into the Great Pyramid. It has long been recorded that the original entrance to the Great Pyramid, at the top of the Descending Passage, has always been open and graffiti dating back to Roman times at the foot of the Descending Passage, inside the Subterranean, attests to this being true. So, if the entrance had always been open why did Ma'mun need to go the extreme effort of tunnelling in. Furthermore, to then be told that he arbitrarily began tunnelling into the pyramid and just happened to strike the junction of the Ascending and Descending passages on his first attempt is incredible. The fact that this junction deep inside the pyramid is actually offset by some 24 feet East of the centreline makes this story all the more remarkable! Put bluntly, this version of the story makes no sense at all. However, if we instead assume that he was forced to carve his tunnel outwards in order to remove something that was too large to pass through the

Descending Passage then events begin to make much more sense. However, by interpreting the story of Ma'mun's explorations in this way we are left with a new problem. How did Ma'mun discover the start of the Ascending Passage that led to the higher chambers in side the Great Pyramid?

Let us go back to the start of the tale and look at it with fresh eyes. Ma'mum would have entered the Great Pyramid by the original entrance. He would have found himself in the Descending Passage and from there would have ventured into the Subterranean Chamber. The entrance to the Ascending Passage was covered at that time with a stone lintel positioned in the ceiling of the Descending Passage. This lintel was indistinguishable from the other blocks forming the roof of the Descending passage and would not only have obscured the plug-blocks behind but also ensured that the Ascending Passage was totally hidden from view. Prior to the removal of this lintel, entering the interior of the Great Pyramid would have been a very similar experience to entering the Red Pyramid at Dashur. You would have descended down one very long passage before emerging into a chamber far below the entrance (there are differences due to the fact that the Red Pyramid's passage is built wholly into masonry but the effect is the same). In those days before Ma'mun, the Ascending Passage in the Great Pyramid would not have been visible at all and every single early visitor to the Great Pyramid would have gone straight past it, completely ignorant of what lay above their heads: the Grand Gallery, the Queen's Chamber and the King's Chamber – no-one knew that these rooms even existed at that time.

Let us assume for a moment that many visitors were also aware of the Trial Passages to the east of the Great Pyramid. How many puzzled explorers had entered these corridors only to ponder why they were there? They led nowhere and there was not a single chamber at their conclusion. Instead they ended in a blank wall. Was Ma'mun the first to realise they bore a resemblance to the Great Pyramid's passages? Anyone measuring the width and height and angle of the entrance to the Great Pyramid and comparing them with the Trial passages would have seen a distinct similarity. Was Ma'mun the first person to do this? Did he then happen to notice that inside the Trial Passages there was a further passage leading up from the roof of its version of the Descending Passage? Did this make him wonder whether a similar passage existed inside the Great Pyramid?

I think it is highly possible that Ma'mun, fresh from this flash of inspiration in the Trial Passages then went back into the Great Pyramid and started to look for a hidden passage in the roof of the Descending Passage. Without knowing it he had noted the builder's first clue and had started the process of unravelling the puzzle.

At this point we have to consider how Ma'mun came to find the exact location of the hidden Ascending passage. History tells us that he did, and the fact that we can walk in the King's Chamber is proof he succeeded, but it is interesting to try and ascertain how he achieved it. Peter Lemesurier in his book *The Great Pyramid Decoded* raises the interesting point that a pair of scored lines carved into the walls of the Great Pyramid's Descending Passage seem to bear a similarity

Fig. 5: Non-descript surroundings of the Trial Passages (photo courtesy Mark Foster)

with a sloped face found at the top of the Trial Passages' Descending Passage. A quick study of both of these features shows that they do indeed seem to indicate a precise point in both sets of passages.

You will remember that the Trial Passages are foreshortened. In other words the lengths of the passages were built at a different scale to those in the Great Pyramid itself. However, it occurred to me that it would have been possible to compare the distance between this precise point and the beginning of each of the two Descending Passages to work out exactly what scale was being used. With this figure it would then be possible to calculate the position of the start of the Ascending Passage inside the Great Pyramid.

I have estimated that if Ma'mun had carried out these simple calculations then it would have enabled him to identify the exact position of the hidden stone lintel in the roof of the Great Pyramid's Descending Passage to within a few inches. This would have been more than accurate enough bearing in mind that the hidden lintel would have resembled one of the large roofing stones. An accuracy of a few inches would have highlighted which stone was actually the hidden lintel and not a roofing slab.

Of course Ma'mun may not have used this method and he may instead just have examined all of thc roofing blocks one by one until he located the right one. The truth is we will likely never know, but it is very interesting to note that it was eminently possible for him to locate the entrance in this manner if he had studied the Trial Passages closely enough, and made the connection between the scored lines and the flat surface of rock inclined at the same angle at the head of the Trial Passages. To further highlight this point it must be mentioned that the purpose of the scored lines within the Great Pyramid has yet to be argued conclusively, so I find it highly likely that they are there for just this purpose, as a marker, a point from which measurements should be taken when compared to the Trial Passages, for the sole purpose of locating the hidden Ascending passage. Once he had found the hidden lintel, Ma'mun would then have removed it. Expecting to find the Ascending Passage, he would have been very surprised to discover that it was indeed there but that it travelled only a few inches before being plugged by huge granite stones.

The blocking up of the Ascending Passage seems to have been designed to intrigue and pique our curiosity even more. First the builders leave us a clue in the form of the Trial Passages. Once this clue is deciphered and the lintel is removed we find to our dismay that the passage is plugged. What would anyone's reaction be in that instance? I don't believe for one minute that anybody could walk away at that point. Ma'mun did what any of us would have done, he tried desperately to get past the plugs. At first Ma'mun tried chiselling through the granite plugs, but the stone proved too tough and the job would have taken forever. So he ordered his workers to dig into the softer limestone that surrounded the granite plugs, in effect digging around the plugs. In doing so he finally breached the Ascending Passage.

The rest is history, as they say. We have Ma'mun to thank for revealing to us the marvels of the upper chambers of the Great Pyramid. Without him we would still be teaching in schools that the Great Pyramid has no chambers within the masonry itself and that the only chamber is the rock-cut Subterranean Chamber. Ma'mun had done his part, the plugs had been breached and modern mankind had progressed to the next stage in the puzzle. He had taken us through the first stage of the riddle.

Puzzles, Puns and Secret Chambers

However, the next part of the puzzle was to remain secret for almost one thousand years, when a man called Waynman Dixon started exploring the Great Pyramid and picked up the scent. At this point I would like to discuss just why the builders left such a key for us. Firstly, readers of my work will have appreciated that I consider it highly unlikely that the Great Pyramid was merely a tomb. Whether

Fig. 6: Entrance to the Trial Passages (photo courtesy Mark Foster)

it was ever the tomb of Khufu is debatable but I do believe from my own research that it is highly probable that the Great Pyramid was standing before Khufu's reign and had a purpose other than being a tomb. For the record, I do believe that the Pyramids of Giza were constructed by Egyptians, it is just that I attribute their civilisation a greater period of time than history currently affords it. Therefore, leaving us a map of the insides of the Great Pyramid becomes slightly more curious. The question now turns to why?

To my mind the Trial Passages are simply a pun carved in stone. Again this is not out of context with what we know of the culture of Ancient Egypt. Scattered throughout Egyptian Texts we come across a variety of puns that were deliberately placed in the spells and lines of *The Book Of The Dead* and other funerary writings. The Egyptians seemed to find great delight in such puns and great pains were taken to place them for dramatic effect. One of countless examples is pointed out by Dr. Ogden Goelet in the *Papyrus of Ani*, Chapter 147 (speaking of Osiris):

> *The one purified by your own efflux (setau) against (r) which the name of Rosetau was made.*
>
> By noting that the word Rosetau sounds much like the phrase 'against the efflux,' the fluids issuing from Osiris' body were thus made innocuous.

While this example is taken from a text dating from circa 1250 BC there are numerous examples throughout Egyptian literature, including the Pyramid Texts inscribed onto the walls of the Fifth Dynasty Pyramids at Saqqara, so it is evident that this kind of word play and punning was prevalent right throughout Egyptian history. While some of these puns were cleverly designed to enhance the power of the particular line, as above, others were much more simply a play on words for everyday objects, superimposing the meaning of one onto another for dramatic and sometimes humorous effect.

So the question is: could they have incorporated such puns into their buildings? I think it is certainly within the realms of probability if the Egyptian culture used them this extensively in their funerary literature.

It would appear that this was indeed the case, as the Trial Passages are not the only example of such a pun being left in stone at Giza. I mentioned that it was almost a thousand years or so before the next clue was found. Waynman Dixon began his survey of the inside of the Great Pyramid with his brother in the year 1872. It is well documented that there were at that time shafts present in the King's chamber but none in the Queen's chamber below.

One day Dixon inserted a piece of wire into a small crack in a wall in the Queen's chamber. He thought there might be a void behind the wall and so, measuring the position of the shafts in the upper chamber he estimated where similar shafts might be found in the Queen's chamber and then asked his man-at-work to bring his chisel to bear on both the south and north walls. Two shafts were revealed, approximately eight inches square.

Incredibly, the shafts leading from the Queen's chamber were not cut through into the chamber itself but were instead hidden some eight inches behind the walls. Furthermore, we now know for certain that both the Southern and Northern shafts do not make it to the outside of the Pyramid. Could it be that the builders have left another pun for us to puzzle over?

I certainly feel that this is in keeping with the minds of the builders. Recent explorations seem to underline this conclusion. Both shafts were explored by the National Geographic in 2002. A new robot, Pyramid Explorer confirmed Rudolf Gantenbrink's original discovery in 1993 of what appears to be a door or portcullis slab at the end of the shaft. Drilling through this door revealed a second door behind the first. Furthermore, explorations of the Northern shaft revealed a third door blocking the end of that shaft. Whatever we find behind these doors, we would not even be aware that these shafts existed if Dixon had not solved this particular riddle in 1872.

I don't think it is irrelevant that the shafts themselves are only eight inches square. This speaks volumes to me concerning the mind of the builders. What better way of frustrating and piquing the mind of the explorer than to build a passage that no man could ever ascend. Dixon tried exploring the shaft and failed, losing part of his iron rods in the process (they can still be seen stuck around a bend in the Northern Queen's shaft). It was only after Rudolf Gantenbrink's exploration by robot that we realised there was something at the end of the Southern passage.

Yet still the pun of the builders is at work because even though we now know there is a door or portcullis slab at the end of the passage we are unable to get up there and open it. We know there is something of importance there because just before we reach the door the passage is suddenly lined with fine Turah limestone, reserved solely for chambers and casing in the Great Pyramid. I can only interpret this one way, that the builders are attempting to show us that there are indeed further chambers high up in the Great Pyramid. But what is the point of showing us there is such a chamber only to then underline the point that there is no way we can reach it? Unless there is another way up?

Could the point here be, that having shown us there is another chamber, we then have to find another way to reach it? Possibly via another passage that at the present time is unknown and hidden from us. To answer this riddle we must try and think the way the builders would have. We have to go back to the original key, the Trial Passages, and look to see if anything has been missed. When I did this I was instantly surprised by what I found. It became clear to me that the purpose of the Trial Passages is to focus attention on one particular part of the Great Pyramid only; the junction of the Ascending Passage with the Descending Passage. This becomes clearer the closer you look. Everything centres on this feature, and other details such as the Grand Gallery are only sketched in so we that we are able to work out that we are indeed being shown a map of the internal passages of the Great Pyramid. Features like the Subterranean chamber are not shown at all, neither is the Queen's chamber. Furthermore, if you examine it closely, it is evident that this is the only portion of the whole set of passages that is completely to scale, other features are foreshortened but the junction does not suffer from this problem of scale, it is there, complete.

This suggests that we should look long and hard at the junction of the Ascending with the Descending for some very important reason. Taking my lead from the passages themselves, I studied this junction until I realised that I had been staring at the solution all along without actually seeing it. The answer is there right in front of our eyes, screaming for attention, but we have failed to see it up until now. There is a passage in the Trial Passages that does not appear in the Great Pyramid. Or rather, there is a passage represented in the Trial Passages which we have yet to uncover inside the Great Pyramid. Remember that before Ma'mun discovered the Ascending Passage in the Great Pyramid nobody knew it was there. Could it be that there is another passage that we are walking past everyday, one that leads into the upper reaches of the pyramid?

Take another look at the layout of the Trial passages, reproduced in Figure 7 (next page). You will notice the vertical passage slightly to the North of the beginning of the Ascending Passage in the Trial Passages. We have yet to find a passage inside the Great Pyramid that corresponds to this feature in the Trial Passages. I believe that this fact has been overlooked because it has been assumed that it represents the Well Shaft. Petrie certainly believed that this is what it represented, saying;

> The vertical shaft here is only analogous in size and not in position, to the well in the Pyramid gallery; and it is the only feature which is not an exact copy of the Great Pyramid passages, *as far as we know them.* [Petrie's own emphasis.]

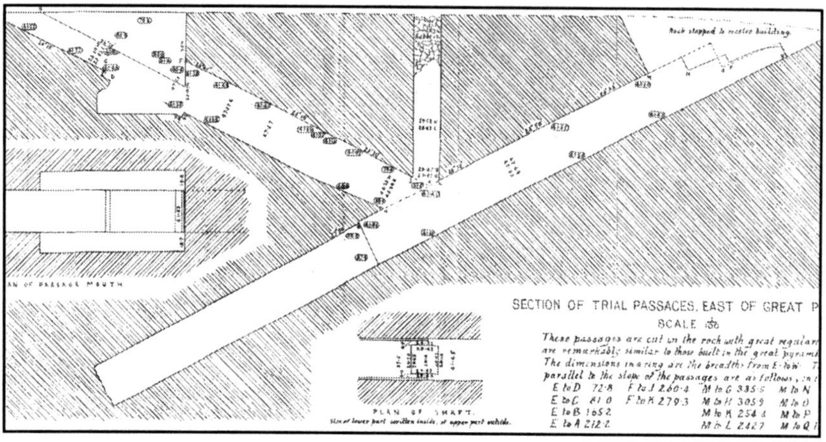

Fig. 7: Layout of the Trial Passages (from *The Pyramids and Temples of Gizeh*)

I have to take issue here with Petrie and, while I have the greatest respect for his work, in my opinion he has made a serious error here in comparing this shaft with the Well Shaft. If we look at the position of the Well Shaft in the Great Pyramid (see Figure 2) it can be seen that it begins in the Descending Passage and, after many twists and turns, climbs through the pyramid to emerge at the base of the Grand Gallery, arriving beneath a loose stone that formed part of the West ramp of the Grand Gallery. Look again at the vertical shaft in the Trial Passages. How can this passage be comparable with the Well Shaft in the Great Pyramid? The position of the two shafts is not even remotely close. A vertical passage in such a place in the Great Pyramid would be nowhere near emerging at the base of the Grand Gallery. To my mind to state that the two are analogous is stretching a point too far. I can only conclude that they relate to separate features and can in no way be thought to be the same feature.

However, in reading Petrie's words again, I am forced to consider the fact that he actually suspected himself that they were not the same feature. What does he mean by the words "*the only feature which is not an exact copy of the Great Pyramid passages, as far as we know them*"? Did he suspect that this vertical shaft might indeed be found in the Great Pyramid? We will never know but what we can do is take his lead.

Having surmised that it is highly likely that this is not actually the Well Shaft, we have to take onboard the message the Trial Passages seem to be pointing out to us here. There is another passage in the Great Pyramid, one we have not uncovered yet. Furthermore, we should expect it to rise up vertically into the body of the pyramid from thc junction of the Ascending Passage with the Descending Passage. If this passage was indeed to be found inside the Great Pyramid where could it lead? It does not necessarily have to remain a vertical passage. It could quite simply lead anywhere. It could develop into a separate passage system and lead us to new chambers. The truth is, it is impossible to predict. The Trial Passages leave the question unanswered. Only the beginning of the vertical shaft is represented in the Trial Passages, in much the same way as only the beginning of the Grand Gallery is depicted. I believe this is so for reasons outlined above, it is the *junction* of these passages *only* that the Trial Passages are attempting to bring to our attention. They seem to want us to make a breakthrough and discover the passage for ourselves. Where it leads will become evident at that time. So does this passage really exist in the Great Pyramid and if so why has it been missed?

I believe it is highly probable that it really is there. The reason it has remained hidden for so long is due in part to the ingenuity of the architect. Look again at the plug-blocks in the Great Pyramid. Now refer back to the vertical passage in the Trial Passages. It is clear that the plugs start at exactly the location where we would expect to find the beginning of the vertical passage, yet the plugs do not entirely cover the entrance to the vertical passage. Why then can we not see the passage? I believe that the vertical passage was designed not to be found by accident and, therefore, it is hidden in a similar way to the shafts found in the Queen's chamber. Remember that those shafts were always there, hidden just behind the wall. It was only the foresight of Dixon that revealed them. I do not believe it is unreasonable to suppose that the vertical shaft really is there, exactly where the Trial Passages show it to be. It is simply the case that the lower end has been made to look identical to the roof of the junction between the Ascending and Descending passages. Again, this is not too far-fetched given that we have already encountered a similar method of hiding a passage within the Great Pyramid itself (the Queen's Chamber shafts). So, there could be such a vertical passage inside the Great Pyramid. How much stone prevents us from gaining access to this new passage? Could it be as little as eight inches as was the case in the Queen's chamber? It is an exciting prospect.

Returning for a moment to look at the granite plugs, it is clear that their prime purpose is to block the Ascending Passage only. However, this is unlikely to be their only purpose. Originally, only the first three plugging stones were granite. Ma'mun also found several limestone plugs behind the granite stones. So why are only the first three granite? This seems to have been an intrinsic part of the design. If all the plugs had been limestone then Ma'mun could have removed them all fairly easily (as he did the ones further up the Ascending Passage) and he would not have needed to tunnel around as he did with the granite plugs. To my mind, using granite for the first three plugs ensures that the correct sequence is followed by anyone following the clues left inside the Trial Passages. They tell the explorer who has found them that there is a passage to find and he then digs around them to break into the Ascending Passage. In following this pattern of behaviour, the granite plugs remain intact and the hidden lintel behind which the vertical passage is concealed remains partially protected by the plugs.

I hinted earlier at where such a passage would lead us to. If there are chambers and other passages leading from such a vertical passage, it follows that these would impact upon the passages and chambers we already know about, causing various stresses and strains within the fabric of the Great Pyramid itself. In fact a few pieces of evidence do present themselves here.

Fig. 8: Junction within the Trial Passages (photo courtesy Mark Foster)

Clues to a Hidden Mystery?

Firstly, some way up the Ascending Passage the construction of the passage changes in several places, and it has been shown that there are three girdle-stones fixed in place, stones where the crosssection of the passage has been cut through one massive stone block rather using several smaller stones. These are obviously designed to strengthen the passage at these points. If we look at a diagram of the Ascending Passage (Figure 9) it is obvious they only occur in one section of the passage. Why is only this point of the passage strengthened? Why was it not necessary to place girdle-stones along the whole length of the Ascending Passage? There is no evidence of similar girdle-stones in the upper part of the Descending Passage, or in the corridor leading to the Queen's chamber, or in fact anywhere else within the Great Pyramid, so why do we encounter them here, at this precise point in the Ascending Passage?

Could it be that it was necessary to strengthen the corridor at this point because there is something above this part of the passage? A chamber directly above the Ascending Passage would cause the weight of the surrounding core blocks to be shifted unevenly around it, possibly to such an extent that girdle-stones were needed to keep the Ascending Passage below intact. It seems very possible to me that the presence of girdle-stones at this particular spot in the pyramid indicates the position of an, as yet, unknown chamber. The position of the girdle-stones is very close to my suggested vertical passage. I do not think it is outside the realms of possibility to suggest that the two features share a connection.

Our second piece of evidence comes from Rudolf Gantenbrink's survey of the shafts found in both the King and Queen Chambers. In particular, it is a peculiar set of anomalies he found some way up both the Southern shafts that we need to focus on. Here is an extract from his exploration of the Queen's Southern shaft:

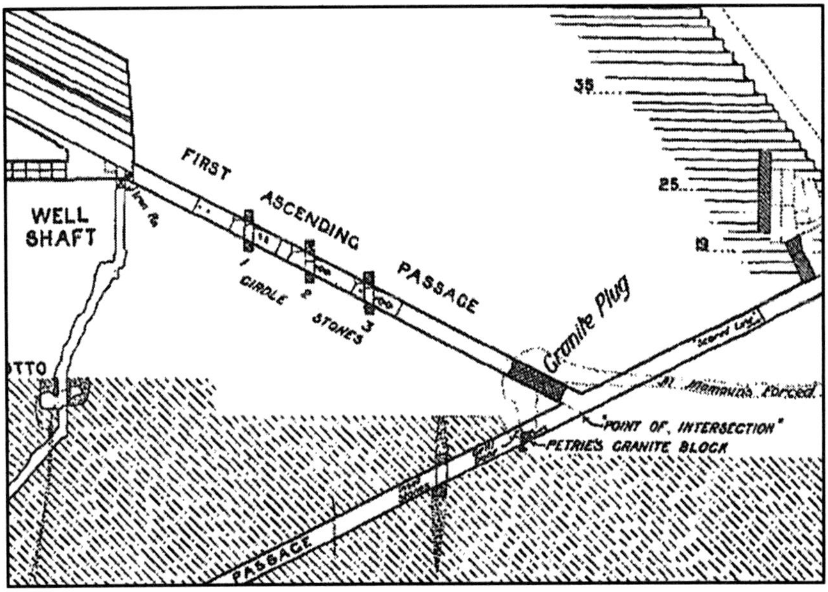

Fig. 9: Girdle-stones in the Ascending Passage in the Great Pyramid

At the beginning of Block No. 26, a large section of the floor has broken away. This is the worst damage we observed anywhere in the shaft sequences so far investigated. At this point, however, the pressure on the shaft amounts to only one-third of the maximum value. Near the Queen's Chamber, 115 meters of pyramid material press downward on the shaft. But only 35 meters of material press down on this spot, where we observe the greatest shaft damage. This highly unusual finding can have resulted only from one of two possible causes:

1. Extremely inept construction work below Block No. 25 and 26. It must be remembered, however, that it is this final section of the shaft which otherwise displays the highest quality workmanship observed anywhere in the shafts system.

2. The existence of an as yet undiscovered structure below or above this shaft section. Such a structure could produce a pressure peak,

> which could in turn focus considerable additional force on the shaft and possibly cause the observed damage.

Additionally, Gantenbrink later finds more evidence further up this shaft that seems to reinforce the idea that there might be an undiscovered structure in the pyramid somewhere in this vicinity when cutting marks are found on the floor of certain blocks forming the shaft:

> Based on the grooves found in the shaft, we can assume that, before their insertion as floor slabs, these blocks served as a base for the cutting of precision joints. This gives rise to a crucial question: exactly which precision joints were cut here?
>
> The shaft blocks themselves were only dressed with the chisel. We observed ample evidence of this in the Caviglia Tunnel, on the lower sides of the shaft blocks, as well as at several sites of block displacement, which exposed the abutting edges. At the upper southern shaft outlet, both outer sides of the blocks are visible. These, too, were worked only with the chisel. Thus, as 9 of a total of 10 surfaces of a shaft block were definitely chiselled, we can well assume that the shafts were constructed without recourse to sawing. The pyramid's nearest casing stones, which lie 19 meters distant from this spot in the shaft, were cut in their final position. We know this because the stones located directly beneath the casing stones display cutting grooves. The pyramid's corridor and chamber system, which also displays precise, cut joints, had been completed long before this shaft construction level was reached.
>
> Taken together, these findings constitute a compelling case for a possible, as yet undiscovered structure – for which precision joints were made – in this upper region of the southern, Queen's Chamber shaft.

To add yet more weight to this hypothesis are his findings in the King's Southern Shaft, at a point directly above the anomalies found in the lower, Queen's Southern Shaft;

> Between Block No. 15 and 16 we discovered a vertical joint. In the shafts such joints, which have a distinct static function, otherwise occur only proximate to the chambers.
>
> It is a complete anomaly to find a vertical joint fully isolated in the nucleus of the pyramid. Since it requires much greater effort to shape and fit the blocks in such an arrangement, we can assume that the builders must have had significant structural justification for going to the trouble of deflecting forces into the horizontal plane.
>
> This vertical joint is located about 12 meters above a point in the lower southern shaft which is subject to extraordinary static influences. The overall statics in this area seem to differ from those in the other shaft segments. For a construction engineer this is a significant clue to the possible existence of an as yet undiscovered structure in the vicinity of these static anomalies.

This, coupled with the evidence I have put forward concerning the girdle-stones in the Ascending passage, shows, I believe, that we should expect to find further chambers within the Great Pyramid, possibly even a whole set of new passages and chambers leading from my proposed vertical passage. As for the question of whether this new set of passages leads ultimately to the other side of the doors found at the end of the Queen's shafts, I am afraid that I will have to leave that question to the first person who enters the vertical passage. However, it is not beyond the realms of possibility to imagine that such a vertical passage leads ultimately to these locations, especially when we bear in mind that we cannot possibly reach them via an eight inch passage.

Thankfully, we live in an age where it is no longer necessary to destroy large parts of the Great Pyramid's internal passages in order to answer some of these questions. Had Howard Vyse stumbled upon what I have revealed here, he would have undoubtedly had his men dynamite the junction of the Ascending Passage with the Descending Passage to establish what lay beyond, simply because they were the only means available to him at the time. Today though we have developed less intrusive methods and I believe it should not be beyond modern technology to confirm whether this vertical passage is really there or not.

For my own part, I trust the message of the Trial Passages and believe that there is a very strong likelihood that this passage can be found if we only take the trouble to look. Exactly what we will find and why the builders of the Great Pyramid went to such lengths to lead us on this voyage of discovery are questions that are beyond me at this time. If the passage exists, as I think it does, then all will become clear once we follow where it leads us. I am confident that even if we do not heed the clue at this moment, in time somebody will at a later date. Maybe, as it was in Ma'mun's time, it will be another thousand years before someone takes the next step.

Mark Foster became obsessed with the mysteries of Ancient Egypt a long time ago and he has since conducted over twenty research trips to Egypt. He has contributed articles to numerous books and periodicals over the years as well as co-authoring two non-fiction books; *An A to Z of Atlantis* and *An A to Z of the Occult*. In 2011 he published his first novel, *Everywhere But No Place*.

Mark lives in London, UK, and divides his time between writing and running a graphic design agency. He can be found on the internet at: http://www.artifice-design.co.uk and http://everywherebutnoplace.com.

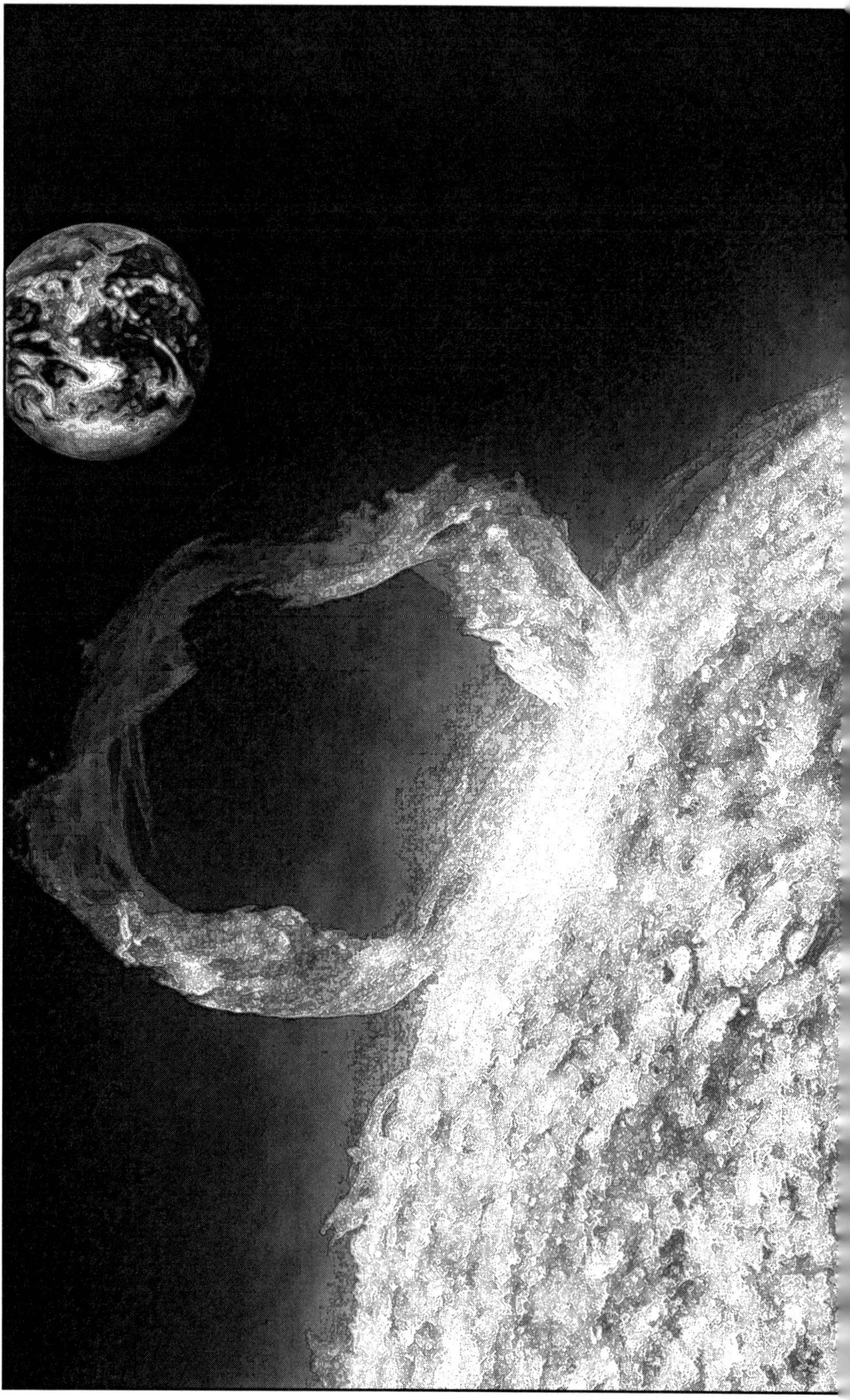

DEATH STAR

☉

The Sun gives life to our planet. Could it just as easily one day take it away?

by *Robert M. Schoch, Ph.D.*

Despite popular misconceptions, the Sun is not a stable, unchanging, eternal, ball of fire in the sky. Indeed, from an astrophysical and geological perspective, the Sun is quite the opposite. Fueled by nuclear fusion reactions, it is unstable, continually seething and churning, in disequilibrium, discharging not only visible light, but also a large energy array across the electromagnetic spectrum, and belting out charged particles as well. While the Sun may have little hiccups from time to time, it can also suffer from major bouts of coughing, spewing massive "solar storms" Earth's way. Such storms, thousands of times more massive than anything recorded in modern times, have left their marks in prehistoric records. It is inevitable that major solar storms will hit us again, and although there is no consensus as to exactly when, the evidence taken as a whole suggests that we are in for something major very soon – in fact, we may be overdue! While experts may disagree on the details, it is clear that a major solar storm will have catastrophic consequences for our modern technological society.

The Carrington Event

On Thursday, 1 September 1859, the British astronomer Richard C. Carrington was observing and sketching an unusually large and dark group of sunspots at his personal observatory at Redhill, about 32 kilometers south of central London.[1] Carrington, although technically an "amateur" (his family was in the brewery business), was an expert on the Sun and had devoted his time and resources to unraveling the mysteries of our star. Suddenly, on that fateful day, at 11:18 a.m. local time, Carrington observed intense white flashes of light coming from two locations within the sunspot group he was drawing. He was so startled by this unusual phenomenon that he wanted a witness to corroborate his observations. In his own words, he...

> ...hastily ran to call some one to witness the exhibition . . .[but he could find no one nearby], and on returning within 60 seconds, was mortified to find that it was already much changed and enfeebled.[2]

The flashes were now "vanishing as two rapidly fading dots of white light"[3] and by 11:23 they had disappeared. Carrington had observed firsthand an incredibly intense, but short-lived, solar flare. As it turns out, there was another witness to the event. Richard Hodgson was observing the Sun at the same time from his house and observatory at Highgate (about 8 kilometers north of central London), and he too saw the white flashes.[4]

At Kew Observatory about 16 kilometers east of central London self-recording magnetographs, owned by the Royal Society, were in operation monitoring Earth's magnetic field. At the very time of Carrington's observation of the solar flare a relatively small but abrupt disturbance was detected in the tracings of the magnetographs. The magnetic field seemed to return to normal, but then about seventeen and a half hours later all hell broke loose and the magnetometers went off the scale. We now understand that this is what happens when a huge coronal mass ejection (CME) – a giant bubble of ionized gas ejected by the Sun – hits Earth's magnetosphere. Given how bright the flare was, modern estimates suggest the surface temperature of the Sun at the point of emission was close to 50 million degrees Celsius. An enormous amount of energy was released, not only as visible light but also as intense X-rays and gamma rays, that traveled at the speed of light and thus hit Earth eight and a half minutes later. A CME was simultaneously discharged by the Sun, but the charged particles took considerably longer than the electromagnetic radiation to cross from the Sun to Earth.[5]

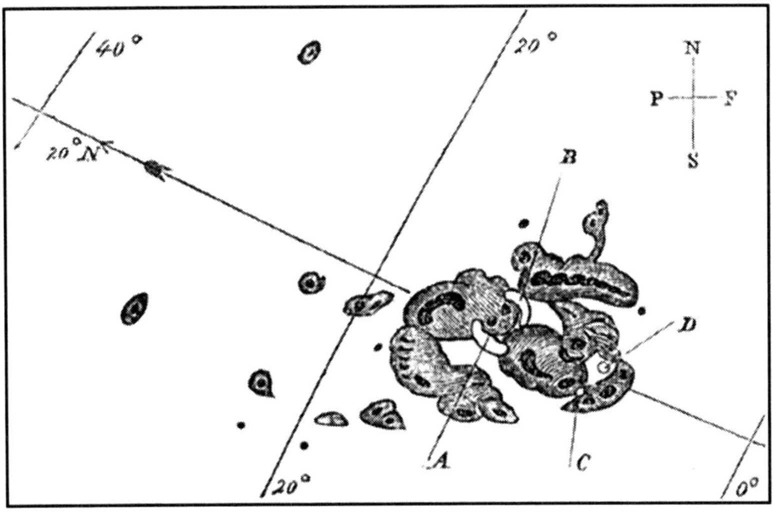

Sunspots of September 1, 1859, as sketched by Richard Carrington. A and B mark his initial flare sighting at 11:18am, which moved over the course of 5 minutes to C and D before disappearing.

Protons ejected by the Sun were accelerated by the solar flare and CME to incredibly high energies, and penetrated our atmosphere creating what is known as a solar proton event (SPE).[6] According to one estimate, this reduced the stratospheric ozone layer by five percent, and it took years to fully recover. Furthermore, energetic protons hitting the nuclei of nitrogen and oxygen atoms created a shower of neutrons that rained down onto the surface of Earth. In 1859 there was no technology to detect the solar proton event or the shower of neutrons and their associated elevated levels of radiation. Today, among other effects, we would likely see the widespread failure of computers and other electronics.

The CME was seen around the world over the next several days as incredible auroral displays in the night skies, and at unusually low latitudes. More importantly, and tellingly, the telegraph systems of the time were widely affected. The 200,000 kilometers of telegraph lines then in use suffered major disruptions and failures, becoming unusable as unwanted electric currents flowed through the wires.[7] In some cases the telegraph operators found that they could disconnect the batteries they normally used and instead send messages via the induced current. In other cases the induced currents sent "fantastical and unreadable messages".[8] There were instances where sparks flew from telegraph receiving instruments, some operators were nearly electrocuted, and several telegraph stations reportedly burned down.[9]

The 1859 geomagnetic storm (the general name given to a major disturbance in Earth's magnetic field/magnetosphere caused by factors external to Earth, such as a solar outburst), which actually consisted of two separate CMEs and associated phenomena occurring over the period from approximately 28 August through 5 September 1859, is referred to as the Carrington Event. It is not just an historical oddity, but of extreme importance to both our understanding of the dynamics of solar outbursts and our ability to predict the ramifications of future solar events. In 1859 civilization suffered little more than a bit of inconvenience and damage to the telegraph system. Such would not be the case if a Carrington-level Event occurred today!

Modern Ramifications of a Carrington Level Event

It is difficult to imagine the socioeconomic impact of a Carrington Level Event (or greater) in the twenty-first century. I believe that the clock is counting down until the next such event, and the longer the Sun retains its pent-up energy, the larger the next major solar event could be. At the same time, we as a society, with our increased reliance on ever more sophisticated and fragile electronics, are becoming ever more vulnerable to even relatively small-scale solar events. These two trends are placing us on a collision course with disaster.

To make matters worse, modern global systems have become incredibly interconnected and interdependent. This results in efficiency when everything is running smoothly, but comes at the price of extreme vulnerability relative to what would have been minor disruptions in the past. To give one example,

> Barry Lynn of the New America Foundation has been studying industrial supply shocks since 1999, when he noticed that global computer chip production was concentrated in Taiwan. After a severe earthquake in that country, the global computer industry nearly shut down, crashing the stocks of large computer makers. This level of concentration of the production of key components in a globalized economy is a new phenomenon. Lynn's work points to the highly dangerous side of globalization, the flip side of a hyper-efficient global supply chain. When one link in that chain is broken, there is no fallback.[10]

Applying this to a solar outburst, such as a Carrington Level Event or greater, imagine if during the catastrophe the only factory producing a particular critical part, vaccine, or medicine was put offline.

In 2009 the staid British journal *New Scientist* published an article with the provocative title "Space storm alert: 90 seconds from catastrophe", which opens with the following lines:

> It is midnight on 22 September 2012 and the skies above Manhattan are filled with a flickering curtain of colourful light. Few New Yorkers have seen the aurora this far south but their fascination is short-lived. Within a few seconds, electric bulbs dim and flicker, then become unusually bright for a fleeting moment. Then all the lights in the state go out. Within 90 seconds, the entire eastern half of the US is without power.
>
> A year later and millions of Americans are dead and the nation's infrastructure lies in tatters. The World Bank declares America a developing nation. Europe, Scandinavia, China and Japan are also struggling to recover from the same fateful event – a violent storm, 150 million kilometres away on the surface of the sun.
>
> It sounds ridiculous. Surely the sun couldn't create so profound a disaster on Earth. Yet an extraordinary report funded by NASA and issued by the US National Academy of Sciences (NAS)... claims it could do just that.[11]

In fact, this scenario is not so ridiculous at all, as the *New Scientist* article goes on to relate.[12] Indeed, if things do not change, it may well be inevitable.

Our modern technological society is, without exaggeration, totally dependent on a constant supply of electricity. An immediate worry concerning a major solar outburst is the vulnerability of modern electricity grid systems – the wires that crisscross nations, and indeed the entire world. The high-voltage systems will essentially act as huge antennae picking up and channeling direct current (DC) as a result of a solar outburst. The power transmission lines are designed to carry alternating (AC) currents, and although the geomagnetically induced current may be relatively weak compared to the currents that normally flow through the transmission lines, since the geomagnetic current is a DC current it can saturate the transformers and system.[13] Among other effects, the all-important transformers along grid lines could heat up and melt, causing massive blackouts. This famously happened in Quebec Province (Canada) when on 13 March 1989 a solar storm disrupted Hydro-Quebec transmission lines and in less than two minutes a blackout occurred affecting six million people for nine to twelve hours.[14] In this particular case a billion-ton cloud of gas and plasma was released from the Sun with the energy of thousands of nuclear bombs exploding simultaneously and headed toward Earth at a speed of approximately 1.6 million kilometers an hour.[15]

Besides the Quebec blackout, the solar flare accompanying the March 1989 solar storm (which was nowhere near the size of the Carrington Event) caused short-wave radio signals to be disrupted, including the jamming of Radio Free Europe that was being broadcast into Russia – initially the Kremlin was suspected as the culprit. Such geomagnetic storms can affect the entire globe, especially the stronger storms (at the level of the Carrington Event and greater), but the immediate risk is most severe at higher latitudes due to the fact that the incoming electric currents are funneled or sucked into Earth's poles. Thus northern latitude Quebec was hard hit by the March 1989 solar storm, and during the solar storms that occurred around Halloween in 2003 there were blackouts in the city of Malmö, Sweden, and transformers failed in South Africa.[16] But, returning to the March 1989 storm, not only Quebec was affected. Spectacular aurora were seen as far south as Florida and Cuba, indicative of the strength of the storm. In the United States no blackouts occurred, but this was perhaps simply a matter of good fortune. Over 200 power grid problems were reported across the U.S. within minutes of the solar storm hitting.[17] And there were still more direct consequences, as reported by astronomer Sten Odenwald:

> In space, some satellites actually tumbled out of control for several hours. NASA's TDRS-1 communication satellite recorded over 250 anomalies as high-energy particles invaded the satellite's sensitive electronics. Even the Space Shuttle Discovery was having its own mysterious problems. A sensor on one of the tanks supplying hydrogen to a fuel cell was showing unusually high pressure readings on March 13. The problem went away just as mysteriously after the solar storm subsided.[18]

A May 1921 geomagnetic storm, caused by a solar outburst, was intermediate in size between the 1859 Carrington Event and the March 1989 solar storm that affected Quebec. In 1921 electrical grid systems and associated technology were neither as extensive nor as susceptible to geomagnetically induced currents as our systems are today. According to recent studies, a 1921 level solar storm could cause 300 to 350 or more large extra high voltage (EHV) transformers to fail or be permanently damaged in the United States, resulting in major electrical grid collapses with resulting blackouts for 130 million people, and the blackouts could last for years.[19] Likewise, transformers would fail around the world. Large transformers, once damaged by overheating, burning, and melting, cannot be repaired but must be replaced. There are few crews trained to replace the transformers, and few spares of these large and expensive transformers on hand. Once the supply of spare transformers has been exhausted, new transformers will have to be manufactured. Even in normal times it can take a year or more to have a large transformer built and delivered. How will it even be possible to build transformers in areas without electricity to power manufacturing facilities?

The scenario described in the last paragraph is based on the May 1921 geomagnetic storm. A Carrington Level Event would be much worse. Plus, in either case, not only the United States would be hit, but nations around the world. Globally electrical grids would be damaged, with attendant blackouts. And it would be the most developed, technologically sophisticated, modern, industrialized countries that would be most affected. Less developed countries and regions, less dependent on modern infrastructure, would experience fewer disruptions, but given the interconnectedness of the global economy, surely they would ultimately feel the impacts too. Loss of electric power for any length of time, say more than a day or two, is not a minor nuisance in the developed world. Our entire modern societies run on, and are dependent on, a ready and reliable supply of electricity. Without electricity, such necessities as water and sewage treatment would be affected, and in short order water would stop flowing in our public water systems. Those living in high-rise apartment buildings, where water has to be pumped to reach their floors, would lose water straightaway. All electrical appliances would

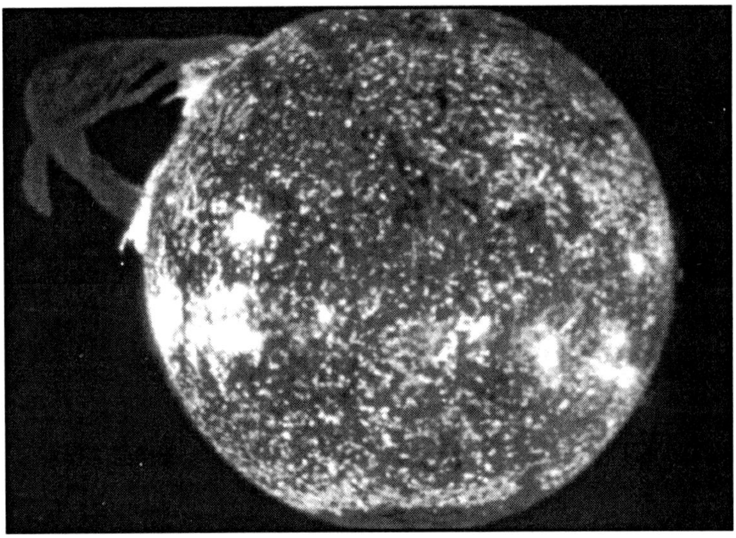

Enormous Coronal Mass Ejection (CME) in 1973

stop working, from computers, lights (imagine the dark nights!), refrigerators, microwaves, televisions, and just about everything else associated with our electronically based society. Battery-powered devices would last only as long as the batteries hold, and then what?

Office buildings, apartment complexes, factories, government buildings, certain small communities, and so forth have backup generators in place, but such generators will last only as long as there is fuel to power them. Depending on what measures may be in place, within days or weeks the fuel will run out. Even if more fuel is theoretically available, without electricity there may be no way to deliver it. Pumps at service (gas) stations will not work without electricity; transportation by petroleum-powered vehicles will come to a halt. Furthermore, without electricity traffic lights (so essential to keeping order in large modern cities) will stop functioning. Much public transportation in some cities, such as trolleys, subways and electric bus lines is directly dependent on electricity that will no longer be available. Underground tracks, such as for subways, may become flooded from penetrating rain and groundwater without electric pumps to keep them dry.

Buildings will lack air-conditioning, which is directly dependent on electricity. In hot areas, people will die from heat stroke, especially after the drinkable water runs out. In cold regions buildings and people may freeze. Some heating systems use electricity directly. Others, which use oil or natural gas as the fuel, still depend on electricity to pump the fuel, to circulate water or air through the building, to ignite the fuel in the furnace, and to regulate the temperature through electric thermostats. No electricity, no heat!

Without refrigeration, many foodstuffs will quickly go bad. Even as peoples' food spoils, fresh supplies will be unavailable. With most or all transportation shut down, any food in supermarkets, or food stockpiled elsewhere, will quickly run out and not be replenished. The same holds true for other items, from toilet paper to prescription drugs, which many people simply take for granted. Likewise medical supplies that need to be kept under controlled temperature conditions may be ruined, and as supplies are exhausted no more will be available. Indeed, any hospital, once the fuel supply for its emergency backup generators is exhausted, will be in very bad shape.

Ultimately, due to the devastation caused by a Carrington Level Event (or greater) hundreds of millions of lives could be lost.

Ironically, many of the very things that make our modern society so "efficient", such as lack of redundancy (why keep old-fashioned bulky paper copies of records when they can be stored electronically?), not wasting space warehousing materials and supplies locally, and the concept of just-in-time delivery that is so dependent on steady and reliable transportation networks, make us especially vulnerable and even helpless in the face of massive grid failures and blackouts.

Beyond disruption of electricity grid systems, electronic communication and satellite systems could be significantly disrupted. With a major solar outburst, satellites could literally leave their designated orbits as the density of the atmosphere they travel through changes, causing them to change speed. High-frequency (HF) radio communications, such as those routinely used by aircraft, and HF navigation signals from Global Positioning System (GPS) satellites, will be scrambled and disrupted. A major breakdown in communication systems could lead to literal anarchy. Even a government is dependent on reliable communications to govern and control the distribution of services and goods, and maintain law and order.

A very specific and serious worry involves the roughly 440 nuclear power plants worldwide. As was demonstrated by the March 2011 Fukushima Daiichi nuclear power plant disaster, when electricity is lost and cooling pumps can no longer keep the reactor cool, the reactor can overheat, potentially meltdown (or explode), and radioactive materials will be released to the environment. In the face of a major solar outburst, we could have hundreds of Chernobyl type situations around the planet simultaneously, and with massive blackouts to boot, no foreseeable way to even attempt to realistically deal with the situation. It is difficult enough to attempt to address a Chernobyl or Fukushima level nuclear disaster in isolation!

One of the major results of a Carrington Level Event could be the collapse of electronic based financial and monetary systems. In the twenty-first century more and more of our financial transactions are carried out in terms of electronic money; that is in terms of simply numbers in computers. There is for the vast majority of "money" in modern industrialized countries actually nothing beyond the electronic accounting system. The money has no physical backing – certainly not gold or other valuables, and not even paper bills or token coins. Quantitative finance expert Espen Haug points out that in 1991 the United States Federal Reserve determined that 69% of all United States dollars were in purely electronic form.[20] Over two decades later this number has surely increased; Haug estimates that 90% of the U.S. money supply currently is purely electronic, and a similar situation occurs for many other countries.

In the case of a major solar outburst, one that would overload power grids, burning out transformers, causing widespread blackouts, disrupting communication systems, and damaging and destroying computers and all sorts of electronic systems, the basis for the global monetary system, as well as national monetary systems, could be destroyed. Not only would transactions be "temporarily" impossible (where temporarily could encompass not just days or weeks, but months or years), but also in many cases electronic financial records could be severely compromised or completely destroyed, such that it would be impossible to reconstruct the system as it was prior to the impact. The only saving grace might be if financial institutions and companies had their records securely backed up in safe havens well protected from the solar onslaught. Possibly the best bet would be storage in self-contained (certainly not connected to an external power grid) secure caves and tunnels deep inside mountains with tens of meters of solid rock to provide shielding from radiation.

Frying the Earth at the End of the Last Ice Age

Historically the Carrington Event is the largest such event in the last 450 years (based on nitrate concentrations in ice cores going back to 1561).[21] However, much larger solar outbursts have occurred in the past. A record of solar activity has been reconstructed using fluctuations of isotopes 14C and 10Be recorded dendrochronologically (in tree rings) and in polar ice cores respectively. This has been done with considerable accuracy back to circa 9500 BCE (essentially the end of the last ice age), and the results are rather startling – our Sun has been more active over the last few decades (since about the middle of the twentieth century) than it has been for thousands of years.[22] Depending on how the data is interpreted (the translation of the isotope data to solar activity is not straight-forward, but requires various forms of analyses), the overall level of solar activity is the highest it has been since about 9500 to 9000 BCE, the end of the last ice age!

Paul LaViolette has marshaled evidence that a major solar flare accompanied by a super solar proton event (or events) at the end of the last ice age[23] fried the Earth (to use the description of LaViolette's hypothesis put forth in the popular *Space Daily*[24]).

LaViolette bases his conclusions on meticulous analyses of radiocarbon concentrations in sediment cores from the Cariaco Basin (off the coast of Venezuela) correlated with acidity spikes, high NO_3^- concentrations, and rises in 10Be deposition rates in the Greenland ice record, all of which he argues are indicators of a sudden cosmic ray influx, in turn correlating with solar activity as expressed specifically through solar flares and SPEs. Additionally, there would also have been accompanying coronal mass ejections (CMEs) on an enormous scale. LaViolette dates the SPE event, which is the major focus of his 2011 paper, to "12,837 +/- 10 cal [calendar] years BP"[25] and equates it with major faunal extinctions in North America at this time. LaViolette also notes that there may have been other SPE events at the end of the last ice age, stating,

> This suggests that an overly active Sun may have played a significant role also in causing abrupt climatic change at the end of the ice age.[26]

In his paper LaViolette discusses some of the effects of a massive SPE and attendant solar activity for the Earth. The ozone layer, our protection from deadly UV rays, would have been greatly depleted with major ozone holes forming in some areas, that is if the ozone layer was not altogether destroyed completely! Increased doses of damaging, and potentially lethal, UV radiation could have posed a major hazard for organisms on Earth, especially in high and middle latitudes. Besides the increased UV radiation, high-energy cosmic rays that are part of a major SPE would penetrate the atmosphere and raise radiation levels on the ground.

According to LaViolette's calculations, unprotected organisms at sea level during the major SPE event he studied could have accumulated radiation doses of three to six Sieverts (a unit of radiation exposure) over a period of two or three days. Lethal radiation doses for humans are in the range of about 3.5 Sieverts, and for many large mammals in the 3 to 8 Sievert range. The best mode of protection at the time, both from the UV radiation and the cosmic ray radiation, may have been to seek safety in caves and other underground shelters.[27] Interestingly, Austrian archaeologist and speleologist Dr. Heinrich Kusch and his wife Ingrid Kusch have documented hundreds upon hundreds of tunnel systems under Neolitihic settlements found throughout Europe and Turkey, some dating back to around 12,000 years ago.[28]

LaViolette also determined that an enormous SPE would significantly disturb the geomagnetic field of Earth and induce a partial (or possibly complete, at least for a short period of time?) collapse of the magnetosphere. Earth is surrounded by a dust cloud, composed of interplanetary debris plus particles that the solar wind blows off of the surface of the Moon. These particles are trapped in the magnetosphere, held and essentially protected there. But with a partial or complete collapse of the magnetosphere, cosmic rays, SPEs, and CMEs could heat the particles up, causing them to melt, and subsequently they would re-solidify, forming spherules. Furthermore, dust particles and spherules could be jettisoned into the atmosphere, and eventually fall to the surface of Earth – as has been found at numerous sites dating back to the end of the last ice age.

I believe that LaViolette puts together a very powerful and compelling argument that our Sun was much more active, by orders of magnitude, at the end of the last ice age. The core of LaViolette's meticulous work is that our Sun is not stable, but goes through periods of major instability and increased activity (whatever the cause of such instability and increased activity may be), and the last major (there have been ups and downs since then) occurrence of such increased solar activity was at the end of the last ice age – that is, unless we are willing to acknowledge that the Sun is ramping up right now and again going into a period of instability and increased activity after a lull of thousands of years.

Will it happen again, and soon?

A truism of geology is that if something has happened in the past, it can happen again in the future – and all the indications are that a major solar outburst will occur sooner rather than later! Writing in the prestigious journal *Nature*, S. K. Solanki and colleagues state,

> According to our reconstruction, the level of solar activity during the past 70 years is exceptional, and the previous period of equally high activity occurred more than 8,000 years ago.[29]

James A. Marusek, a physicist and engineer who until his retirement worked for the U.S. Department of the Navy, argues that the Sun is currently undergoing a state change.[30] That is, the inherently unstable Sun is readjusting and re-equilibrating, as it must do periodically through geological time. We may already have had a precursor of what is to come in the very near future, namely the solar storms of 1859.

During the summer of 2011, there were reports[31] that the Sun is showing signs of going into a period of low activity when just the opposite had been expected. It is not clear if this is really the case, but even if it is, it does not preclude the possibility there could be some very unusual activity of the Sun on the other extreme – that is during a period of relative dormancy or hibernation there could be an incredible solar outburst. At the end of the ice age some 12,000 years ago there were wild fluctuations in sunspot activity, wide swings between highs and lows, and it seems that during periods of low sunspot activity the energy builds up and erupts as massive solar outbursts rather than being given off as more numerous and smaller flares and CMEs. The 1859 Carrington Event occurred during an overall "quiet" period. As plasma physicist Paul Kintner (Cornell University) has stated,

> The Carrington event happened during a mediocre, ho-hum solar cycle... It came out of nowhere, so we just don't know when something like that is going to happen again.[32]

Being a geologist, I like the analogy of a major active tectonic/earthquake zone where stress is building up – the stress and energy can be relieved either by many small earthquakes in succession over time,[33] or the stress and energy can build up and continue to build up until it is finally released as one or a few major earthquakes (and the accompanying foreshocks and aftershocks). A short-term lull in sunspot activity says to me that energy is building up in the Sun and it will be released, probably sooner rather than later, in one or a few massive outbursts. My conclusion is that we better be prepared!

It seems that some governments are taking the threat of a major solar outburst seriously. During the summer of 2011 there were reports that the British government...

> ...has been warned that a massive surge of energy from the sun could hit the Earth in the next 18 months. In a worst-case scenario, it could blow out the national grid and leave parts of the country without electricity for months.[34]

Therefore, according to the same article, the British government is making plans to deal with such a scenario, including invoking emergency powers to shut down the electricity grid (purposefully causing massive, though hopefully temporary, blackouts) in an attempt to protect the infrastructure from the worst effects. On the other hand, it was reported that in Australia (which is at lower latitudes than Britain, and arguably therefore less vulnerable to some types of solar outbursts) "electricity experts are not convinced the solar flare will have anywhere near the catastrophic effects predicted in Britain and think any electromagnetic surge will go largely unnoticed".[35] One wonders, however, if the attitude expressed by the Australian officials – and the same holds true for government leaders and spokespeople elsewhere around the world – is actually a cover so as to avoid concern and potential panic among an ignorant public, even as those in the know secretly make plans to protect themselves and their institutions.

Robert M. Schoch received a Ph.D. in Geology and Geophysics from Yale University, and since 1984 has been a full-time faculty member at the College of General Studies of Boston University. His books include the trilogy with R. A. McNally: *Voices of the Rocks, Voyages of the Pyramid Builders,* and *Pyramid Quest.* His most recent book is *The Parapsychology Revolution: A Concise Anthology of Paranormal and Psychical Research* (Compilation and Commentary by Robert M. Schoch and Logan Yonavjak, Tarcher/Penguin, 2008). Dr. Schoch's personal website is located at: www.robertschoch.com.

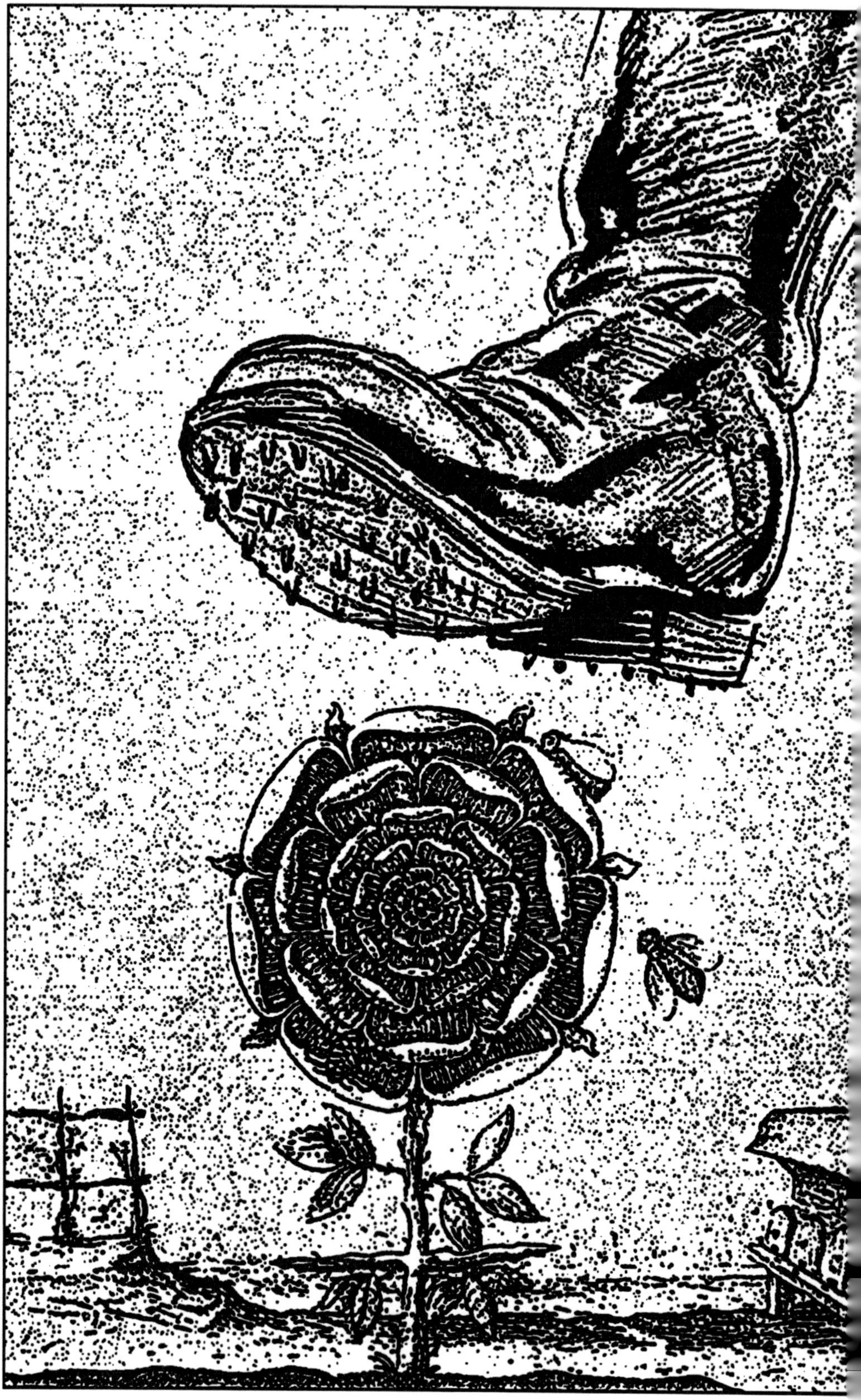

When Science Lost its Soul

The Real Story of the Birth of The Royal Society

by *Lynn Picknett and Clive Prince*

Many thousands of words have been written about the undeniable connection between Freemasonry and the foundation of the Royal Society in the 1660s, usually invoking the mysterious 'Invisible College' mentioned by one of its founders, Robert Boyle, some fifteen years earlier (see for example Robert Lomas' *The Invisible College: The Royal Society, Freemasonry and the Birth of Modern Science*, 2002). However, after researching our latest book *The Forbidden Universe*, we have come to the conclusion that the famous Invisible College was heavily involved with a different stream of the esoteric entirely – Rosicrucianism or Hermeticism. In fact it seems that the formative years of the Royal Society suffered from a conflict between this and the Masonic faction – and that even James Bond wouldn't have been ashamed of the secret reason behind the Society's creation...

As Lomas acknowledges, Boyle declined the presidency because his religious scruples prevented him from taking oaths – and oaths are the lifeblood of Masonic practice.[1] So since Boyle still considered himself a member of the Invisible College, it could hardly have been Masonic, or at least not exclusively so.

John Gribbin pointed out in his history of the Royal Society, *The Fellowship* (2005), that the institution emerged from the coming together in post-Restoration London of two groups of leisured gentlemen with an interest in natural philosophy (as science was then known), neatly representing both sides of the royalist-parliamentarian divide. The royalists had returned from exile with Charles II at the Restoration in May 1660, while the other was a 'philosophical club' formed by clergyman and scholar John Wilkins in the late 1640s that had continued to meet in London and Oxford throughout Cromwell's republican rule. But more fascinating to *Darklore* readers will be the fact that these cabals also represented Masonic and Rosicrucian esotericism.

The two factions found themselves in the same audience of a series of lectures at Gresham College in London in the summer of 1660. On 28 November 1660 a group of twelve natural philosophers led by Viscount Brouncker, and including Wilkins, Boyle and luminaries such as Christopher Wren, met to form a society to promote the new 'experimental philosophy'. A year and half later it was granted a royal charter by Charles II, and the Royal Society of London for the Improving of Natural Knowledge came into being, with Brouncker as its first president.

The evocative term 'Invisible College' appears in several letters written in the mid-1640s by the young Robert Boyle (1627-91) to other scholars. The intellectually gifted son of the Earl of Cork, he was to enjoy a glittering career and the accolade of being the father of modern chemistry – besides, of course, being a founder member of the Royal Society.

'The Midwife and Nurse' of the College

The identity of the other members of the 'College' is still debated. Was it just a collective term for like-minded intellectuals, or a code for another organisation or society, perhaps Masonic? Boyle's letters are pretty clear about what he, at least, meant by the College, especially his correspondence with one Samuel Hartlib (1600-62), a prodigious intellectual star, now sadly largely unknown.[2] A polymath with a wide range of interests in all the arts and sciences as well as social and political matters, Hartlib was born in Germany, of Polish parents. In 1628 he had fled to England from the Thirty Years War between the Catholic and Protestant nations that was ravaging Europe. But like all natural philosophers of the time, he was also deeply immersed in the esoteric, being a Hermeticist and an enthusiast of the works of Paracelsus and John Dee. And as is often the way, this occultist was also an 'intelligencer', the man behind a Europe-wide network to exchange information on a huge variety of topics.

Robert Boyle

Boyle clearly thought Hartlib was the power at the hub of the Invisible College, writing to him on 8 May 1647: "you interest yourself so much in the Invisible College, and that whole society is so concerned in all the accidents of your life." In another letter (undated but from internal references, April 1647) Boyle even calls Hartlib the "midwife and nurse" of the college – essentially its creator and continuing guardian. It is a fair assumption that at least a cabal within his scholarly network was itself the Invisible College. The term, however, also reveals the mystical stream that motivated Hartlib and which flowed under seventeenth-century philosophy...

'Europe Is With Child'

The Rosicrucian story famously began with the publication in Germany, in 1614 and 1615, of two tracts – generally known as the 'Rosicrucian manifestos' – announcing the existence of a secret brotherhood that possessed great esoteric secrets. It described itself as the Fraternity of the Rose Cross, dedicated to a passionately transcendental and personal relationship with Christ that by its very nature challenged the authority of the Roman Church. Declaring that "Europe is with child", the manifestos called for, indeed anticipated, a radical reform of all levels of society based on spiritual and metaphysical principles. As a means to further this agenda, various institutions would be set up to study all the arts and sciences and share scientific, medical, occult and philosophical knowledge.

The manifestos ran through the souls of Europe's intelligentsia like hot metal through butter: it is difficult for us today to appreciate just how radical and exciting they were, and how they would literally entrance with their promise of a golden future for the heart and soul of every man and woman. Although the precise intended symbolism of the Rose + Cross has been hotly debated for centuries, it is not difficult to see that the image of Christ's suffering is presented as equal to the potent, more feminine symbol of love and redemption. Unsurprisingly, the uncompromisingly pro-Protestant manifestos also caused the Catholic Church great anxiety. (For a start, the Vatican had always stressed the importance of pain in every life, not the balancing with mystical love.)

There was another reason that the manifestos so threatened the Catholic Church. The Rosicrucian movement also aimed at a root-and-branch reform of European society based on the principles of Hermeticism, the occult philosophy encapsulated in ancient texts attributed to the legendary Egyptian sage Hermes Trismegistus ('Thrice-great Hermes'). We argue that these books derived from the theology of the great city of Heliopolis; they had provided the inspiration for the pyramid builders whose works are still indisputably wonders of the world.

(As we point out in our book, the Hermetic texts were a strange blend of practical, scientific wisdom and intensely occult (meaning esoteric, not satanic) philosophy and practice, and were the single inspiration behind *every* big name of the Scientific Revolution, from Copernicus to Isaac Newton. What really distinguished them, even at first sight, from the prevailing Catholic ethos was that the Hermetic works insisted that human beings, rather than being sinful worms, are magnificent potential gods to whom nothing is impossible. The attraction to great minds of the day is obvious, what is less so is the legacy of the Hermetic tradition: put bluntly in a phrase, the modern science of the west.)

The linking of a strand of Christianity and ancient Egyptian belief was then by no means as weird as it might seem today – as we explain at length in our book. Rosicrucianism must have seemed to the Vatican like some two-headed monster from the Book of Revelation.

The manifestos generated a controversy that has continued ever since. Were they really the work of a highly-organised secret society, or was the whole thing some kind of hoax? Perhaps, despite what conspiracy theorists would have us believe, and as is often the way, the truth lies somewhere in between. Although the situation is notoriously difficult to unravel, the manifestos were indisputably the work of a group centred on the theologian and playwright Johann Valentin Andreae (1586-1654).

The attempt at Hermetic reform is usually linked with Italian movers and shakers such as the great Giordano Bruno (1548-1600) and his successor Tommaso Campanella (1568-1639), both Dominican monks turned heretics. However, not only had Bruno spent time in Germany in the 1580s – where he organised a secret society, the Giordanisti, which some historians believe was the direct antecedent of the Rosicrucians – but Andreae's circle was also in direct contact with Campanella. (See our *The Forbidden Universe* for more details.)

"The Invisible College of the Rosy Cross Fraternity", by Theophilus Schweighardt

Historians such as Dame Frances Yates, in her *The Rosicrucian Enlightenment* (1972), have shown that the manifestos were essentially flag-waving for a much wider campaign for radical change in both European politics and religion. Hopes focussed on the golden couple of Frederick V, Elector (hereditary ruler) of the Palatinate of the Rhine and Elizabeth Stuart, daughter of James I of England, who were married in 1613, the year before the first of the manifestos appeared. Especially when Frederick became King of Bohemia in 1619, Protestants believed they would lead an alliance of like-minded nations to victory over Catholicism, uniting Europe and ushering in the new age of Hermetic reform. But this was not to be: events swung in the opposite direction. In 1620 a Catholic alliance invaded Bohemia and drove Frederick and Elizabeth into exile. This raised the curtain on the Thirty Years War that ripped Europe apart for a generation – and the overt manifestation of Hermetic reform was rapidly sidelined, one of the sad historical ideas that might have been.

However, if its political ambitions were thwarted, the Rosicrucian-Hermetic ideal continued to exert a strong influence over what was then a smooth blend of the esoteric, scientific and philosophical worlds. They were particularly keen to establish centres of learning to nurture not just intellectual but also spiritual, ethical and political ideas based on the Hermetic principles. And this is where Hartlib – a former protégé of Elizabeth of Bohemia – becomes a major player.

Not So 'Invisible'

Inspired by the Rosicrucian ideal and Andreae's writings, Hartlib desperately sought to establish a 'pansophic college' to promote all forms of knowledge, which he called 'Antilia' or 'Macaria'. He wrote to his close friend John Worthington, Master of Jesus College, Cambridge:

> The word Antilia I used because of a former society, that was really begun almost to the same purpose a little before the Bohemian wars. It was as it were a tessera of that society, used only by the members thereof. I never desired the interpretation of it. It was interrupted and destroyed by the following Bohemian and German wars.

Obviously this refers to the Rosicrucian movement – or perhaps more accurately to Andreae's inner group – which was indeed interrupted by the conflicts that segued into the prolonged agony of the Thirty Years War. Andreae and Hartlib seemed to take 'Antilia' to designate an inner elite that directs events from behind the scenes. Indeed, that was what Andreae called the prime movers in his utopian work *Christianopolis* (1619), detailing his vision of an ideal society based on Rosicrucian principles.

This is also implied by Hartlib's use of the term 'tessera' – part of a larger mosaic, or alternatively, a token or voucher implying that 'Antilia' was a kind of code- or pass-word. And, of course, this implies Hartlib was himself a member. As for the origins of 'Antilia' itself, since it derives from a legend about Spanish Christians fleeing the eighth-century Moorish invasion of Spain to an island of that name in the Atlantic, it obviously represents the secret survival of a religion in the face of attempted suppression.

There is no doubt that Hartlib's Antilia and Boyle's Invisible College were simply new terms for the Rosy Cross. After all, the first of the manifestos referred to the Rosy Cross as an 'invisible society' – and in the 1620s its Jesuit opponents, especially in France, derisively called the brotherhood 'the invisible ones'.

However, Hartlib's plans came to naught as, like many scholars who had flourished during the English Commonwealth, he lost favour at the Restoration of the monarchy. He wrote disconsolately to Worthington in October 1660 that "We were wont to call the desirable Society by the name of Antilia, and sometimes by the name of Macaria, but name & thing is as good as vanished."[3]

But a month later a chance of reviving the project presented itself when what was to become the Royal Society had its first meeting, attended by Hartlib's protégé Boyle. Just three weeks later Hartlib wrote excitedly to Worthington:

> Thus much is certain, that there is a meeting every week of the prime virtuosi, not only at Gresham College, in term time, but also out of it, at Mr Ball's chambers in the Temple. They desired that his Maj leave that they might thus meet or assemble ymselves at all times, wch is certainly granted. Mr Boyle, Dr Wilkins, Sr Paul Neale, Viscount Brouncker are some of the members.

It is also clear that some of those involved hoped to use the new society as the springboard to the fulfilment of Hartlib's dream. He told Worthington:

> ...I have recd some other papers, that have been confided to me, holding forth almost the same things as the other Antilia (for be not offended if I continue to use this mystical word) but, as I hope, to better purpose.

These papers about the 'mystical word', he explains, had been sent to him by Baron Skytte, in London as an emissary of the King of Sweden to promote a Protestant Alliance. Skytte, who was passionate about the new learning, was another eager attendee of the Gresham College lectures. Clearly part of Hartlib's network, it appears it was Skytte's idea to petition Charles II for the group's royal recognition, as the groundwork for the pansophic college. Hartlib told Worthington that the papers sent to him by Skytte included:

> ...the propositions which were made to his Majesty by the Lord Skytte, and... a draught for the royal grant or patent wch is desired for the establishment of this foundation.

Although, unsurprisingly, Skytte's plan was supported by Boyle, other members of the group opposed it and once again poor Hartlib's hopes were dashed. By April 1661 he was writing to Worthington that "There becomes nothing of Lord Skytte's business, & I believe the other virtuosi will not have it that it should go forward."

Tragically, Hartlib never lived to see his great project 'go forward'. He died in March the following year and Skytte returned to Sweden.

The Society Takes Shape

The early years of the Royal Society were characterised by a struggle between the 'Antilian' faction who wanted it to further Hartlib's Rosicrucian dream and those who took a less idealistic, more practical approach to 'experimental natural philosophy'. Eventually the society rejected the esoteric aspects to concentrate on the experimental angle, laying the foundations for modern science. Very quickly, the Antilians were eclipsed.

This basic struggle was epitomised in the story of the man who had started it all. This was the clergyman John Wilkins (1614-71), warden of Wadham College, Oxford – and later Bishop of Chester – in whose rooms in 1648 the Society began in informal meetings of his 'philosophical club'.

A great polymath, Wilkins was both the inventor of the metric system and a pioneering science fiction writer, whose *The Discovery of a World in the Moone* was published in 1638. He was also firmly a devotee of the Rosicrucian movement (not nearly as strange for an Anglican cleric then as it appears now). His books – especially his masterpiece *Mathematicall Magick* (1648) – actually cited the manifestos and the works of esotericists such as Cornelius Agrippa, John Dee and Robert Fludd.

Before being appointed Wadham's Warden he had been chaplain to Charles Louis, the Elector Palatine – son of the erstwhile golden

Portrait of John Wilkins, by Mary Beale.

couple Frederick and Elizabeth – embodying another strong connection with the Rosicrucian reform movement. (Charles Louis, perhaps oddly given that he was Charles I's nephew, had been invited by Parliament to live in London during the Civil War.)

During the Commonwealth, in an astute move that did his career no harm at the time, the 42-year-old Wilkins married Oliver Cromwell's 63-year-old widowed sister. However, his contrived assimilation into that particular family was not destined to endear him to the powers that be when the monarchy was restored.

As the driving force behind the Commonwealth faction that joined the royalists at Gresham College to create the Royal Society, Wilkins naturally took the major role of secretary. However, within a short time he had been sidelined, his place taken by another fellow, Henry Oldenburg – at first joint secretary (responsible for the overseas membership) but then replacing the hapless Wilkins entirely.

Although the sidelining of Wilkins and others may simply have been due to political expediency – the King's supporters having the upper hand over those who had been happy to work under Cromwell (and even marry his sisters) – there is also a sense of the society consciously, and even brutally, purging itself of the hardcore Rosicrucian element.

That was certainly how John Worthington, Hartlib's confidant in the 'Antilia' project, saw it. In 1668 he lamented that the Society was "materialistic and for nothing but what gratifies externall sense." He was concerned that it had rejected the philosophical and metaphysical elements that could have made it even greater.

Worthington's comments were a reaction to the publication a few months earlier of the Royal Society's first official history, written by the clergyman Thomas Sprat – later Charles II's chaplain – in which he allegedly detailed the society's origins. More cynically, it was the version the Society intended posterity to believe: that it had always been exclusively about the promotion of the experimental scientific method. The underlying Rosicrucian ambition was simply airbrushed out. There is nothing, for example, about Baron Skytte's role in obtaining the royal charter – the credit is given entirely to another founder member, Sir Robert Moray. In fact, Skytte's initiative was unknown until the relevant papers came to light in the 1960s.

Enter the Usual Suspects

Just four months after Hartlib's death – on 15 July 1662 – Charles II finally signed the longed-for royal charter. However, the prime mover was not Skytte, Boyle or any of Hartlib's followers, but a man who represents the other esoteric stream in the founding of the Royal Society: the Freemasons. This was the enigmatic and colourful Scot, Sir Robert Moray, who, at the second meeting of the society in December 1660, proudly reported he had discussed it with the King – who heartily approved of its aims – thus kick-starting the process that led to its official royal patronage. It is generally assumed that being so close to the king, Moray was simply in the right place to elicit his support. But there is another possible reason...

It took a long time for the Royal Society to become the hallowed and internationally respected institution it is today. At the start it was merely a gentleman's club with the vaguest of criteria for membership, and for the first few decades boasted only around 100 fellows. Its rise in prestige and prominence was largely due to the reflected glory of the quarter-century presidency of Sir Isaac Newton, from 1703 to 1727. In the years afterwards the Society tightened up its rules of membership (being a fellow began to bestow real status) and – some eighty years after its foundation – took on the role of scientific adviser to the government that continues to this day.

Quite why the society in its original form should have been so keen to boast royal patronage, and why Charles II should have bestowed it remains something of a puzzle. After all, what was in it for him? The pervasive feeling that something must be missing

Frontispiece of Sprat's *The History of the Royal Society*, with dedication to Charles II prominent

has prompted Robert Lomas to propose that Moray sold the idea to Charles by hyping the potential usefulness of the scientific and technical expertise within the Society. In particular it could be harnessed to rebuild the Royal Navy, an urgent requirement that was beyond Charles' budget. In fact, Lomas suggests that endorsing the Society was a canny way of getting the work done on the cheap. However, we can suggest another reason, especially when Moray's previous career is taken into account.

Robert Moray (1619-74) is one of the most fascinating and enigmatic figures of the period, whose turbulent life among the highest in several lands begs the question of why he was thought of so highly. His precise origins are obscure, but he first appears in the historical spotlight in 1633 as a member of the Scots Guard of Louis XIII of France, when he was also a spy for Cardinal Richelieu, the king's chief minister. He then became the quartermaster of the Covenanter's Army raised in Scotland in 1638 – to combat England's control of the Church in Scotland – which marched on England two years later. The Covenanters occupied Newcastle for a time, and it was there, on 20 May 1641, that Moray's initiation into a Masonic lodge became famously the first ever recorded on English soil.

A year later Moray was back at the French court, from where, in December 1642, he was official messenger to England, taking the news of Richelieu's death to Charles I, who knighted him. However, Moray found himself out of favour with Richelieu's successor Cardinal Mazarin, so he rejoined the Scots Guard. Taken prisoner in Bavaria in 1643, Mazarin ransomed him as part of a deal in which, according to some historians, Moray agreed to use his contacts in Scottish Freemasonry for purposes of espionage.

Mazarin sent Moray to England, where with his suspiciously charmed life, he became Charles I's secretary. After the king's execution Moray returned to Scotland, where he took part in an unsuccessful uprising against Cromwell in 1654. As a result, he fled to Paris where he joined Charles II's court in exile. He was a key player in the negotiations that brought his great friend Charles back to England in 1660. (Moray was given a 'grace-and-favour' residence in the Palace of Whitehall, where he conducted alchemical experiments. In his later life he became eccentric, reclusive and impoverished, but was buried among the elite in Westminster Abbey on Charles' instructions.)

Moray managed to combine a colourful and remarkable career as soldier, diplomat, spy – and Freemason – with an interest in science, engineering and alchemy. It is usually assumed that the latter inspired his enthusiasm for the Royal Society – but the evidence suggests his more 007-like activities also played a not insignificant role.

As we have seen, the idea of securing royal endorsement originated with Baron Skytte, one of Hartlib's circle, and a devotee of the Antilian or Rosicrucian agenda. Moray seems to have seized on Skytte's initiative, but – judging by the eclipse of the Rosicrucian element and Skytte's airbrushing out of the official history – for quite other motives. What were they? And, again, what was in it for Charles II?

Whether by accident or design, one of the outcomes of the struggle for the direction of the Society – and of Hartlib's death – was that the Royal Society inherited his Europe-wide network. Its records and the task of running it fell into the hands of Henry Oldenburg, the secretary responsible for handling the foreign correspondence (and editor of the Society's *Philosophical Transactions*) who, as we saw, elbowed John Wilkins out.

Oldenburg (1619-77) was a German-born theologian and diplomat, as well as a gifted linguist, who, sent to London as an emissary of the city-state of Bremen in 1653, had settled in the English capital. There is, however, no doubt that he used his role as 'intelligencer' within the Royal Society not only to acquire scientific information but also for intelligence-gathering of a more sensitive kind – all on behalf of His Majesty's government.

Besides the exchange of scientific and philosophical information – the 'civil news' as it was known – the correspondence also included political and diplomatic material, or 'state news'. The latter was obtained by Oldenburg for Lord Arlington, the Secretary of State who Charles II had assigned to foreign affairs. The Royal Society's incoming mail from abroad was actually delivered to the office of Arlington's undersecretary, Sir Joseph Williamson, where Oldenburg collected it, copied the 'civil' news and returned all the originals to Williamson. (The arrangement suited everybody, as the government was responsible for the postage – which in those days was paid by the recipient.)[4]

A sign that the government knew about Oldenburg's espionage was his imprisonment in the Tower of London as a precaution during the Anglo-Dutch war of 1667. Clearly his access to sensitive diplomatic information, as well as his foreign background, prompted Arlington and the King to be extra cautious. An added incentive was the fact that Oldenburg also had a private sideline in selling the information that flowed in through the Royal Society.

In a letter to Boyle he blatantly touts for business, asking if he comes across anyone who wants "weekly intelligence, both of state and literary news" he should point them in his direction. Oldenburg offers these weekly reports for the bargain price of £10 (in the region of £10,000 in today's money) a year – or, if hard pressed, £6-8 (£6000-£8000 today) "will also do the business".[5] Such venality outraged Robert Hooke, the physicist and chemist in charge of the Society's experiments, who complained that Oldenburg "made a trade of intelligence".[6]

The inescapable question is, was the Royal Society always intended to be primarily a cover for espionage? After all, Oldenburg unquestionably used his position for intelligence-gathering, and so did that other prominent spymaster – Moray – in establishing the society and securing the prestige of a royal charter. While the other founders, such as Viscount Brouncker, would have genuinely focussed on the natural philosophy agenda of the club, Moray immediately recognised its more clandestine value to the Crown.

In the end, all the Rosicrucian dreams of the likes of Samuel Hartlib were jettisoned in favour of hard-nosed practicalities, both in the form of rationalist experiments and cloak-and-dagger activities. But in electing to follow such a path, the Royal Society did not only lose its pro-Protestant roots, which most people today would now consider merely an interesting historical footnote. It also lost the wisdom of the Rosicrucian's inspiration, the transcendental vision of the ancient Egyptian Hermeticism, arguably the greatest jewel in the crown of all philosophy and scientific theory. Modern science was born, with all its enormous strides and discoveries, but these days it seems to have lost its soul, heart – and to some extent perhaps even its understanding, especially in the light of the new realm of quantum realities. The strange blend of practical insight and metaphysical awareness that is Hermeticism would, we argue, have helped scientists comprehend the world they are only now uncovering in all its weird glory so much more comprehensively – and so much more joyously.

Lynn Picknett and Clive Prince first met in 1989, and have since collaborated on researching and writing a number of books which investigate various mysteries, from the esoteric history of secret societies to the real origins of Christianity. Their book *The Templar Revelation* was one of the key sources used by Dan Brown in his research for *The Da Vinci Code*. Lynn and Clive's latest book is *The Forbidden Universe: The Occult Origins of Science and the Search for the Mind of God.*

There's Something STRANGE in the Sewers

'Below me is a sight that few living eighth graders have ever seen.'

- The Autobiography Of FBI Special Agent Dale Cooper

by *Neil Arnold*

When I was a child I was always warned about a non-specific bogeyman. Whether it was a monster said to lurk under the bed, in the cupboard, or in the woods, it didn't matter. For parents it was always important for a 'monster' to exist somewhere, whether in the form of those 'things' that come in the night – i.e. Tooth Fairy, Sandman, and even Father Christmas, or the creature/dark apparition said to inhabit the local lake, pond or thicket, a great way of making kids behave and to make sure they kept out of treacherous terrain and other places they should not venture. Of course, as the kids grow up, the things which lurk in the shadows no longer exist, and such fears and mystery dissipate as maturity takes over. However, some scare stories down the years have had some element of truth, even if much of what occurred was simply the product of hysteria in most cases. I always imagined shadowy monsters inhabiting gloomy places closer to home – sewers, tunnels, subways, viaducts – because even in such urban areas these places provided enough shadow to conceal something beyond the imagination and yet within arms reach. Whether as social panics, or mere hoaxes, sewer monsters and their ilk prove that not all monster scares need be confined to remote forests. Stephen King's movie *It* told the tale of an evil clown said to exist beneath the grates of Maine and more recently a Korean monster movie *The Host* presented a leviathan dwelling beneath the city of Seoul in the network of tunnels. In reality it's highly unlikely that sinister clowns and serpents dwell beneath our towns and cities, although the following batch of tales may force you to consider not letting your children play near those subterranean locations.

Pennywise the monster clown, hiding in the sewer (from Stephen King's *It*)

From the Bogeyman to Bigfoot!

On February 23rd 1983, a *Sumter Daily Item* headline read 'Sewer Monster scares children in Florida Town',[1] after it was claimed that a strange individual was inhabiting a maze of underground pipes, and occasionally popping his head out to tempt children to his lair. The newspaper stated that "a heavily armed detective donned a pair of knee-high rubber boots and cautiously waded through a mazc of dank drainage pipes to search for a man who supposedly pops out and rasps, 'Hey, c'mere' to passing children".

> Clutching two knives, two guns and a flashlight, Pasco County Detective David Helfrich climbed into the drains on Wednesday. For more than an hour he crawled around – sometimes on his hands and knees – hunting for the mysterious man who children believe haunts the storm sewers. He discovered some footprints that seemed fresh, and a pile of soaked blankets and sheets covered with debris. But that was all.
>
> "Well, the sewer monster ain't here now" Helfrich said as he poked his head out from under a manhole cover several blocks from where he entered the storm drains. A 10-year old boy from this small community near Tampa told investigators he was riding his bicycle near a secluded county park last week when the drain dweller suddenly appeared and chased him, flashing a hunting knife. Paul Manson, 12, also claimed to have seen the sewer man.
>
> "I was walking to school and I heard somebody say 'Hey, c'mere', said the youth. "I thought it was one of my friends up in a tree or something." Paul described the man as wearing dirty jeans and a brown jacket but his face was hidden.

> Helfrich, and fellow detective Keith Price believed that the incident bore a resemblance to a recent episode of the US television show *Hill Street Blues* where police officers spooked rookie cops with tales of a monster said to lurk in the sewers. However, Sarah Manson, mother of Paul, stated that the show was on too late for her son to watch and she added, "All I can tell you is the story started Monday evening after the kids were told about someone finding a human skull over there".
>
> The old skull had been discovered by 18-year old student Mike Carleton and had been sent to the Florida State University Department of Anthropology for analysis. Sarah Manson was so spooked by the stories of the sewer ghoul that she phoned the police and since the rumour children have been advised to travel to school in groups.

Two days later the *Ocala Star Banner* ran the headline "Teen may be cause of sewer scare",[2] stating that a 16-year old named Andy Eshan had come forward to say he'd heard about the young boy who had seen a man in jacket and jeans, and that in fact the sewer 'monster' may have been him as he'd spent time down by the drains setting traps for raccoons. A spokeswoman for the Pasco County sheriff stated, "I think this is turning out to be a real tempest in a teapot". One officer claimed that there had possibly been someone down in the drain, for some unknown reason, who emerged and unknowingly spooked a group of children playing nearby.

During the summer of 1978 in Toronto, Canada, a man named Ernest living on Parliament Street couldn't find his missing kitten and his search eventually lead him to a small tunnel near his apartment. Peering into the gloom of the passage which lead eventually to the sewer system, the 51-year old couldn't see his pet and so climbed into the tunnel and got the shock of his life when he encountered what he could only describe as a "living nightmare". The terrified witness saw a monkey-like creature, around three-feet in length and covered in grey fur. The beast had a long thin tail and as the man neared the form hissed at him to "go away, go away".

Further investigations were carried out in the sewer. The remains of the kitten were discovered in one area and fuelled rumours that a strange entity was occupying the pipes but no mystery creature was ever found.[3]

On May 13th 1982 the *Lakeland Ledger* reported "Sewer monster stinks up neighbourhood",[4] asking "What's eight-feet tall, dark and hairy from the waist up and smells "worse than a sewer?"

According to locals in Buena Park, California, some strange beast had been crawling up the drainage pipes of a night, silencing frogs and crickets, leaving a foul odour and huge footprints in the mud. Buena Park police refused to take the sightings seriously but resident Frank Missanelli claimed to have heard something big roaring in the vicinity of the sewer. The brave man searched the area with a flashlight and found massive footprints but didn't get a glimpse of the beast.

Panic Under the Streets of London!

The city of London has its fair share of sewer stories in reference to monsters and other strange beasts. Whether the following tale is true (unlikely!) we may never find out but *The London Chronicle* of Saturday August 12, 2006 were keen to report…

> Beast of the depths strikes again… Another sewer worker has disappeared leading to more reports of a deadly creature in the sewers of London. Paddy Patterson, an employee of Thames Water, was working on a pipe repair when he failed to report back in after his shift. A search party is underway. He is the third person to vanish after venturing into the sewers of London.

> For some months now there has been rumours spreading over the 'Beast of the Depths' and its possible involvement in the disappearances. No one has ever confirmed the existence of the creature however theories and sketches can be found all over the internet. Many of the pictures show the creature as having a long extended snake-like body, a huge gaping jaw and long fangs.
>
> Thames Water have denied the presence of any living creature in the sewers. A spokesman for the company stated "We have carried out extensive surveys of the sewer tunnels in the vicinity of the reported incidents but have found no evidence that the so called Beast of the Depths exists." However, no explanation has yet been provided for the disappearances. Until the mystery is resolved, the Beast of the Depths lives on.[5]

It's more than likely that the story, written by 'Administrator', was nothing more than fictional. On a less monstrous, but equally interesting note, during the 1800s rumour was rife that wild pigs were inhabiting the sewers of Hampstead. Now, for many years there have been legends in cities such as New York that alligators, once cute pets then disposed of down the toilet, were inhabiting the underground, but how on earth could pigs live beneath London? Well, despite the comical edge, such a rumour was in fact true as I wrote in my 'Saturday Strangeness' weekly column for website *Londonist* under the title "Urban Legends of the Underbelly",[6] commenting:

> There is a rumour that in 1851 beneath Hampstead, feral pigs, or hogs were prowling the depths of the sewers! Legend has it that a pregnant sow somehow ended up trapped in the gloomy tunnels, giving birth to a happy litter of excrement swilling, offal consuming offspring, even more ferocious than their known relatives that may have inhabited some nearby yard.

> Sceptics argued that such animals had never been seen or heard to grunt through the drain gates, but believers in such quirky tales claimed that the reason for this elusive behaviour was simply down to the Fleet ditch, which once encountered from the mouth of the sewer at the riverside, would have flushed the piggies back to their lair after failed attempts to swim against the rapids.

Although some three-quarters of a million cats were said to exist in London in 1898, the rising population of rats from the 1940s suggested that domestic felids were all too well kept to be feasting on rat populations. Mind you, I doubt a cat would want to take on the legendary King Rat! This was a creature recorded in Rickard and Michelle's *Living Wonders*[7] book of 1982:

> Workers in the London sewers tell of rare sightings of the King Rat, a huge creature, paler than the rest, attended by a bodyguard of other large rats. On his appearance the ordinary rats become silent and motionless. The earliest reference to this creature is in the *Historia animalium* of the Swiss zoologist, Conrad Gesner, written in 1555.
>
> Some say that the rat, in its old age, grows enormously large and is fed by the younger rats; it is called a Rat King by our people.

A legend is also mentioned in which the younger rats steal red cloth to adorn the King Rat in a robe-like garment. Such weirdness brings to mind the *Doctor Who* episode 'The Talons Of Weng Chiang', in which Tom Baker investigates reports of several murders in the foggy London streets, which lead him to an underground lair which feeds into the sewer systems which are said to be haunted by a monstrous human-sized rat – albeit a man dressed up rather badly in a rat costume!

See You Later Alligator - In A While Crocodile!

For several decades there have been rumours across the United States, particularly in New York, that alligators inhabit the sewer systems which run deep beneath the streets. These stories have been classed as urban legend since the 1930s yet remain the most popular monster tales in reference to sewer systems – and there are several documented cases, as recently as 2010, of alligators being discovered. Of course, whilst alligators do live in certain areas of the United States, some of the following cases prove that if a particular animal can live in a sewer near its native habitat, then maybe it's a possibility a 'gator can exist in a sewer somewhere else. The *Herald Sun*, along with several other newspapers of August 23, 2010 stated "Alligator appears in New York City, may have crawled from sewer",[8] in reference to an incident involving a witness who, whilst walking down Newtown Avenue, near 29th St, Astoria, Queens, began to yell, "Crocodile", after the appearance of the 46cm creature. Despite the fact that local authorities could not prove as to where the animal had come from, the incident merely added to the folklore that such beasts are believed to exist beneath the city. However, despite the longevity of such tales, they have often been dismissed. On May 21st 1983 the *Sarasota Herald-Tribune* ran a short story pertaining to the legends under the heading, "New York Sewer Expert Dispels Crocodile Myth",[9] stating "Like Captain Hook, John T. Flaherty is dogged by crocodiles, and in addition, alligators. Flaherty is chief of design in the New York City Bureau of Sewers, but he is also the resident expert on the most durable urban myth in the history of cities, reptiles or waste disposal":

> "Dear Sirs", writes a correspondent from Stockholm, where sewers are called cloaks. "I take the liberty to write to you, since I from many sources have been informed that, for many years, a substantial number of krokodiles (sic) have found themselves a suitable atmosphere of living in the cloak tunnels of New York."

"Dear persons", begins the letter from a high school student in Wilkesboro, N.C., "Recently I have become very interested in an uncommon subject. Alligator population in the New York City water system."

A man from Celeron, N.Y., writes, "I disagree with a co-worker who insists that an alligator which had lived in a sewer system over a long period of time does not change colour. I said I believe the pigmentation of the alligator would become much lighter and in some cases turn almost white."

To all these Flaherty, a good-humoured man with an alligator cigarette lighter on his desk, must reply "No Virginia, there are no alligators in the New York sewer system."

Alligators have become Flaherty's sideline, and he handles them with flair. The myth is that travellers to Florida adopted the baby reptiles, tired of them and flushed them down the toilet into the city sewer system, where they grew to immense size. To a woman from Denver who asked if it was true that sewer workers carried guns in case of alligator attack: "As the resident expert of all matters relating to subterranean saurians, I can state with authority that there ain't no such animal. Rumours! How do they start ? It is ironic, for instance that you should write of sewer maintenance personnel here in New York carrying .38s to protect themselves from the ravages of rapacious reptiles. Did you know that there are many New Yorkers who believe that all residents of Denver carry .38s at all times ?

The *Miami News* of October 21st 1921 happily announced "Alligator clogs sewer in Fort Myers Street",[10] after it was reported that the previous day a nine-foot long alligator had crawled up a pipe and made its home at the rear of a café. A gang of workmen managed to wrench the reptile from the pipe and it was eventually placed into a pool at Tonnelier Court. Sadly, the alligator proved to be too big for the pool and the creature was taken to the outskirts of the city and shot dead.

The February 10th 1935 edition of the *New York Times* reported the discovery of an alligator in an Uptown sewer.[11] The lengthy article noted that youths "having a rather grand time at dusk yesterday shoveling the last of the recent snow into a gaping manhole" had suddenly noticed signs of clogging some ten feet below them, where the manhole merged with the conduit to the river. Sixteen-year-old Salvatore Condulucci dropped to his knees to see what was causing the blockage:

> What he saw, in the thickening dusk, almost caused him to topple into the icy cavern. For the jagged surface of the ice blockade below was moving; and something black was breaking through. Salvatore's eyes widened; then he managed to leap to his feet and call his friends.
>
> "Honest, it's an alligator!" he exploded. There was a murmur of skepticism. Jimmy Mireno, 19, of 440 East 123d Street, shouldered his way to the rim and stared. "He's right," he said.
>
> Frankie Lonzo, 19, of 1,743 Park Avenue, looked next, he also confirmed the spectre. Then there was a great crush about the opening in the middle of the street and heads were bent low around the aperture. The animal apparently was threshing about in the ice, trying to get clear.

The boys fetched some rope and dangled a noose into the sewer, "and after several tantalizing near-catches, looped it about the 'gator's neck." The group worked together to pull the reptile up to the street, "where it lay, non-committal; it was not in Florida, that was clear."

However, when one of the boys approached the alligator to loosen the rope, the creature opened its jaws and snapped furiously at him.

> The boys jumped back. Curiosity and sympathy turned to enmity. "Let 'im have it!" the cry went up. So the shovels that had been used to pile snow on the alligator's head were now to rain blows upon it. The 'gator's tail swished about a few last times. Its jaws clashed weakly. But it was in no mood for a real struggle after its icy incarceration. It died on the spot.
>
> Triumphantly, but not without the inevitable reaction of sorrow, the boys took their victim to the Lehigh Stove and Repair Shop. There it was found to weigh 125 pounds; they said it measured seven and a half or eight feet. It became at once the greatest attraction the store ever had. The whole neighborhood milled about, and finally, a call for the police reached a nearby station. But there was little for the hurrying policemen to do. The strange visitor was quite dead; and no charge could be preferred against it or against its slayers. The neighbors were calmed with little trouble and speculation as to where the 'gator had come from was rife.
>
> There are no pet shops in the vicinity; that theory was ruled out almost at once. Finally, the theories simmered down to that of a passing boat. Plainly, a steamer from the mysterious Everglades, or thereabouts, had been passing 123d Street, and the alligator had fallen overboard.
>
> …At about 9 P.M., when tired mothers had succeeded in getting most of their alligator-conscious youngsters to bed, a Department of Sanitation truck rumbled up to the store and made off with the prize. Its destination was Barren Island and an incinerator.

Two years later on the 1st of June the *New York Times* reported on an alligator encounter at Brooklyn Bay which concerned a Captain Fisk who had moored his boat at Pier 916.[12] Fisk was amazed to see the four-foot long reptile swimming towards him and eventually captured the critter with the help of some local boys. The following week a prowling alligator was observed by many witnesses on the eastbound platform of the railway station at Brooklyn Museum. Terrified women reported to police that they'd seen a mysterious man put a large, covered item into a refuse can. Shortly afterwards the alligator appeared from the can. The alligator was caught by two patrolmen.[13]

The headlines continue throughout the decades. The *Windsor Star* of June 8th 1963 claimed that four young boys fished an eight-foot long alligator out of a storm drain in Miami, Florida.[14] The article was accompanied by a photo of the four boys restraining the creature. On September 8th 1977 the *Free Lance Star* commented that a six-foot specimen was found in a sewer system after a severe storm in Baton Rouge, Louisiana.[15] The *Ocala Star Banner* of June 29th 1978 commented that an alligator found in a rain sewer at Deerfield Beach, Florida, had been killed by officials of the Florida Game and Fresh Water Fish Commission. A week previous the animal had attacked an eight-year old boy.[16] The *Altus Times* of March 10th 1982 reported that residents of Wilmington, North Carolina, had been spooked by an eight-foot long alligator living in a sewer close to an apartment complex.[17] On May 3rd 1984 the *Daily Times* ran the headline, "Alligator in sewer line a surprise", after a three-foot long individual was discovered in Winchester, Kentucky.[18] Three years later a two-and-a-half foot long caiman was snared near a storm sewer in

Philadelphia.[19] In 1994 an alligator was found in a sewer in Buckley Towers, North Miami.[20] A year later it was rumoured by several press agencies that an alligator had been found in a lake in New York City. The animal was said to have measured three-feet in length.[21]

More recently the American television show *Monster Quest* sent cameras into the murky pipes of New York and discovered a salamander perched on a ledge. Despite the abundance of reports of alligators inhabiting sewer systems across the United States, the New York 'gators were once again dismissed in the February of 2011 when Luis Baerga, who is the longest-serving sewer inspector, stated quite categorically in an article for the *New York Times* that the alligator legend in New York had originated solely from an old photo which was once pinned on the wall of the Bureau of Sewers (situated at 40 Worth Street, in New York), and depicted workmen pulling an alligator from a sewer.[22] The photo was taken in Florida, but many New Yorkers were confused and believed the photo had been taken in New York.

Half a world away, in 1987 an alligator crawled out of a sewer system beneath Madras, in India and terrified locals who tried to bombard the beast with stones. The seven-foot long animal was eventually overpowered by authorities.[23] In 1998 a crocodile was found in a sewer in the Queensland suburb of Cairns, Australia.[24] The six-foot long beast was observed in a storm water drain close to an area where a young girl had been mauled. Meanwhile, *The Milwaukee Journal* of June 23rd 1912 reported a Japanese crocodilian sewer dweller,[25] stating that "loungers in the museum garden at Osaka were astonished to see a long snout protrude from a drainpipe by the side of the pathway and two huge jaws commence to snap at the legs of the passers by. The snout belonged to a crocodile. The reptile was recognized by the director as one which had escaped from its cage in the museum in September 1910. It is supposed that since that date it has been exploring the drainage system of the city."

What Else Lurks Below?

In 2009 it was claimed that a slimy, pulsating creature had been found in a sewer in Raleigh, North Carolina. Several bizarre headlines made the news, including, "Raleigh sewer monster may clog pipes", and the more dramatic "Satanic blob menaces North Carolina". A *Daily Mail* headline of 2nd July 2009 read "Is it a hoax? Video of 'alien' life form found in sewer becomes internet hit",[26] after a construction firm in North Carolina came forward to say they'd filmed a bizarre, blob-like creature. Malphrus Construction were carrying out a routine inspection of the sewer networks, which had been built in 1949. The creature, according to Ed Buchan, environmental coordinator at the Raleigh Public Utilities Department stated that the 'creature' was in fact a colony of worms – possibly annelid worms – and not one, single unidentified monster.

On the 5th April 1990 *The Times* of New York reported on the "real-life turtles" said to inhabit the New York sewer system.[27] Snapping turtles, possibly purchased as pets after the hype of the children's movie *Teenage Mutant Ninja Turtles*, were probably flushed down the toilet after owners could no longer look after their animals – in the UK parents purchased terrapins for their children and many have been seen basking in the sun in local ponds. Another theory suggests such creatures were backwashed into outlet pipes from the Bronx or East River. Other researchers argue that it more likely that turtles hatch in ponds at local zoo parks and make their way into the sewer system. Networks of tunnels beneath the Bronx and Manhattan were proving to be ideal habitat for turtles weighing up to fifty pounds. Tina Casey, spokeswoman for the Department of Environmental Protection commented, "They're big enough to do serious damage to any hoodlum!" In 1988 Casey had discovered two huge snapping turtles in New York's sewer system. Ironically, she originally came across the turtles whilst searching for the legendary blind albino alligators once rumoured to exist beneath the city.

In 1979 *The Milwaukee Journal* of April 19th reported that a rare turtle, known as the bog turtle, measuring just four-inches in length, was jeopardizing a $5 million sewer pipeline project in New Jersey. The endangered turtle, unique to New Jersey, New York and Pennsylvania, was put on the list of endangered species in 1975. After a handful of sightings near to where the sewer pipeline was being constructed, a scientist was called in to carry out a two day survey of the marshy area.[28]

Eels and pythons have been discovered in the pipes also. Sewers are also the most likely of places to find monster rats and cockroaches. However, one of the most bizarre stories of an out-of-place creature in a sewer comes from Birmingham, in England of all places. The *New York Times* of 20th October 1889 covered the bizarre story:[29]

> In the small hours of a recent Sunday morning a second desperate lion hunt was conducted through one of the sewers, but without the knowledge or presence of the general public. "It seems", says a correspondent of the London *Times*, "that the Nubian lion which was recaptured at the sewer outlet in Ashton Brook on the previous Friday afternoon was not the only one that escaped on that day from Wombwell's menagerie, but the proprietors of the show thought it inadvisable to take the public into their confidence on this subject, and they took measures privately to intercept and recapture the runaway animal."
>
> Beyond placing a watch at the sewer outlet, however, nothing was done until a late hour on Saturday night, when, with the assistance of the police having been obtained, active operations were begun for recovering the lost lion. In the first place, the fair ground near the sewer outlet was cleared of people shortly after midnight, and a trap cage was placed over the outlet. The manager of the expedition then proceeded to the nearest manhole. As the lion tamer Orenzo did not care to repeat his daring exploit of

> the previous Friday, two young men belonging to the working staff of the menagerie volunteered to descend into the sewer, which they did, armed each with a six-barrelled revolver and a policeman's lantern. Traces of the lion were soon found, and his roar was distinctly heard, but at a distance further up the sewer. The young men then reascended and the party proceeded to a manhole further inland; but here, again they were on the wrong side of the lion, and it was not until they came to the junction of the sewers in Bracebridge Street that they got fairly on its track. It was then determined to trap it on the spot instead of driving it into the outlet, and with this object the manager of the party lowered a stout looped rope with a slip-knot in such a manner that the lion, in issuing from the neighbouring sewer would inevitably run into it. Then the two young men descended into the next manhole and proceeded to drive the lion through the narrow pipe toward the looped rope. This was not accomplished until they had discharged all their ammunition and had been compelled to take a boot with which to strike the sides of the sewer and frighten the animal in the direction required.
>
> Presently a prolonged howl informed them of the success of their tactics. The lion had stepped into the noose, which fairly encircled his loins. In the meantime the people at the top of the opening pulled desperately at the rope until the animal was raised nearly to the level of the road, when a trap cage was placed over the manhole, and the lion, more dead than alive, was dragged body first into it.

In 2009 a baby hippo was found dead in a sewer in Bangkok after it had gone missing from a nearby zoo.[30] In 1941 a cow was caught after a fourteen-hour ramble through a storm sewer in New Jersey. The animal had walked between Irvington and East Orange but was eventually lead back to its farm.[31] In October 1992 a cow was found in a drainpipe in Texas.[32] A cowboy named Steve Cox had told many people about his sighting of the creature but no-one believed him until the animal stuck its head out of the drainpipe. Officials eventually fished the poor cow out. It had suffered a minor scrape to its tail bone. In the September of 1992, staff writer Vicki Smith, for the *Press Of Atlantic* City website, listed a piece of unusual news under the real estate section, reporting "Sewer workers saved from vicious lizard".[33] According to the report a crew cleaning out an Absecon wet well spotted a strange creature floating among the sewage. A safety co-ordinator was commended for daring to capture the reptile – which turned out to be a Nile monitor lizard which had apparently, "threatened the safety of his co-workers."

The *Spokesman Review* of 22nd April 1957 reported on a remarkable find in a sewer in Kamiah, Idaho, USA.[34] A monstrous skeleton of a prehistoric creature was unearthed by a contractor named Sigurd Grove a quarter of a mile from the town in Idaho. Grove was digging a sewer trench when he found the bones twenty-feet down. The yellow-grey remains belonged to an animal larger than an elephant. In 1989 workers in Oregon found animal bones dating back to the Ice Age whilst they were digging a sewer line.

In 2005, at West Didsbury, in Manchester, England, a ten-foot long boa constrictor was thought to be living in sewer pipes beneath Clyde Road. The reptile was eventually caught after it slithered out of someone's toilet and made its way across the bathroom floor.[35] Five years later a snake was found in a sewage system in Scotland.[36] This tale echoes several sewer snake stories. In 1984, in Rosenberg, Texas, an eleven-foot python was found in a sewer line after it had gone missing from the property of owner Thomas Houston.[37] In 1963 a young boy, playing in the area of Lower East Side, New York, claimed that a snake crawled out of the sewer and bit him in the hand.[38] Two years later an anaconda measuring almost seven-feet was caught after four weeks on the loose in Madera, California.[39] In 1975 in Altadena, California, a seven-foot long snake surprised several workers who were about to step into a sewer. The animal was roped and lifted out.[40] In 1981 a ten-foot long python was found in a sewer in Terre Haute by workers who were cleaning out the waterway.[41] Three years later a dead snake was pulled from a sewer lane after it flooded in Montreal, Canada. In 2006 and 2008 snakes were also found dead in Montreal, this time after making their way through sewer pipes into apartments. These accounts are just a handful of a long list of snake stories pertaining to sewer systems across the world.

Sewer Ghosts!

If dank, labyrinthine sewer systems can harbour large animals, then it's no real surprise that such places can harbour ghost stories too. The first comes from Sussex in England.

The Zombie!

In 2008 the *Bexhill-On-Sea Observer*, of Sussex in England, spoke of a zombie-like ghoul said to haunt the water treatment plant at Prince William Parade in Eastbourne. An employee, who'd been stationed at the plant since 2000 claimed he'd seen a strange apparition in 2008 in the control room. A fellow worker commented, "I believe in ghosts and I'm sure there's something in there. I dread doing the night shift. It's not funny going to work and worrying that a zombie might be around the corner."

Eerie voices, fleeting shadows, and even a "humanoid shadow" were recorded at the building during an investigation. A Southern Water spokesperson stated: "He (Mr Wey) organised this psychic investigation as part of his ghostly hobby and we hope the findings weren't too frightening."[42]

Messie

A second story comes from Liverpool, the home of The Beatles and a supposed sewer monster known as Messie! On the conspicuous date of 30th March 2011 the *Liverpool Echo* ran the headline, "Merseyside sewer monster hunt, after mysterious beast seen on CCTV",[43] accompanied by a photo showing a set of glowing eyes peering from the gloom of a sewer:

> Today we reveal the shocking CCTV footage of Messie – a freakish animal which is kicking up a stink in Merseyside's sewers. Terrified staff at North West water company United Utilities, whose close circuit cameras captured the mystery creature, said it was "far too big for a rat.
>
> The public were today urged to sniff out the pipe prowler, dubbed "the most unusual sighting ever." The creature, which can clearly be seen standing upright on strong back legs, was filmed by engineers. It is believed the animal is surviving by tucking in to fat deposits within Merseyside sewer pipes. Mike Wood, United Utilities regional wastewater network manager, said: "The animal could possibly be a domestic pet or feasibly, an animal which has escaped from the zoo."
>
> Sewer workers have jokingly dubbed the creature 'Messie' likening it to a dirty version of the Loch Ness Monster. Ian Appleton, operating the CCTV unit said, "I physically jumped when I saw the thing". Dr Pauline Yorleg (get it?), a Liverpool lecturer specialising in sewage sightings said: "I've not been this excited since red herrings were found in Wallasey last April."

Joking aside, sewers, although rarely frequented by the public are spooky places indeed. They wind beneath the streets, out of sight, and pretty much out of mind, but occasionally, the strange inhabitants of this gloomy world like to rear an ugly head and emerge from the realm of legend into reality.

A Spectral Head ?

The Sydney Morning Herald of 28th December 1933 reported on an "Apparition On Christmas Eve – Bondi Sewer Ghost",[44] stating that on Christmas Eve, Mr X – "a solid citizen of North Bondi" – had been wending his way homeward after an enjoyable night out...

> Mr X drew in a long breath of fragrant night air. His legs carried him, almost mechanically, along the familiar footpath Murriverie Road. Suddenly his legs refused to carry him any further. A fearful object stood before him; the head of a horse, standing erect on the footpath. A live head. The thing moved. Mr X jumped. Mr X fled.

Fancy a stroll down here?[45]

> Mr X arrived home a bundle of nerves. He sought the reassurance of a human voice. He awoke his wife and unburdened himself. Mrs X advised him to take something to steady his nerves, go back and have another look. Mr X summoned up the remnants of his courage. He approached the thing once more. His courage nearly gave out, but he mastered himself and walked close to it. Mr X groaned with relief. The horse's head was not resting on the pavement; it was protruding through a hole in the pavement. The body was in a storm water channel. The animal had fallen into the hole when the covering had collapsed under its weight. Bondi police hoisted it out with a windlass. Mr X returned home to sleep in peace.'

A Sewer Legend – Did She Fall Or Was She Pushed?

Some unusual tales have the ability to embed themselves into local folklore whether they are true or not. One urban myth doing the rounds, especially on the internet, concerns the legend of a teenage girl called Carmen Winstead.[46] The teenager, who allegedly resided in Indiana, USA, was, according to legend, pushed down a sewer at school by a gang of bullies. This incident was said to have occurred during a fire drill and the group of five girls, to embarrass Miss Winstead, decided to push her but the prank went disastrously wrong and the young girl died. Police arrived on the scene and wrenched Carmen's broken body from the sewer; she had broken her neck and back. At the time the girls who had pushed Carmen claimed that she'd fallen, and the police believed their story.

Shortly after the incident a male teen who'd read the post was allegedly found dead in the sewer. The legend of the story circulates as a type of chain letter and it is said that if you do not repost the email/letter stating Carmen was pushed, then she will come for you. These type of stories are potent particularly in Asian folklore and have been the subject of terrifying films such as *Ring*.

A Mystery Explained By A Mystery

For more than ten years a five storey building situated in the GuangXi province of China has had a reputation of being haunted. In fact, such was the paranormal activity of the building that four different sets of owners had fled the place fearing its ghosts, mainly in the form of things that were making bumps in the night. When first put on the market the property sold for $34,000 but after a series of inexplicable events two brothers eventually purchased the apartment for just $6500. Despite not believing in ghosts the two brothers were tormented by many strange noises, but being down to earth people they attempted to investigate the source of these sounds. One night they heard a strange flapping noise in one of the bathroom pipes and decided to break it open. They were shocked to find a small catfish weighing approximately five pounds. When the noises continued the brothers unearthed a further nine catfish, some weighing up to ten pound in weight. So, the strange noises had been explained but now they were faced with another mystery – how had these catfish ended up in the pipes ? Rumour has it that a chap who resided in the block in 1995 purchased some catfish and left them in a bucket in the bathroom. Two allegedly escaped and made their way to the sewer pond. The catfish produced young which eventually made their way into the pipes of the building.[47]

One particular sewer story which cannot be explained took place on the evening of November 23rd 1904 and concerned a Godfrey Anderson of Edinburgh, Scotland. A sinister pillar of black smoke appeared to rise from a drain – the apparition measured around four-feet in length and was two-feet in thickness. The spectre oozed towards a stationary horse and in one vaporous swoop engulfed the horse. The victim emerged with a ripped open throat and the smoke monster reverted back to the sewer.[48]

When we consider the amount of rubbish that sits in the murky depths of the sewers it's no real surprise that some creatures could survive down there. In 2010 the London press reported that "enough lard to fill nine double-decker buses is being removed from sewers under London's Leicester Square", and when coupled with the morbid fact that there are hundreds of headlines the world over reporting on the discovery of human remains down in the sewers, it's no wonder that your parents warned you away from such hazardous realms. What lies beneath ? We'll never really know.

Neil Arnold a full-time monster hunter and author of several books including *Monster! The A-Z Of Zooform Phenomena* (CFZ Press 2007), *Paranormal London* (The History Press 2010), *Mystery Animals Of The British Isles- Kent* (CFZ Press 2009) and *Mystery Animals Of The British Isles – London* (CFZ Press 2011). Neil has appeared on NBC News, Sky News and BBC News, and written for magazines such as *Fate*, *Fortean Times* and *Paranormal.* His websites are: www.beastsoflondon.blogspot.com, www.kentbigcats.blogspot.com, and www.zooform.blogspot.com.

SACRED
to the Memory of
WASHINGTON
PLURIBUS

THE MYSTIC HISTORY OF AMERICA

The occult philosophies that transformed a nation

by *Mitch Horowitz*

U.S. Senator James Shields loved a good fight. A former general, he was known to challenge rivals – including future president Abraham Lincoln – to duels. But at the start of a Washington spring day in 1854, Shields startled his Senate colleagues with a gesture that seemed bold, even for him.

On April 17, the Illinois Democrat rose on the Senate floor to speak on behalf of one of the strangest petitions in American history. Signed by a reported 15,000 citizens, the document was, he acknowledged, of a "very singular and novel subject." At this moment his colleagues began to lean forward in their chairs; the hum of conversation on the Senate floor fell silent.

"The petitioners represent," Shields announced, "that certain physical and mental phenomena of a mysterious import have become so prevalent in this country and Europe as to engross a large share of public attention." Citing the neglected work of medieval alchemist Roger Bacon, occult philosopher Cornelius Agrippa, and Hermetic mathematician John Dee, Shields begged his colleagues to take seriously the request of his petitioners to fund a "scientific commission" to study the possibility of talking to the dead – perhaps, Shields offered, even "establishing a spiritual telegraph between the material and spiritual world."

In an era of séances and table-rapping, one senator guffawed that "it would be better to allow the petition to lie on the table." "This is an important subject and should not be sneered away," Shields protested as laughter began to ring from the chamber. Another colleague suggested that the petition be dispatched to the Committee on Foreign Relations. More laughter erupted. Shields, red-faced, agreed to let the proposal drop.

But it was not the last time that Spiritualism had its day in the halls of Congress. In early 1871, the chamber invited the first woman to address a joint congressional committee. That winter day, it was a free-love advocate – and avowed trance medium – named Victoria Woodhull who took the floor (as pictured opposite). Poised and handsome, Woodhull delivered a rousing brief in defense of women's suffrage, which she later said had been dictated to her in a dream by a ghostly, tunic-wearing Greek elder—a spirit guardian who had guided all of her public utterances ever since she was a young girl. By the time of Woodhull's appearance, Spiritualism could not be hooted down, even in the Senate. Its acolytes included Mary Todd Lincoln and a range of industrialists, congressmen, and figures from everyday life. The year following Woodhull's speech, suffragists nominated her as the first female candidate for president.

More than a century later, however, the word "occult" seems like a stranger in American life. Today it is tempting to dismiss

Victoria Woodhull addresses the U.S. Congress

occultism as no more than the crazy auntie tucked away in the attic of America's history. But that kind of dismissal would be a misreading of occultism's role in America, and of America's role in recent religious history. Indeed, the arcane philosophies grouped under the name of occultism represent an unheralded thought movement in America's national life, one that not only placed horoscopes into nearly every daily newspaper, but that transformed a young nation into the launching pad for the revolutions in alternative spirituality that spanned the globe in the twentieth century.

The Occult Renaissance

Today, the concept of a personal spiritual search, one of self-discovery and experimentation, seems like a birthright. But long before such a notion was generally conceived of, and centuries before America and other nations sought to protect a person's inner search as a right, occult tradition was locked in a struggle to survive.

Early Christendom had characterized pantheists and nature-worshipers, astrologers and cosmologists, cultists and soothsayers, in ways that such believers had never conceived of themselves – as practitioners of black magic and Satan worship. This added a new category of villainy, entirely of the Church's invention, to the Western mindset. Once so characterized, the religious minority could be outlawed and persecuted, just as pagan powers had once done to early Christians.

The Renaissance brought on a surprising reversal. The term "occult" – from the Latin *occultus*, meaning secret – took on new use through the work of Renaissance-era magus Heinrich Cornelius Agrippa. He used it in 1533 to define his massive study of pre-Christian rites and esoteric lore, *De occulta philosophia*. Agrippa's overview of occultism – encompassing astrology, alchemy, spirit conjuring, and prophetic or divinatory rituals – reflected the culmination of a series of thought currents, some growing directly from church history: Returning Crusaders brought home myths and tales of exotic lands; church reforms began permitting the study of pantheistic Greek and Latin literature; renewed fluency in Hellenic languages led to an unexpected discovery of Egypt's mysterious philosophies; scholars came to realize that monasteries had preserved some of the ancient Hellenic literature during years of Dark Ages plague and chaos. Feeding one into the other, such developments elevated interest in the allegories, symbols, and magico-scientific ideas of the ancient world.

The proliferation of esoteric philosophies extended into the Elizabethan era and beyond in the work of figures like Giordano Bruno, John Dee, Francis Bacon, and even William Shakespeare, whose Romanesque depictions of gods and myth drew directly on occult Renaissance traditions. But the Elizabethan age also witnessed a backlash, as church partisans began reasserting authority over intellectual life.

In a development that held future significance for America, occult philosophy briefly revived with the advent of a secretive thought movement called Rosicrucianism in the early seventeenth century. Europe marveled at the rumor of an "invisible college" of adepts – master practitioners of hidden wisdom – whose manifestos extolled mysticism and higher learning, while prophesying the dawn of a new age of education and enlightenment. Rosicrucian writings gave powerful expression to ecumenism – a nearly unthinkable ideal at the time and one that likely influenced the religious pluralism of Freemasonry as it later existed in America.

Renewed persecution, however, lay immediately ahead: Church loyalists assailed Rosicrucian ideas. The papal Hapsburg Empire crushed a brief flowering of occult culture in Bohemia when political events tripped the Thirty Years' War. In later generations, the Age of Enlightenment – contrary to the intent of some of its leading intellects – dealt a near-deathblow to occult philosophy. In echoes of the Inquisition, authorities forced astrologers and alchemists, mystics and seers, out of respectable colleges and courts and onto the margins of society, if not underground, to avoid ridicule or persecution.

In the eighteenth century, members of European royalty maintained discrete ties to occult societies and impresarios. But most educated people saw pentagrams, zodiac signs, and mythical images as little more than decorations or guild insignias. And our story of the occult might simply end there – were it not for a young nation across the sea, on whose shores it was just beginning.

An Occult Republic

Even in its colonial history, America was entwined with esoteric spirituality. North America's first intentional mystical community reached its shores in the summer of 1694. That year, the determined spiritual philosopher Johannes Kelpius led about forty pilgrims out of Central Germany – a region decimated by the Thirty Years' War – and to the banks of the Wissahickon Creek, just beyond

Philadelphia. The city then hosted only about 500 houses, but it represented a Mecca of freedom for the Kelpius circle, who longed for a new homeland where they could practice their brands of astrology, alchemy, numerology, and mystical Christianity without fear of harassment from church or government.

Soon more mystical thinkers from the Rhine Valley journeyed to America, building a larger commune at Ephrata, Pennsylvania. A young woman named Ann Lee fled persecution in her native Manchester, England and relocated her esoteric sect, the "Shaking Quakers" – or the Shakers – to upstate New York in 1776. That same year, a Rhode Island girl, Jemima Wilkinson, declared herself a spirit channeler, took the name *Publick Universal Friend*, and began to preach across the northeast. The trend was set: America became a destination for religious idealists, especially those of a supernatural bent.

By the 1830s and 40s, a region of central New York State called "the Burned-Over District" (so-named for its religious passions) became the magnetic center for the religious radicalism sweeping the young nation. Stretching from Albany to Buffalo, it was the Mt. Sinai of American mysticism, giving birth to new religions such as Mormonism and Seventh-Day Adventism, and also to the spread of Spiritualism, Mesmerism, mediumship, table-rapping, séances, and other occult sensations – many of which mirrored, and aided, the rise of Suffragism and related progressive movements. The nation's occult culture gave women their first opportunity to openly serve as religious leaders – in this case as spirit mediums, seers, and channelers. America's social and spiritual radicals were becoming joined, and the partnership would never fade.

The robust growth of occult and mystical movements in nineteenth-century America was aided by the influence of three mighty social and spiritual movements: Freemasonry, Transcendentalism, and Spiritualism. Each helped transform the young nation into a laboratory for religious experiment and a springboard for the revolutions in nontraditional and therapeutic spirituality that eventually swept the globe. Consider:

- Freemasonry is, perhaps, a direct remnant of the most radical thought movement to emerge from the Reformation, and it instilled a strong anti-authoritarian streak in America's early religious culture. Masonry's penchant for occult and esoteric symbolism suggests how some of the nation's Founders – many of whom were Masons – understood religious truth as emanating from a common source that could be found in different cultures throughout history, including those of a mystical and pre-Christian past. American Masonry emphasized religious tolerance, which its highly placed members, including George Washington (pictured on next page in Masonic garb) and Benjamin Franklin, modeled and interwove throughout American life. Early in his presidency, Washington took matters a step further. In a letter to the congregation of a Rhode Island synagogue, the first president wrote: "It is now no more that toleration is spoken of, as if it was by the indulgence of one class of people that another enjoyed the exercise of their inherent national gifts." In other words, minority religions were no longer guests of the new republic, but full members. Whatever Freemasonry's aura of secrecy and images of skulls, pyramids, and all-seeing eyes, it is in this principle where one finds the order's truly most radical, even dangerous, idea: the encouragement of different faiths within a single nation.
- In New England in the mid-nineteenth century, the writings of Ralph Waldo Emerson, Henry David Thoreau, and their contemporaries extolled the individual's capacity for spiritual self-discovery beyond the boundaries of established religion. Their thought movement called itself Transcendentalism and introduced mystical concepts from Eastern and Western

Portrait of George Washington in his Masonic garb

esoteric traditions into the bloodstream of American life. As defined by these "Yankee mystics," Transcendentalism believed the seat of worship – the place of communion with the Divine – existed within. As the Transcendentalists saw it, the individual mirrors a larger cosmos, which bestows a natural order, or ebb and flow of life, and a sense of objective truth. This truth can be verified by lived experience, as it has by seekers throughout history. Transcendentalists drew freely on "Hindoo" texts, such as the *Upanishads* and *Bhagavad Gita*, as well as the ethical and religious traditions of antiquity. Echoing the Hermetic concept of *As Above, So Below*, Emerson depicted man as a microcosm of the universe. ("The world," he wrote, "globes itself in a drop of dew.") Indeed, some saw within Transcendentalism the idea that man shapes the outer world as much as it shapes him. Philosophy, wrote Emerson, "proceeds on the faith that a law determines all phenomena... That law, when in the mind, is an idea." In this sense, Transcendentalism aided the rise of the "positive thinking" and self-improvement movements of the twentieth century.

- In the late 1840s, there dawned a movement that popularized belief in the supernatural like nothing the young nation had ever seen. It was called Spiritualism. Through table-rapping, séances, and mediumistic trances, millions of Americans became convinced that communication with the "other side" was available to each individual. Spiritualism also became the first religious movement that Americans exported abroad, inspiring séance circles in London and Paris. Yet the movement had another, largely unknown side. Spiritualism possessed a surprising culture of egalitarianism and social concern. The movement attracted the interest and participation of social reformers because, among other things, it provided a setting in which women – for one of the first times in modern history – could serve as religious leaders, at least of a certain kind. Many spirit mediums were women – active suffragettes among them. Spiritualism's thought leaders, which included the formidable Anglo-American religious thinker Emma Hardinge Britten, saw the movement as the basis of a new religious and social order. Suffragism, free love, talking to the dead, transcendental visions, communal living – each found expression within Spiritualism.

The Theosophical Dawn

While Spiritualism reached its peak of influence in the United States – and exported its ideas abroad – there appeared in America an occult organization whose influence would be felt across the globe. Neither quite Eastern nor Western, it was named the Theosophical Society. Its stated aim was to recover forgotten esoteric ideas at the heart of the world's religious traditions. Theosophy's leading light, a brilliant and mysterious Russian noblewoman named Helena Petrovna Blavatsky, explained that in 1873 she journeyed to America, the land of Spiritualism, "with feelings not unlike those of a Mohammedan approaching the birthplace of his Prophet." The opening created by Spiritualism made the young nation into a magnet for every kind of spiritual experiment.

With retired Civil War colonel Henry Steel Olcott at her side, Madame Blavatsky founded the Theosophical Society in New York City in 1875. Within three years, however, Blavatsky and Olcott departed for India, where their organization grew increasingly active in the early 1880s. At the time, Theosophy dedicated itself to reintroducing Hindu and Buddhist ideas in India and Sri Lanka, whose religious traditions were under twin assault from British colonial rule and missionary campaigns. A core part of Theosophy's mission was to re-ignite interest – in Europe, Asia, and America

– in the mystical teachings of the East. The consequences were as enormous as they are today forgotten.

A young, starch-collared law student named Mohandas Gandhi came into contact with Blavatsky's followers when he was studying in London in 1889. In a remarkably overlooked fact of twentieth-century history, Gandhi very openly credited Theosophy with bringing him back to Hinduism, to the study of its holy book, the *Bhagavad Gita* (which became the guiding text of Gandhi's life), and to the ideals of universal brotherhood. Madame Blavatsky's *Key to Theosophy*, Gandhi wrote in his autobiography, "stimulated in me the desire to read books on Hinduism, and disabused me of the notion fostered by the missionaries that Hinduism was rife with superstition." Theosophy, Gandhi later told his biographer, "is Hinduism at its best." Hence, it was not in America alone that occultism and social reform crossed paths.

Helena Petrovna Blavatsky

Indeed, the mystical experimentation that had been cut short by the Thirty Years' War seemed everywhere to flourish anew in Europe in the second half of the nineteenth century. On the continent as in America, the theories of Darwin had the dual effect of undermining old ecclesiastical certainties while creating a new hunger for mystery in a biologically ordered world. For avant-garde artists and intellectuals who had lost faith in old-line religion, esoteric philosophies offered a new light. In 1855, French writer-magician Eliphas Lévi, in his *Transcendental Magic*, proclaimed the existence of an occult philosophy hidden at the base of all "ancient doctrines" and "under the seal of all sacred writings in the ruins of Nineveh or Thebes, on the crumbling stones of old temples and on the blackened visage of the Assyrian or Egyptian sphinx...in the cryptic emblems of our old books on alchemy, in the ceremonies practiced at reception by all secret societies." In Lévi's vision, occultists discovered a renewed sense of mission and drama.

What came to be seen as a European occult revival attracted formidable intellects and earnest seekers, though with a peculiar twist: leading European occultists of the late nineteenth century often adopted airs of secrecy and pageantry, as if mimicking the outer appearances of ancient temple orders and mysterious sects would assist their quest to revive lost or fragmentary knowledge. Often on the thin pretext of concealing hallowed doctrine, they cloaked their study groups and fraternities in mystery and exclusivity. In America, by contrast, occult spirituality was about to make its deepest inroads into the settings of mainstream daily life.

The Power of Mind

By the late nineteenth century, America was suffused with influences from Freemasonry, Transcendentalism, Theosophy, and Spiritualism. Each, in its own fashion, imbued the nation's spiritual culture with the conviction that the Divine existed not at the top rung of a cosmic ladder, but within the settings of ordinary existence.

And ordinary existence was undergoing remarkable changes. As the nineteenth century closed, the fruits of modern science appeared everywhere: telegraphs, motor engines, electricity, and automated production. In medicine, Pasteur's germ theory was explaining illnesses that for years had resisted understanding. In biology, Darwin had theorized a gradual order in the development of all forms of life. In politics, Marx had classified economics as a matter of "science," in which inevitable outcomes could be foreseen. In psychology, Freud had begun to codify childhood traumas that triggered adult neuroses, and hypnotists (more-respectable versions of Mesmerists) claimed the power to alter behavior through autosuggestion and conditioning. Caught in this onrush of currents, intellectual leaders from all walks of life – academia, clergy, business – reasoned that scientific principles were applicable to every aspect of existence. Why couldn't there be a "science" of success, or even a "science" of religion – that is, a protocol of definable, rational steps that would produce a desired result?

Inspired by the possibilities, a group of religious thinkers and impresarios formed a loosely knit spiritual movement around this "scientific" religious concept. Thoughts, they argued, could be seen to manifest into actual events, such as health or sickness, wealth or poverty. They claimed Ralph Waldo Emerson as their founding prophet: "We know," the Concord mystic wrote in 1841, "that the ancestor of every action is a thought." The Bible, in their reading, seemed to agree, particularly in the Proverb: "As a man thinketh in his heart, so is he." In an enthused leap of reasoning, the movement that came to be known as New Thought maintained that the individual's creative mind was one and the same as the creative force called God. As such, a person could literally think his dreams to life. It was America's boldest – and most influential – attempt at what one religious scholar called "a practical use of the occult powers of the soul."

As thought movements often do, New Thought began with the experience of one individual. A stolid New England clockmaker named Phineas Quimby noticed that his tuberculosis seemed to ease whenever he took a refreshing carriage ride in the Maine countryside. Quimby discovered that as his spirits lifted, so did his illness. Eventually, he was completely cured. Quimby began to study the practice of Mesmerism – in which a subject could be placed into a suggestive trance – and grew fascinated with the health effects of the mind. By 1859, he had devised a philosophy of "mental healing" and began using it to treat the ill. While Quimby focused primarily on the mind's power over disease, he increasingly came to view the subconscious as an extension of the Divine, through which a person could, with the proper training and understanding, construct outer circumstance. His ideas quickly found influence: Quimby treated a patient named Mary Baker Eddy, who went on to establish one of the nation's most significant new religions, Christian Science.

But it was not within any single religion that Quimby's ideas took flight. Indeed, the taciturn Mrs. Eddy (as followers called her) soon denounced her old mentor as little more than a carnival Mesmerist. Nonetheless, his "mental healing" philosophy seemed to ride the winds all across America, winning far-flung adherents and evangelizers who in turn brought their own novel twists to it. It was these inheritors who morphed into the loosely bound psycho-spiritual school known by the late nineteenth century as New Thought. In later decades, this belief system attained mass popularity in the form of Norman Vincent Peale's "power of positive thinking." As such, it reached into nearly every church, living room, and bookstore in America.

Ironically, few Americans today have heard the term or of the movement called New Thought. Its ideas have been so widely adopted that the movement itself – which persists in metaphysical churches throughout America, sometimes under the names of Unity or Religious Science – has become almost unseen. Americans like ideas, but not necessarily movements, which they discard like outer wrapping once an idea has been embraced. Moreover, secularized elements of the New Thought philosophy had already appeared by the last decade of the nineteenth century and successfully vied for influence with the more religiously inspired variants. By the mid-twentieth century, non-religious figures like Dale Carnegie (*How to Win Friends and Influence People*) and Napoleon Hill (*Think and Grow Rich*) rode the wings of New Thought to worldwide fame. Today, every life coach, motivational speaker, and self-help program uses the concept of an attitudinal approach to success, of mind over circumstance, and so on. It is easy to forget that this now-familiar concept was very much a mystical philosophy at its birth.

The New Age and Beyond

Amid the material boom of post-World War II America, the occult seemed sidelined for a time. But by the 1950s, its rumblings were heard again – partly through the influence of a man who had died just as the war was nearing an end. From 1901 to late 1944, a Kentucky-born Sunday school teacher named Edgar Cayce entered near-daily clairvoyant trances from which he produced more than 14,000 psychical "readings." The Cayce readings mostly diagnosed and prescribed cures for ill people who wrote to him, but also expounded on topics ranging from reincarnation to astrology to earth-change prophecies. This voluminous (and deeply intriguing) material inspired a new generation of metaphysical writers and explorers. They made Cayce's topics – from clairvoyance to mind-body healing – the focus of a wide range of bestselling books and popular magazine articles.

In this sense, Cayce is probably more responsible than any other single person for introducing esoteric ideas into mainstream American life. He was, for example, the first American to prescribe meditation for medical purposes; his readings probing "past lives" inspired the 1956 mega-bestseller *The Search for Bridey Murphy*, which ignited a craze over reincarnation; and Cayce introduced the now-ubiquitous term *channeling* into the American vocabulary. But the psychic did more than set the template for New Age spirituality. The tone and ethics found in his trance readings suffused the burgeoning alternative religious culture with a sense of inclusiveness and religious universality. In his readings, Cayce made frequent reference to "the hopeful energies" – or, put another way, the force that calls us to love (or at least tolerate) our neighbors, eschew conflict, and help others.

With the dawn of the sixties, Cayce's influence contributed to a growing interest among young people in unseen realms of consciousness. For some, the early uses of psychedelics appeared to promise the existence of another world just beyond the periphery of our ordinary vision. The onrush of social experiments – combined with the youth culture's distrust of staid belief systems – created a resurgence of interest in Eastern spirituality and occultism. The sixties rebellion shook up all aspects of America's religious geography, feeding alternative religious systems from witchcraft to Zen Buddhism to Taoism. In short order, the vast, sprawling term "New Age" entered the popular lexicon, with a meaning malleable to every acolyte and critic.

A core tenet of the New Age was a belief in the fateful convergence of all religious systems, resulting in an era of boundless human potential. Above all, however, the religious opening of the late 1960s and early 70s demanded that spiritual teachings be personally *useful*. The growth in "transpersonal" or meaning-based psychology signaled a bridging of the rupture declared by Freud between the psychological and the religious.* Psychology could no longer limit the aims of life to love and work; rather, the questions of purposeful existence had entered the therapist's office – and were there to stay. Likewise, religion was no longer expected to prepare followers for the afterworld, but had to satisfy the flock's needs in the present. First at the margins and increasingly within the mainstream, religion was compelled to address the psychological needs and aspirations of the individual seeker. Even evangelical movements in the early twenty-first century embraced this role. Christian ministers and writers routinely counseled readers and congregants on everything from debt relief to relationship woes to the mental laws of success.

---

* Freud could also reveal a greater openness to the metaphysical than is commonly assumed. In his 1922 paper *Dreams and Telepathy,* he noted: "...psychoanalysis may do something to advance the study of telepathy, in so far as, by the help of its interpretations, many of the puzzling characteristics of telepathic phenomena may be rendered more intelligible to us; or other, still doubtful phenomena be for the first time definitely ascertained to be of a telepathic nature."

In the public mind, psycho-spiritual philosophies and therapies blended one into another. By the seventies and eighties, there could be no easily discerned "occult" or "Eastern" or "yogic" movement; but rather America experienced the rise of a vast metaphysical culture that appeared ever-expanding, ever-accommodating, and perpetually ready to adapt to any foreign or homegrown influence that met the needs of those who yearned for self-discovery.

Even tough-skinned skeptics who dismissed the New Age as flimflam turned to "woo- woo" methods, often unknowingly. When faced with chronic illness, addiction, or stress, rationalists from every reach of life used alternative approaches in medicine and relaxation – ranging from meditation to hypnotherapy to positive thinking to practices in yoga, herbs, and acupuncture that had entered America through the channel created by arcane subcultures.

The encounter between America and occultism reconciled itself in the creation of a vast spiritual-therapeutic culture that extolled religious egalitarianism and that responded, perhaps more than any other movement in history, to the inner needs and search of the individual. At work and at church, on television and in bookstores, there was no avoiding it: Occult America had prevailed.

Mitch Horowitz is the editor-in-chief of Tarcher/Penguin and the author of *Occult America* (Bantam), which *The Washington Post Book World* called: "Fascinating...a serious, wide-ranging study of all the magical, mystical, and spiritual movements that have arisen and influenced American history in often-surprising ways." The book received the 2010 PEN Oakland/ Josephine Miles Award for literary excellence. Horowitz has written on alternative spiritual topics for *The Wall Street Journal*, *The Washington Post*, *U.S. News & World Report*, and *Boing Boing*, and has appeared on CBS Sunday Morning, NPR's All Things Considered, Dateline NBC, and Big Think. He lives in New York City, where he and his wife raise two young sons. Visit him online at: www.MitchHorowitz.com

Aroniel Speaks: illustration by Norman Harrison'

ALIEN Messages and Impressions

If the Space Gods were to speak to us, what would they say?

by *Nigel Watson*

When I was interviewing people in northern England about their encounters with aliens during the late 1970s, I came into contact with a young man called Norman Harrison.* He revealed to me that the Earth "is now under close surveillance and profound scrutiny by alien intelligences from distant star systems. I am not being silly, I know what I am saying and doing as well as you."

He wrote those words in a letter sent to *MUFOB* (now *Magonia*) editor John Rimmer on 6th January 1978. Norman, who at that time lived in Sheffield, Yorkshire, went on to outline the different races of beings which inhabit this galaxy. The first race populate the fourth and fifth planets of Epsilon Eridani (a star that was targeted by the SETI Project Ozma in 1960), and are "4ft. tall on average, spindly and yellowish skinned and totally devoid of any hair. Their heads are disproportionately large due to further evolved brain capacity."

According to Norman, a second race inhabits three planets orbiting Canopus; a third race derives from Proxima Centauri III and IV. A fourth inhabits the two planets of Capella. Describing these latter races, Norman wrote that they are quite similar to each other and that they are "over 7ft tall on average, powerfully built and extremely agile, [have] fine blonde hair and [are] musically and artistically gifted. These three are of one Root Race type, corresponding to Earth Nordic."

The stars of Betelgeuse IV, V and VI in Orion were said to be the location of the fifth race of aliens, and a sixth populates the constellations of Ursa Major and Cassiopeia. In particular, this race occupies the solar systems of Merak, Alcor, and Dubhe in the Ursa Major constellation. The whole race is linked in a confederation and their colonies are densely populated. Other than being humanoid, Norman did not describe the appearance of these two races, but he had other interesting insights to share:

> All these aliens have spacecraft capable of exceeding light velocity several times over and have the facility to set up impenetrable force fields as well as invisibility shields. They make use of unimaginably advanced energy propulsion technology and have extremely powerful electromagnetic- gravitic (sic) devices at their disposal, all capable of effecting vital changes in this world. Force fields and rays are extensively utilised at enormous distances: in spite of the long distance these are resolved to fine focus and can be intensified as required to influence the course of events on Earth.
>
> Many of their Earth contingents are military task-force or scientific field operatives. The remainder engaged in collating or compiling vital information, making regular operational shuttle trips and submitting data reports to their base planets.

Norman said that he received this information about our galactic neighbours by way of telepathic communication from aliens, beginning in 1975 and occurring with increasing frequency over the next three years. In a letter to me dated 17th March 1978, he wrote that, "these 'contacts' can occur virtually at any time... I still hardly know what to think about the whole business – if these are hallucinations, I don't see how they could contain information about the Universe which I never had before." Apparently he does not hear or see things when having a 'telepathic' communication, instead the information "comes through direct without any sensory impressions, vision or delusions whatever."

He said that much of the information he received came when he felt rather tired and hungry, and when he wrote it down "my mind wasn't preoccupied with anything, I just felt more or less 'neutral' or indifferent. The words just flowed without any conscious direction on my part. This is always the case with either writings or drawings set straight down 'automatically'. Very often the physically weaker or hungrier I feel, the more clearly the contacts are received."

He notes that there are a group of aliens that he calls the 'Observers', who have similar views to Norman:

> Human Western society is rapidly falling into catastrophic decline and Mankind is now falling into chaos and absolute folly. They believe there is virtually zero survival probability as a result of mental degeneration and moral decay combined with political corruption, greed and militarism. These and other factors, they feel sure now will destroy all human civilization within another half-century.
>
> This isn't just pessimism or gloom-and-doom alarmism – these people are infinitely more intelligent, more truly civilized and more mature than any race on Earth, and have reached their conclusions via strict mathematical extrapolative calculus based in historical, social, psychological and economic FACTS. Most of these races

> have had an intimate exhaustive knowledge of Man for tens of thousands of years and the wisdom of their logic is undeniable.
>
> I have little to add, except that I am notified that a final terrible war will definitely take place (whether atomic or not) between East and West within three decades, and pollution poisoning will soon endanger all vegetation and animal species of the globe. All the most recent incidents positively indicate to me personally that the aliens are correct. We ignore and gloss over such dire warnings at our peril, and we have no-one but ourselves to blame for the destruction of our own world-home by our madness, ignorance and blind folly.

These communications, transmissions, or impressions – whatever we might label them – were preceded by a UFO sighting, some time in 1974. Norman was then staying with a friend of his in the Beeston area of Leeds for a few days, when he saw his first and only UFO. His friend had just gone outside for a few minutes; the time was between 8 and 9 pm when Norman had a "distinct urge to get up and look out of the door."

Opening the door, he saw between the doorframe and the rooftops of the houses across the road, a box-like shape silhouetted against the night sky. Upon it were banks of multi-coloured lights. The object was slanted at an angle towards the ground, and was moving from right to left in the direction of its central axis at slow speed. He heard no sound from this phenomenon, which he estimated to be gliding at a height of 1000 feet. After twenty seconds, it drifted out of view, although "why I did not step out into the street for a better look I don't know."

Norman's reaction to the sighting was interesting, as he wrote: "I wasn't in the least bit frightened of it, but it did disturb me in an eerie way, as if hypnotic". He went on to speculate as to what it might have been:

Extraterrestrial, as drawn by Norman Harrison*

> It must have been a huge carrier vessel of tremendous motive power, capable of containing a number of smaller saucer type craft or several hundred passengers. By proportion and distance, I feel sure it was anything up to 300 feet long. A massive vessel like that must be able to traverse the whole galactic radius at speeds far in excess of light velocity who would logically build that big for merely planet to planet journeys. Who would employ that much propulsion and that scale of motive energy? My belief is that this 'ship' was from a giant planet in the hub of the Milky Way (Bigger than Texas!!!).

Early Psi Experiences

Having read Norman's correspondence with John Rimmer and having arranged to meet him, I wondered what I could expect on visiting his household. Norman anticipated this question by explaining his circumstances in one of his letters, saying that he lived in a working-class area and that his house was "not too beautiful" and "rather decrepit". He also said he was embarrassed about it not being the ideal place for social contact.

When I first met Norman on 26th February 1978, he told me about how he had experienced distinct impressions from 1968 through to 1969. He felt he had been picking up thoughts that were being powerfully projected towards him. However, he could not pick up any words or language, instead it was a "kind of thought expression that doesn't rely on language. And not a true voice that you could hear...but the sensation of words virtually spontaneously".

Usually he had these experiences when in a state of meditation, when sitting down, or before going to sleep. Norman described his condition as in a "diminished state" when he had these experiences, but not a condition like a trance or under the influence of drink or drugs. On most occasions, he was on his own when this phenomenon happened, though once he was walking along a city street when he felt that he could tell what people were thinking.

On another occasion during this period, he and a friend visited a Spiritualist Church in Sheffield, when he was "awakened to Christian faith". The Church was quite full when they entered and the minister was delivering a sermon. As the minister spoke, Norman felt a knot of tension build up in himself. They stood to sing a hymn and half way through it, he felt a distinct physical sensation of a twisting knot of tension in the area of the solar plexus.

"I felt this oppressive, almost hostile, presence in the church, I felt a strong hostility, a threat...", he explained. At this juncture, a nearby usher approached Norman and his companion, and said in a quiet voice to them: "Would you mind leaving please, I'd like you to go".

> Just before he approached me this thing was building up to a real climax ... as if something was tearing me inside out, literally... This man sensed that there was something amiss.

Norman's friend experienced nothing untoward in the church, and was no doubt puzzled as to why they were asked to leave.

In 1966, Norman knew a girl called Angela who lived in London. He took her out for about four months, and was very serious about her, and "cared an awful lot for her". However, in due course they went their separate ways. Later in a period when he was feeling emotionally low, very depressed anxious, physically depleted and under-nourished he saw Angela's face distinctly in front of him, as he was lying down one evening. She seemed to be speaking to him, but he cannot now remember what she was saying, except that she might have been asking him what he was doing, where he was, had he been thinking about her, had he missed her, etc.

Alien Intervention

Norman explained how he received extraterrestrial communications, saying that...

> ...I've had occasions, not just recently but I should say over the last two or three years, when I've been walking outside in the open, in a sort of park or recreation area something like that. The more open air the better. If I was in a large crowd of people...nothing. But on occasion I thought 'Oh, that's a daft idea, where did I get it from?', and then I'd suddenly realise that it's not an idea, but it's information. I'd have a sort of powerful influence to get a pen and notepad and jot it down. On some occasions I did this; I didn't keep the notes, but there have been times...when I've drawn pictures, and I've had these images which were very clear when I draw them, what I myself perceived was not very clear at all, but in the act of drawing it came through with clarity. And it seemed to me that I'd sort of acted as an unwitting unconscious intermediary and I've had this distinct sensation that someone is using me in order to transmit knowledge.

In particular, Norman noted, he has frequently had recurring impressions of three figures:

> None of them sort of stand on the ground, they all seem to be just suspended in space, and there are no buildings or anything recognisable around them at all. As though they were suspended in vacuum. They all have a powerful projection and I've not been personally intimidated, it doesn't seem to me that they are threatening me or in any way warning me, but they have an air of warning or admonition, if you like. Sort of 'take care', or 'watch it', pay attention.

The three figures are Aroniel, Mik-Ael and Uriel, whom Norman described in more detail:

Aroniel:

This personage is a "tall figure very straight, dressed in a long yellow robe, a flowing yellow robe with a high collar and he looks oriental. He wears a medallion in the centre of his forehead, and his own colour, his skin colour, is yellowish or shall we say golden and he's like a sort of gold appearance generally... He carries a book in one hand and the other is raised as if in greeting. The book looks like some sort of old book"

Mik-Ael:

"This is an image of what you might call something like a Crusader or armoured knight figure; chain mail with a tabard or tunic. It's a white tunic with a broad belt which looks metallic and has buttons on, and the tunic has a...red cross on it. He's like a Crusader, but the helmet is rather strange...it completely conceals the features, you can't make out the face. It's not like an ordinary visor but it's a solid, transparent sort of plate with a division in the middle. At the bottom (of it) there is a little round disc thing with a wire. He has...full sleeves and gauntlets, heavy gauntlets and he's carrying a sword in one hand.

"He sort of stands very powerfully with his legs apart. He presents either a challenging or shall we say an extremely aggressive, intimidating strength or just an image of strength. Its an intimidating sort of an aggressive image. His sword has a sort of red radiance... and he himself is surrounded with red, a deep scarlet or crimson. I should say it is crimson actually. It's like an aura or radiance all around him."

Aroniel, Michael and Uriel: illustration by Norman Harrison*

Uriel:

The third figure "has long, flowing robes, blue and green, and has like a blue or greenish-blue sort of radiance around him...this third one has white hair and apparently normal skin colour or slightly blue tinge and a white beard and white hair, and he also looks big, powerful but not in a military or a Crusader knight-in-armour fashion, but he looks as though he's sort of...tremendously ancient, tremendously, you know, tremendous power at his disposal. He doesn't seem to carry anything, he's got like a sash around the waist and he wears something like...one of the old fashioned robes of the Middle East."

Messages from Beyond

Later during the interview, he explained that the colours of the figures were directly linked with the type of energy they were emitting. He also claimed that he saw these figures in a kind of sequence, sometimes he would 'see' them fleetingly for only two – three seconds, other times they would appear for two or three minutes. Usually the first figure to appear is the one who has supremacy over the other two. Then maybe a few letters or geometrical symbols will appear: "They seem to be attempting to express relationships, but as I say, some of it isn't in any sort of expressed language, but there seems to be a logical sequence or progression. It's not logical to me, I don't know it, but it's logical to them."

Many of the letters he has seen are from Greek and Hebrew sources: "I've seen the triangle over and over again," he said about the recurring image he has seen over the past four or five months, and has included in many of his drawings, "I've seen a triangle with an eye in the centre, and I've seen this as a visual image, quite literally as though it was suspended in front of my eyes, in broad daylight when I was fully wide awake and stone cold sober – I hardly ever drink." This triangle is seen as red coloured with an eye in the centre, which is not like a real eye, but looks effectively like a bright red line drawing of an eye.

He then went on to describe the population of the galaxy, how at the hub there are regions of incalculable amounts of radiance and electromagnetic energy, where discarnate, disembodied 'beings' of ultimate intelligence reside. Radiating outwards from the hub, the state of evolution, culture, civilization and society diminish until we reach the very fringes of the galaxy where Neanderthal type beings populate the planets. These lesser planets, including Earth (as our Solar System is much closer to the fringe than the hub) are watched closely by the more superior races who take a parental interest in their evolution. Apparently, at the present time there has been a resurgence of interest in our planet.

This renewed interest might be because: "Man is a very disobedient wretch and keeps veering off, and getting side-tracked one way or another. The guiding hand keeps bringing him back to dead centre... there's this guidance all the way. There is one definite path of evolution of the spirit and mind."

According to him, humanity is being constantly helped by outside, alien forces. It was their influence, which partly established some of the most ancient of all the Oriental religions. He claims that many early religious figures such as Buddha and Moses were inspired by the influence of the extraterrestrials. Even today, a small number of adepts, who have a profound understanding of metaphysical philosophy, and live in very remote regions of the world, are in direct telepathic communication with alien people.

Through alien intervention – and according to Norman there are dozens, hundreds of alien races, some of which are almost immortal – the human mind has been triggered off to experience ESP, telepathy, clairvoyance, prophecy, predictions, etc. However, we have misused the forces and energy sources available, claims Norman, and distort things for our own greedy ends. We have probably, in the past, been punished for it afterwards. He quoted the examples, among others, of Atlantis and Babylon, and stated that global disasters are initiated from the outside and convey the alien moral standpoint. These purges occur because the behaviour of humanity can become offensive and noisily wrong:

> Man has destroyed himself as a living specimen at least six times in a row, cataclysm after cataclysm. There have been several cycles of biological life, gradually slowly, painstakingly developing, then flourishing, reaching an apex then declining... The Golden Age has long passed, none absolutely none of the 20th Century is anything like the Golden Age. It is a period now of the pinnacle of machinery, it's a pinnacle of mechanical contrivance, ingenuity is totally materialistic, physical things. It's a period of total stagnation and decadence in what you might call things of the spirit. There is

Michael Battles the CCCP: illustration by Norman Harrison*

> a complete decline in the ability to understand higher matters... in religious doctrine or philosophical things. Where are the people like Plato, Socrates, Aristotle? Where is the architecture, sculpture and art of Leonardo or Michelangelo?

He answers himself by explaining that the difference between them and modern contemporaries is "self evident."

Premonitions

In February of 1974, Norman had his first premonition. This was of a plane exploding in mid-air with people from the city of Leeds on board – an event which occurred three weeks later over France. During August 1974 he was living in London when he had a premonition of the Moorgate tube disaster, which happened in April 1975. He also 'knew' that the IRA would be posting letter-bombs to people in London in 1975. "All these premonitions seemed to me personally that they are being transmitted to me from an outside source," said Norman, who related that he felt no conscious control over these premonitions.

He also felt certain that humanity would have some crucial contact with extraterrestrials in the near future. It will be with somebody like the Archbishop of Canterbury, or some other such celebrity, and their reaction to the encounter will have far-reaching consequences.

After my visit and interview with Norman, he wrote to me on the 17th of March, and stated: "I feel quite sure now that these telepathic communications are only the beginning – there must be something more to follow in the future; I have a 'hunch' about it". In the same letter he noted another precognition of an impending disaster:

> Although there have been no new telepathic transmissions or impressions since you came over, I have received a warning in the

> form of one pen sketch which showed a big explosion. It involves highly inflammable chemicals and will happen in Britain within another month. I have no more exact location than that, but I do know this much – it will involve loss of life and will be caused by criminal negligence and carelessness. This foreboding is very strong and I know it comes from an outside source. The accident must be connected with a big chemical company like ICI or one of the fuel firms like Esso, or North Sea oil. I hope it doesn't happen because it will be a horrible tragedy – it could be averted if only there were proper precautions taken.

With this state of affairs, it is not surprising to learn that he had suffered four nervous breakdowns and was obsessed by the fate of humanity. Having met him on three occasions I can vouch for the fact that he is very verbose, and passionately intense about what he believes to be the gloomy and cataclysmic future of humanity. This fear is not generated by any love he might have for humanity; on the contrary, his fear is for himself. Living as someone who regards himself as being isolated and different from the rest of humanity, it is not surprising that Norman has transposed his ideas and imagination into an 'extraterrestrial' framework. His concept of the galaxy – pure energy and ultimate intelligence at the hub, Neanderthal beings on the edge – corresponds to concepts of heaven and hell, Jekyll and Hyde or unconscious and conscious, with the mortal Human pivoted between the two.

Even worse, we do not have full control over our destiny: the aliens have intervened throughout human history in order that we follow the "one definite path of evolution of the spirit and mind". Yet humanity cannot come up to this 'parental' expectation so we are punished for our morally offensive behaviour.

After my meetings with Norman at his home in Sheffield during 1978, I had a final meeting with him on 18th November 1979 at his new home in Leeds. This bed-sit was even worse than his previous address, but Norman seemed slightly more optimistic about the intentions of the aliens – but still felt that humanity was doomed. He was still receiving communications from beings that "have the power to project their own intelligence, identity and personality, out into interstellar space, and they can communicate this way. They have no need for space ships, because they use like, astral travel, or out-of-the-body projection. This is the result of advanced mental powers..."

My view was that Norman's communications were metaphorical and symbolic expressions of his feelings of guilt, isolation, alienation and emotional stagnation, which emanated from his own psyche. In addition, that it was no wonder that he feared the impending cataclysm. Norman responded by stating that I was guilty of "a glib, dogmatic, 'psychological' brand of easy rationalizing. (Nigel's) assumption is that I am a psychoneurotic down-and-out underdog, misfit, trying to compensate for my inferiority by erecting fantasies, and so on."

His opinion is valid, but from a ufological point of view, Norman offered no positive proof for the existence of extraterrestrial space vehicles or aliens. Nonetheless, he reflected the view of many ufo contactees and abductees: that the aliens are here to warn us of an apocalyptic end to humanity.

Since 1980, I don't know what has happened to Norman. If you are still out there, are the aliens still communicating with you? And, what is the fate of humanity today?

Nigel Watson is the author of *The Alien Deception* (2009), *Portraits of Alien Encounters* (1990), *Supernatural Spielberg* (with Darren Slade, 1992) and editor/writer of *The Scareship Mystery* (2000). He has written for numerous publications, including *Paranormal Magazine, Fortean Times, Beyond, Wired, History Today, Flipside, Strange Magazine, Magonia, The Unexplained, Flying Saucer Review, Alien Worlds,* and *UFO Magazine.* He produces the media website Talking Pictures (www.talkingpix.co.uk). He has a BA degree in Psychology (Open University) and a BA (Hons) degree in Film and Literature (University of Warwick). He lives in Plymouth, UK, with his wife and three children.

Courtesy of Liverpool Records Office

The Calderstones of Liverpool

Forgotten history hidden in the parks of Great Britain

by *John Reppion*

After living in the district of Toxteth for ten years, my wife and I have recently moved – along with our son and cat – back into the area of Liverpool where I grew up. We now reside in deepest Beatle country. The unremarkable childhood homes of Lennon and McCartney within easy walking distance; Harrison and Starr's each just a short bus ride away. Strawberry Field is just around the corner, and I regularly shove a pushchair up and down Penny Lane. Indeed, much of the area is practically unchanged since long, long before the days when moptops walked the earth – a good chunk of it being made up of parks, playing fields, cemeteries and other green-spaces. One of the most impressive of these parks stands next to the institution formerly known as Quarry Bank High School which

Lennon attended and named his proto-Beatles skiffle group The Quarrymen after.[1] After numerous mergings with other schools the institution was eventually renamed in 1985. Calderstones Community Comprehensive School took its new name from the adjacent Calderstones Park which is in turn named after the most ancient and perhaps easily overlooked monument in the city of Liverpool: The Calderstones.

Formerly a private estate, the land which makes up the park was purchased by Liverpool Corporation in 1902 for the sum of £43,000 from shipping magnate brothers Charles and David McIver. Calderstones Park was officially opened to the public three years later in 1905.[1] The 94 acre (0.38 km2) space is well kept and always busy, boasting as it does a walled garden, a children's play area, an historic Mansion House, a café, a former boating lake turned wildlife haven, a miniature ride-on railway, and even a thousand year old Oak Tree known as "the Law Oak". It is beneath the spreading branches of this majestic tree that crime and punishment are alleged to have been discussed in the days before court buildings. Local folklore has it that, although the Law Oak (also known as the Allerton Oak) looks for all the world as though it has been struck by lightning at some point in its long life, the damage was actually done by the explosion of a gunpowder ship in the Mersey in the 1860s.[2] The fact that the park and the Law Oak are more than a mile inland rarely, if ever, get in the way of the telling of the tale. Then there's the tennis – the park is home to the annual Liverpool International Tennis Tournament in which globally renowned players such as Martina Navratilova, John McEnroe and Martina Hingis regularly participate. Buried amongst this myriad of amusements, attractions and events – set back from the pathway which leads from the park's heavily ornamented main gates - is

[1] Other Quarry Bank alumni include horror novelist Clive Barker and actor Doug Bradley, most famous for playing Pinhead in the *Hellraiser* films which are (increasingly loosely) based on Barker's books.

an unassuming, semi-derelict looking conservatory. This weather-beaten structure is known as "the vestibule" and once served as the entry point to a network of greenhouses belonging to the Harthill community allotments beyond. Though the allotments are still in use, the greenhouses are long gone. Today the padlocked vestibule is home to half a dozen curiously ornamented sandstone relics ranging in size from almost 8 feet (2.4 m) to 4 feet (1.2 metres) tall, whose history was already all but forgotten when the Law Oak was still an acorn.

The Calldwaye Stones

The oldest written record of the stones dates back to 1568 where they are marked on a map relating to a boundary dispute between the districts of Wavertree and Allerton thusly:

> The Calldwaye Stones, called by the Quenes tenantes. And called bye y tenantes of Rich. Lathame the Dojer Stones, otherwise Roger Stones, or Calldwaye Stones.

The map shows only five upright "Calldwaye Stones" – four of which appear to be on a circular or oval mound. It also indicates another, solitary, standing stone marked "The Roger Stone" nearby. Furthermore there is a green circular hillock marked "The Pykklaoo Hill" which seems to be marked with a spiral-like pattern, possibly illustrating a pathway cut into its surface. It is worth noting that in much of the literature published since, Pykklaoo Hill is mentioned as being "flanked by two upright stones about 30 metres [98.4 feet] apart".[4,5,6] These stones are, however, not shown on the 19th century copy of the map I have before me today. The Caldewaye Stones, The Roger Stone, and Pykklaoo Hill are shown in a row hugging the South East edge of the land around which the dispute centred and which was later to become the boundary of the modern day park. The documentation accompanying the map records testimony from "Robert Mercer, of West Derby" – a district about 5 miles (8 km) north of the stones location – in which he states that a sixth Calderstone was removed from the site circa 1550.[7]

Written evidence of the stones over the next two hundred or so years is fairly scant. In 1700 the documentation accompanying another boundary dispute mentions just three stones set out on a little ascent or rising ground called "Dogger Stones, Caldway Stones". In 1804 or thereabouts the "high and extensive mound on which stones formerly stood" is all but destroyed to provide sand for the mortar of a house being built nearby.[8] Then we get a very interesting and revealing entry in Baines's Directory of 1825:

> Close by the farm on which the famous Allerton oak stands, and just at the point where four ways meet, are a quantity of remains called Calder stones [...]. From the circumstance that in digging about them urns made of the coarsest clay [and] containing human dust and bones have been discovered, there is reason to believe that they indicate an ancient burying place [...]. Some of the urns were dug up about sixty years ago, and were in the possession of Mr. Mercer of Allerton.[9]

A young farmhand's recollections of the destruction of the mound on which the Calderstones stood were recorded in 1833:

> When the stones were dug down to, they seemed rather tumbled about in the mound. They looked as if they had been a little hut or cellar. Below the stones was found a large quantity of burnt bones, white and in small pieces. He thought there must have been a cart-load or two.[10]

The stones were removed and stored on a nearby farmstead, with the exception of one which was taken by a Mr Booker for use as a rubbing stone for his cattle.[11]

By this time the land which was to become the Calderstones Park was owned by wealthy lead shot manufacturer Joseph Need Walker (builder of the park's extant Georgian-style Mansion House, completed in 1828). It was Walker who had the idea of making a feature of the stones – relocating them to a site at the South East entrance to his estate, not far from their original position. The Calderstones were retrieved from the nearby farmland and arranged in a circle, as they were assumed to have originally stood. A low wall was constructed around the Calderstones and still stands to this day at the junction of Menlove Avenue, Calderstones Road and Druids Cross Road. The stone plaque built into the barrier is now partly below street level so that only the top line of its inscription is clearly legible. Beneath "The Calderstones" the sign once read "Enclosed and Planted 1845".[12]

Roundabout where the Calderstones once stood (courtesy Moore & Reppion)

Stone plaque on roundabout, now slightly buried: "The Calderstones. Enclosed and Planted 1845" (courtesy Moore & Reppion)

Evidence from Antiquity

In a talk given for the Historic Society of Lancashire & Cheshire, later reproduced in their 1865 Transactions, the noted Scottish physician Sir James Young Simpson spoke eagerly about the "small megalithic circle" he had examined in Liverpool.[13] Sir Simpson is most famous today for discovering the anaesthetic properties of chloroform but he was also something of an antiquarian, speaking and writing on various archaeological and historical topics. The most fascinating, though perplexing, detail of the Calderstones, so far as Sir Simpson was concerned, were undoubtedly their markings:

> Many suggestions, I may observe, have been offered in regard to the intent and import of such lapidary cup and ring cuttings as exist on the Calder Stones; but none of the theories proposed solve, as it seems to me, the hieroglyphic mystery in which these sculpturings are still involved. They are old enigmatical 'handwritings on the wall,' which no modern reader has yet deciphered.[14]

The "cup and ring cuttings" referred to by Sir Simpson are a form of rock-art found chiefly in Europe, although similar markings have been discovered elsewhere including Mexico, Brazil, Greece, and India. They consist of a concave depression (cups, cupmarks, or cupules), carved into a rock surface and are often surrounded by etched concentric circles (rings).[15] These markings upon the surface of the Calderstones literally date back millennia.

Cup and ring marks are often found on rock outcrops, standing stones, and on cists (small stone-built coffin-like boxes) but they are also commonly associated with passage graves.[16] Passage graves consist of a narrow passageway made of stone leading to one or more burial chambers enclosed in more stone. A circular earthen mound is set over the chamber(s) giving them a hillock-like appearance. The nearest such surviving tombs to the Calderstones are Barclodiad y Gawres ("The Giantess's Apronful"), and Bryn Celli Ddu ("The Mound in the Dark Grove") 100 miles (160 km) to the West on the isle of Anglesey, in Wales.[17] Both of these passage graves are virtually intact and some of the stones at Barclodiad y Gawres have very similar carvings (known as petroglyphs) to the Calderstones, most notably the double spiral design on the Welsh tomb's "Stone 6".[18] Comparable patterns are also found on the stones of Irish passage graves at Newgrange and Knowth, which Barclodiad y Gawres and Bryn Celli Ddu also share similarities in their construction, size and layout with. These similarities have lead archaeologists to conclude that the Calderstones – rather than being a "small megalithic circle" – are in fact the remnants of a Neolithic passage grave constructed 4000 to 5000 years ago.

Given that it has already been mentioned that "urns made of the coarsest clay [and] containing human dust and bones" were discovered among the Calderstones some time prior to 1825, the revelation of the tomb might not seem quite so… revelatory. However, the urns in question would almost certainly date from the Bronze Age and could in fact be as much as 2000 years younger than the passage grave itself. The later record of the farmhand's testimony of excavation with its mentions of "a little hut or cellar" beneath, and "a large quantity of burnt bones" should, however, have made it very clear to Sir Simon and his fellow antiquaries that they were not dealing with a simple stone circle. In fact, it may well have done so when they eventually read it because, although recorded in 1833, the account was not published until 1896 in W.A Herdman's *A Contribution to the History of the Calderstones, near Liverpool.*

The presence of the Bronze Age cremation urns is now seen as evidence that the Calderstones Tomb remained in use as a sacred site for many thousands of years after its initial construction. This was a place where generation after generation after generation performed now long forgotten rituals. Where they committed the remains of the chosen few to the already ancient earthen sepulchre which must, to them, have seemed as old as the world itself.

The Language of the 'Liths

In 1954 the Calderstones were moved from where Walker planted them but much damage had been done in those one-hundred and nine years. The stones were "covered by a black patina or film, as well as by a growth of moss".[19] Removed under orders of Liverpool Corporation, the stones were cleaned and latex impressions taken of their surfaces, revealing details of carving which had previously been all but invisible to the naked eye. A survey was made of the stones based entirely upon these (now lost) moulds by J. L. Forde-Johnson, the results of which were published in his 1957 paper "Megalithic Art in the North West of Britain, The Calderstones, Liverpool." In his document Forde-Johnson allocated a letter to each of the six surviving stones and gave each carving on that stone a number. The stones were on display within the park for close to a decade until it was eventually decided that they should be moved - for their own protection - to their current location in the vestibule to the Hearthill greenhouses. Forde-Johnson's survey remained the definitive work on the Calderstones petroglyphs up until 2007/2008 when a high resolution digital photography survey of the stones was undertaken by Messrs George Nash and Adam Stanford. Key to the success of Nash & Stanford's survey was their use of oblique lighting techniques to optimise shadows cast on and by the designs. Their paper "Recording Images Old and New on the Calderstones in Liverpool" was published in 2010 and is an exhaustive chronicle of every visible motif upon the stones' surface.

In addition to the cup and ring markings already mentioned, the six surviving Calderstones also bear many other petroglyphs including spirals (single and conjoined), curved and straight lines (single and in groups), footprint images, and shoe, or boot, prints.[20] Many of these symbols provide further evidence of Calderstones Tomb's continued significance and use throughout aeons, while some simply represent a callous profaning of objects which may predate the oldest of Egypt's pyramids by a millennium.

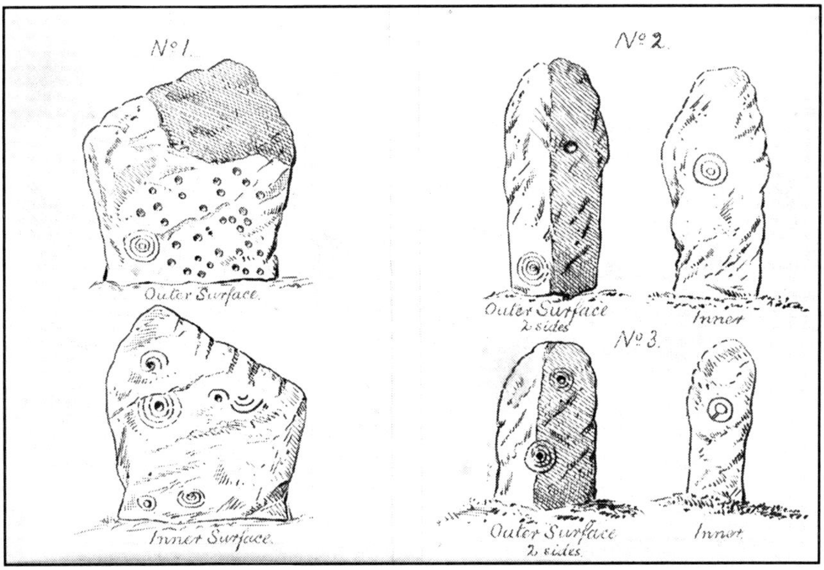

Markings on the Calderstones (courtesy Liverpool Records Office)

The Caldestones' spiral patterns are thought to be their original markings, carved circa 3000 BCE. The previously mentioned Irish passage graves at Newgrange and Knowth, and the Welsh Barclodiad y Gawres feature stones engraved with similar complex spiral designs. The meaning of these designs is still a matter of some debate. On the most basic level they are clearly decorative, marking out the stones and the tomb as a special place. Depending on the original location of these designs, some may also have acted as an externally visible indicator for the tomb. In his 1993 work *Subjective Vision and the Source of Irish Megalithic Art* Jeremy Dronfield puts forward a theory that spirals in passage graves such as the one at Knowth may be representations of visions seen with the aid of psychoactive substances.[21] Spirals have been variously interpreted as representing everything from local topography to astrological maps to cloud forms but are increasingly considered to be connected with the Sun and solar events. In short, though their exact meaning is unknown, the advent of spiral carvings is thought to represent a pivotal moment in prehistory – a time when humans were trying to find a way of expressing their thoughts and beliefs in a meaningful and lasting way.

The cup and ring markings and the curved and straight lines are the next oldest, possibly dating from as late as the Early Bronze Age. They are also the most easily recognisable petroglyphs in terms of their occurrence elsewhere. However, these carvings are also almost impossible to interpret accurately – "old enigmatical handwritings on the wall" indeed. Speaking in a 1970 BBC television documentary called *Cracking the Stone Age Code*, the Scottish engineer and megalithic expert Alexander "Sandy" Thom put forward his own theory:

> I have an idea, entirely nebulous at the moment, that the cup and ring markings were a method of recording, of writing, and that they may indicate, once we can read them, what a particular stone was for. We have seen the cup and ring markings on the stone at Temple Wood [for example] but we can't interpret them... yet.[22]

The footprints (more correctly referred to as petrosomatoglyphs, rather than petroglyphs) are also thought to be Bronze Age. There are eight well defined individual footprints, seven of which have five forward facing toes, while one print on Stone B has six. Each footprint has a blunt, squared heel giving them a slightly flipper-esque quality.[II] There are only a few British stones and artefacts with similar carvings, most notably a cist which originated from the Pool Farm barrow in West Harptree, Somerset and features six such footprints. Because the footprints are all singular, each is thought to represent specific individuals.[23] Whether these were people who were entombed there, who oversaw rituals, or perhaps acted as guardians of the site, we can only speculate.

The shoe or boot prints on the front face of Stone D are late 19th or early 20th century, presumably dating from the era when the stones were on display outside the park. Nash & Stanford's "Recording Images..." has the following to say on the carvings:

> Of the seven shoe or boot prints, three are buried beneath the present gravel (D4 – D10). The style of each carving is roughly similar, although four (D4, D6, D7, D10) have [separated] heels. [...] Inscribed into each print, usually on the sole area of the shoe are a series of letter. It is probable that these marks each represent the carver's initials.[24,25]

These Victorian (or possibly Edwardian) vandals were not the last to make their mark upon the ancient stones either. Several of the Calderstones are covered with initials, many of which must

---

[II] The Calderstones' footprint markings are mentioned in Ramsey Campbell's *Creatures of the Pool* as "blurred marks that suggest some bulky person has been fumbling wet-handed at the stones". Joseph Williamson's extensive tunnels beneath Liverpool [see: "The Underground Empire of Joseph Williamson" in *Darklore Volume 4*] also feature heavily in the novel.

have been carved during their unprotected, post-cleaning display in the park between 1954 and 1964. The fact that the initials "JL" are clearly visible on one stone has not escaped the notice of those few visiting Beatles fans who have been lucky enough to see stones up close.[26]

On the opposite face of Stone D to the boot prints, half buried beneath the ground, is perhaps the most fascinating yet easily overlooked of all the Calderstones adornments: an image of a dagger.[27] The alleged knife, or dagger, is very difficult to make out even with Nash & Stanford's expert photography. The carving is described in their 2010 paper as "a south east European-style dagger" dating from the Early Bronze Age.[28] Such daggers do occur in funerary art across Bronze Age Atlantic Europe but are not common in the UK. A notable example, showing three such daggers, is visible on the Castriño de Conxo - a Castro (a kind of ancient settlement composed of a fortified area with round stone huts inside it) in the Galicia region of Spain.[29,30] Actual Bronze Age daggers are occasionally found at grave sites (such as the flat bladed, horn hilted dagger found in a cist at Rameldry, Fife, Scotland, in the year 2000)[31] and are usually interpreted as marking the burial place of a high status individual because of the time and resources which would have been devoted to creating such an object. A carving of a dagger then possibly indicates that a high status individual buried there owned such a weapon but that it was considered too precious to commit to the tomb, perhaps even having been already passed on to another individual. That being the case, could the dagger represent the final person laid to rest in the ancient sepulchre? The dagger is certainly amongst the latest of the BCE carvings and quite possibly the most recent. Could an Iron Age chieftain have been the last interment in Claderstones Tomb? Sadly, it seems highly unlikely that we'll ever know – all of the "human dust and bones" the grave once contained having long since been removed.

Blood from a Stone: The Spectre of the Druid

There is, of course, another interpretation of the graven dagger image on Calderstone D – few of us can read of such an instrument carved on an ancient mystical site and not have some suitably Hammer Horror-esque image of primeval blood sacrifice called to mind. And who is that hooded figure wielding the blade in our shared vision? Why, it is the Druid, of course. The notion of the Druids as bloodthirsty "baddies", however, predates the birth of Christopher Lee et al by several millennia. Greek Historian Diodorus Siculus wrote in the 1st century BCE of some of the barbaric rituals purportedly then being practiced by the Celtic Druids in Britain:

> These men predict the future by observing the flight and calls of birds and by the sacrifice of holy animals: all orders of society are in their power... and in very important matters they prepare a human victim, plunging a dagger into his chest; by observing the way his limbs convulse as he falls and the gushing of his blood, they are able to read the future.[32]

Diodorus's contemporary the Roman writer Gaius Plinius Secundus (better known as Pliny the Elder) went further, suggesting the Celts practiced ritual cannibalism, eating their enemies' flesh as a source of spiritual and physical strength.[33] Such writings have long been taken with a generous pinch of salt by most historians who understand them to be works of propaganda, portraying the British Isles' inhabitants as superstitious, heathen barbarians badly in need of conquering. Nevertheless, the true nature of the Druids and their practices remains a hotly-debated topic within academic circles. The 1st century CE body known as Lindow Man, for example, has provoked much discussion in the decades since its discovery at Lindow Moss bog in Cheshire, England. Lindow Man now resides within the walls of the British Museum and is described on their website thusly:

> The man met a horrific death. He was struck on the top of his head twice with a heavy object, perhaps a narrow bladed axe. He also received a vicious blow in the back – perhaps from someone's knee – which broke one of his ribs. He had a thin cord tied around his neck which may have been used to strangle him and break his neck. By now he was dead, but then his throat was cut. Finally, he was placed face down in a pool in the bog. This elaborate sequence of events suggests that his death may have been ritual killing. Some people have argued that he was the victim of a human sacrifice possibly carried out by Druids.

The sacrifice story has long been put forward as a likely explanation for Lindow Man's death, not just by the British Museum themselves, but in numerous books, and even television programs such as National Geographic Channel's *Secrets of the Druids*.[34] Robert Connolly, senior lecturer in physical anthropology at the University of Liverpool, has very different ideas on the matter. Connolly was quoted in *The Times* newspaper in March 2004 as saying:

> We do not have evidence from this body of ritual sacrifice in Iron Age Cheshire. We mustn't write it into the books until we have evidence. That is disrupting history. That is not historical evidence. It wouldn't stand up in court.[35]

In the article Connolly and Professor Ronald Hutton of the University of Bristol argue that many of Lindow Man's wounds could have been inflicted during peat-cutting activities or from his having been trampled by a horse. They go on to say that Lindow Man's throat cartilage shows no sign of the trauma associated with strangulation and that a decorative necklace, being made of animal sinew, could have shrunk over time, allowing it to be later interpreted as a garrotte.[36]

If we accept that the Celts – whose holy men the Druids were – are not believed to have reached Britain until the Iron Age (circa

500 BCE) it seems impossible that the Druids could have had any influence on the construction of structures and monuments created thousands of years previously. The design of the dagger engraved into the sandstone surface of Calderstone D likewise predates the age of the Druids, not by millennia, but certainly by centuries. How is it then, that stone circles such as Stonehenge and megalithic tombs like Barclodiad y Gawres have come to be associated in so many people's minds with the Druids? William Stukeley M. D.'s work *Stonehenge, A Temple Restor'd to the British Druids*, published in 1740, certainly has something to do with it.

Working with Astronomer Royal Edmond Halley (best known for computing the orbit of the eponymous Halley's Comet), Stukeley came to the conclusion that Stonehenge was aligned with magnetic north and built by the Druids, being completed circa 460 BCE.[37] Writing copiously on other supposed Druid remains (including passage graves) Stukeley became popularly known as the "Arch-Druid" and, indeed, later came to identify himself as a Druid.[38] Other antiquaries devoted more and more time towards the study of what they perceived to be Druidism and soon groups such as The Druid Society of Anglesey, The Society of the Druids of Cardigan, and the London based Ancient Order of Druids (still in existence today) began to spring up all across Britain.[39] Through these societies, and the writings of Stukeley and those who followed, the connection between Druids and menhirs[III] was firmly established in the public consciousness. This association endures to this day, despite much archaeological evidence to the contrary.

Any alleged connections between the carving of the Early Bronze Age "south east European-style dagger" on Calderstone D and the Druids would then, it seems, be little more than a fantasy – albeit one whose origins lie in literally thousands of years worth of propaganda

---

[III] Menhir: "long-stone" in Celtic Middle Breton – a term first applied to standing stones by 19th century antiquarians.

and misinformation. Of course, it is still impossible to prove conclusively that the Calderstones Tomb was never visited by Celtic wise men during its existence. It is perhaps fair to say though, that the only genuine sign of Druids near the former tomb site remains that of the adjacent Druids Cross Road.

Missing Menhirs

A mile or so South East of Calderstones Park, at the junction of Booker Avenue and Archerfield Road an ice-cream van's engine idles as the pupils from the nearby Booker Avenue Infants and Juniors queue for their after-school treats. Neither the over-excited children nor their harassed parents seem to give the curious prehistoric relic in their midst so much as a second glance. Here in the heart of suburbia, enclosed by green painted iron railings, is an ancient sandstone menhir. A weathered bronze plaque within the railings explains the stone's recent history:

> THIS MONOLITH KNOWN AS "ROBIN HOODS STONE" STOOD IN A FIELD NAMED THE STONE HEY AT A SPOT 198 FEET DISTANT, AND IN A DIRECTION BEARING 7 DEGREES EAST OF TRUE NORTH FROM ITS PRESENT POSITION, TO WHICH IT WAS MOVED IN AUGUST 1928.

Robin Hood's Stone seems a rather misleading name since there are no tales of the fabled outlaw and his merry band straying quite so far from Sherwood as Merseyside. The monolith was formerly known as "The Archer's Stone" on account of a series of deep grooves worn into it, once believed to have been used during medieval times for sharpening arrowheads. As fanciful as this idea might seem, it is perhaps worth mentioning that during the 19th century the common

Robin Hood's Stone (courtesy Moore & Reppion)

consensus amongst antiquarians was that these grooves were created by Druids to aid the draining of blood from their sacrificial victims.[40,41] The grooves are now generally considered to have occurred naturally when the rock was formed and been further ingrained as the fragile sandstone was worn away by aeons of wind and rain. Archerfield road is so named because it was built upon the site of the field where The Archer's Stone once stood – the construction of that neighbourhood being the reason for the stone's relocation in the 1920s. Booker Avenue, incidentally, is named after Josias Booker - a 19th century West India merchant and shipping magnate who lived for a time in nearby Poplar Grove. It might be remembered that, prior to the Calderstones being relocated by Joseph Need Walker in 1845, one of the stones was taken by a Mr Booker for use as a rubbing stone for his cattle. Josias was certainly no farmer and actually emigrated to Demerara (now Guyana) in 1815 but, the fact that his family - he was one of seven brothers – lived so close to the field where The Archer's Stone stood seems quite a coincidence.[42] There are, however, those who would point out that the plot where the menhir formerly stood is recorded on a map of 1772 as "Stone Hey" which could well indicate that the stone was already in situ. On the other hand, there is the 1568 testimony of Robert Mercer, of West Derby which states that a Calderstone was taken from its original site circa 1550. So, could Robin Hood's Stone actually be one of these lost Calderstones?

Although the supposed arrow sharpening/bloodletting grooves are now considered to be natural, there are other, more intriguing, markings on Robin Hood's Stone which are currently buried beneath a thick layer of concrete. A 1910 photograph of the now hidden end of the menhir clearly shows cup and ring markings just like those on Calderstones B, C, D and E.[43] The photograph was taken by R. Stuart-Brown and published, along with at least one other of Robin Hood's Stone, in his 1911 work *A History of the Manor and Township of Allerton in the County of Lancashire, Liverpool.* This other photograph shows the stone standing in its field with roughly the same portion of its surface underground as today – the cup and rings still very much hidden from view. Only when the earth was dug out around the base of the menhir were the ancient carvings made visible. This would seem to suggest that the person who placed the stone in that position saw no significance, or perhaps simply had no interest, in the menhir's prehistoric markings which certainly fits in with the cattle rubbing stone hypothesis. Even if we rule out our 19th century Mr Booker, is it perhaps fair to deduce that whoever took the other stone circa 1550 might have wanted it for the same purpose and therefore set it in a cattle field. The type of sandstone used for Robin Hood's Stone and five of the Calderstones is identical, having probably been quarried locally.[44] This is perhaps unsurprising – one might well expect all such stone to come from the same source, but consider then Calderstone F which has a distinctly finer grain than its supposed counterparts. Calderstone F also has a distinct lack of prehistoric markings.[45] In reality, it seems that a much more compelling case can be made for Robin Hood's Stone having originally been a part of the passage grave than can for Calderstone F. Could this be because Calderstone F was actually a lone standing stone (or part thereof) which was later lumped in with the remnants of Calderstones Tomb? In which case, might Calderstone F actually be the remains of The Roger Stone which we know from the 16th century boundary dispute documentation to have been the closest such menhir? Certainly, it seems possible and, given the way we know the Calderstones have been treated in the past four-hundred-and-odd years, not unlikely, that such a mix up might have occurred.

Lost in the Mists of Time

The Calderstones themselves are currently not mentioned on Liverpool City Council's Calderstones Park webpage.[46] On the black painted signs which mark each of the park's four official entrances, a circular symbol depicting a Stonehenge-like dolmen[IV] seems somehow lost amongst others showing ducks, a seesaw, and more typical attractions.

Of the many, many times I have visited the park I can only clearly recall one instance of seeing anyone, other than myself and the people I was with, paying any real attention to the stones. It was 2007 and I was in the middle of researching a book I was writing on Liverpool ghosts. A "spooky" evening tour of Calderstones given by the park rangers seemed too tempting an offer to pass up. Having heard the yarns of a kitchen boy crushed to death by a Christmas Eve coal delivery in the cellar of the Mansion House, a girl drowned in the boating lake, and so on, we gradually progressed toward the Calderstones. When we reached the vestibule its doors were unlocked and myself, my wife, and the dozen or so other tourers were ushered in. The space was warm and damp – electric heaters working against the foggy October air to protect the megaliths from winter's chill. Fine spider's webs spun across the pitted surfaces of the menhirs were frosted with moisture which glistened in the glow of the heat elements. The engravings shimmered fierily as if each stone had a core of liquid magma beneath its brittle sandy surface. Our guide hurried through a truncated history of the stones, explaining that they were once part of an ancient tomb and that pottery urns containing human ashes had been found buried beneath them. For a precious few moments the crowd stared at the battered orphic stones in absolute wonder. But, all too soon, the spell was broken. The ranger had no eerie tale directly connected to the stones to tell, so instead urns supposedly similar to those which once been entrusted to them became the focus of his next story. By the time we left the vestibule, the ranger's colourful yarn about a spectral Iron Age horseman wielding an axe had all but erased the brief, vague history of the circle of crumbling stones from most people's minds. And, with each step away from

---

[IV] Dolmen: from the Celtic Middle Breton "taol maen" meaning "stone table".

the dilapidated structure, the illusionary fire within the ancient sigils seemed to dim.

Despite the fact that the decaying vestibule might seem a less than salubrious home for the prehistoric Calderstones it is still, in many respects, actually the best place for them. The stones need to be under cover to protect them from weathering, and from vandalism. They also need to be kept in an environment where the temperature can be controlled (to some extent) to prevent damage by frost. The vestibule, unattractive as it is, fulfils these criteria amply. Even so, some might wonder why the Calderstones have not, by now, been removed from the park entirely and placed on display at one of Liverpool's numerous museums. Such a removal would, in my opinion, be something of a mixed blessing. On the one hand the stones could be better protected, could be more thoroughly studied, and, above all, could be seen by many, many more people. However, they would also be robbed of

The Calderstones at their current location, within the vestibule at Calderstones Park (courtesy Moore & Reppion)

The Calderstones as they were in 1905, exposed to the elements (courtesy Liverpool Records Office)

their context – becoming mere skeletal remains of some long lost tomb which once stood in the Allerton area.

In their 5000 or so years of existence the Calderstones have moved - with the possible exception of one or two – less than half a mile (0.8 km). The park which is named after them – landscaped and gardened as it now is – has nevertheless been a continuous, inextricably linked green-space for the duration of that time. The Calderstones may not be in the best condition, they may not have as many visitors as they used to, and their home certainly isn't in brilliant shape. However, they're still there. Still in the same neighbourhood, amongst old friends like the Law Oak, and though they need a bit of help now and then, they're doing okay. Ripping them out of their native surroundings, putting them somewhere cold and clinical might well be the best way of preserving their facades. It might well be "for their own good", but what about their function? What about their purpose? What of the prehistoric Britons who carved those labyrinthine spirals whose meaning still eludes us and whose graves the stones once marked? The buried ends of those stones touch that self same soil which was piled up, by hand, millennia ago to form the earthen roof of their tomb. That self same soil in which those bodies – and later those urns of ash – were laid to rest. The park and the stones belong to each other, and long may they remain together.

John Reppion is a freelance writer with an interest in all things Fortean, folkloric and esoteric. In the past he has written for the likes of *Fortean Times, Strange Attractor Journal, Paranormal Magazine* and *The End is Nigh* on subjects as diverse as medieval revenants, exogenesis and Spring-heeled Jack. His book *800 Years of Haunted Liverpool* was published in 2008 by The History Press and covers much of the uncanny history and folklore of his native city. More information can be found online at www.MooreReppion.com

double Trouble

The Science and Superstition of Multiple Suns

by *Martin Shough*

In early March, 2011, Asian television stations carried news of a cosmic spectacle captured on video in Taiwan.[1] Journalists announced breathlessly that the images of twin suns, side by side just above the horizon (Fig.1), were "unexplained by science", and before long the story of the amazing Taiwanese double-sun had gone around the world.

Numerous versions of the story and related spin-off videos appeared on internet sites such as YouTube. People everywhere, it seemed, had been seeing and filming double suns, triple suns and similar astonishing portents in the heavens. In fact the TV story was not seminal, but merely served to fan the flames of an already widespread belief which had been fostering apocalyptic predictions for years.

Fig.1 A frame from the Taiwanese "double sun" video of March 2, 2011

Much of the current popular fascination with these ideas can be traced to end-times myths about destruction of the Earth by the passage of the planet Nibiru, a fictitious giant world supposed to occupy a highly-eccentric inclined orbit about an unseen dark companion of the sun. This orbit is said to intersect that of the Earth at long cosmic intervals, when the proximity of the giant planet triggers global catastrophe. When Nibiru passes Earth in 2012 it will "be seen as a second Sun around the size of our moon", notes one website, which reassures us that this information "is fact using Astronomical and scientific facts as the ultimate proof."[2]

According to the curious numerology of these beliefs, the passage of Nibiru through the ecliptic on December 21, 2012, anticipated with a mixture of fierce glee and lamentation on many websites, will trigger earthquakes, mega-tsunamis, chaotic weather and general devastation, and will fulfill the prophecy implicit in the supposed termination of the Mayan calendar in 2012: The End of the World, accompanied – so the Mayans purportedly also tell us – by the appearance of two suns.

And as if to make triply certain of the dread outcome, fate has arranged that 2012 will be the approximate date of the next regular maximum of the activity cycle of our familiar sun, Sol, at which time there is indeed some risk that an increase in solar flares and coronal mass-ejections could cause geomagnetic fluctuations and particle storms with accompanying effects on orbiting satellites, power and communications systems.

How could mankind possibly hope to escape such a redundancy of apocalypses? As the above-mentioned blog warns us, there is "not much time left to decide what is truly important in your life..."

Should we worry? Well, no. Double suns do not necessarily signify the end of the world, because the legends and folktales of many cultures around the world tell us that the miracle has happened countless times before.

Multiple Suns in Myth and Folklore

In the cosmogony of the Bashkir people of western Russia[3], whose lands lay around the Ural Mountains about 1000 miles east of Moscow, there were originally two suns in the sky, so that it was never dark. The ceaseless brilliance drove men mad, but although many powerful bowmen tried none could shoot an arrow high enough to damage the suns. Until one day a hero called Batyr Ural let fly an arrow made of diamond from his bow of horn, with a twanging that set the whole world reverberating such that mountains fell down and rivers reversed their courses. In the midst of this cataclysm the diamond arrow flew up and up until it pierced one of the two suns, breaking it in half. The people all cried out, "Ai!", as one half fell to the Earth and created the Ural Mountains, whilst the other half remained in the sky but grew dim, becoming the Moon, and the word of exclamation that the people cried out became the name of the Moon, *Ai*, in the Bashkir tongue.[4]

A similar tale of "The Two Suns" appears in the legends of the Udegey people, some 3000 miles further east on the Pacific coast of Outer Manchuria.[5] And a myth of the Meitheis[6] of the Brahmaputra valley region of the Himalayas, south of Bhutan, says that "at first there were two suns which rose and set alternately. A slave, tired of getting no rest, shot one of them."[7] Whilst according to a 1906 book[8] the people of Malacca, Malaysia (on the southern Malay Peninsula) had "a myth of three suns, one of which was always left in the sky. The female sun was induced to swallow her husband and child, and now there was night."[9] And in China, it was told 2000 years ago that there had once been as many as *ten* suns in the sky, their pitiless heat causing terrible drought, drying up rivers and withering all growing things. They would have destroyed the world. But a great – if overenthusiastic – hunter and archer called Houyi shot nine of the ten suns, and would have shot the tenth, too, were it not for the fortuitous theft of his last arrow, thus narrowly averting permanent darkness on the face of the Earth.[10]

No doubt one could assemble a longer list. The image of multiple suns, as a special case of heavenly portents in general (and of solar misbehaviour in particular, exemplified otherwise by such anomalies as the biblical standing still of the sun in heaven), evidently has considerable mythic power. It is associated often with catastrophe, creative or destructive, with a great change in the natural or moral order. Not surprising. The sun is in many ways the pre-eminent power of nature, the pole and axle of the world, and there is in these shocking dislocations of the sun something which especially symbolises an overturning of the pillars and foundations of the natural order.

Moving into semi-historical times, the ideology of the Roman cult of Mithras in the early Christian era contains the notion of two suns, one being Helios the sun-god and the other Mithras in the form of "sol invictus" or the "unconquered sun". The Mithraic ideology is obscure and the function of this motif in relation to the symbolic slaying of the Bull is "perplexing" but has been related to the idea in contemporary Platonism "of the existence of two suns, one being the normal astronomical sun and the other being a so-called 'hypercosmic' sun located beyond the sphere of the fixed stars."[11]

In China, in January of 314 AD "three suns were seen moving from the west to the east… The royal astronomer said, '…Three suns appearing together means that feudal lords are about to fight for the crown within the next three months.' The prediction came true… The whole world was thrown into complete chaos."[12] As usual the display is considered prophetic. Likewise, connoisseurs of apocalyptic auguries have attempted to weave the verses of the 16th century French seer Nostradamus[13] into a prophecy of cataclysm in 2012. In one of his many gnomic quatrains (C2, Q41) he predicted the arrival of a "great star". At this time "the large mastiff will howl all night when the great pontiff changes his abode" and "the cloud will make the sun appear double".

Given that the motif of double suns was anciently embedded in a range of myths across Europe and Asia, it is perhaps no great surprise that when Europeans arrived in the New World they discovered a prophecy of the native American Hopi people foretelling that a new sun, a terrible blue star called Kachina, will appear in the sky, heralding a final conflict between the spiritual and material and ushering in catastrophically a new phase of the world.[14]

And it seems that for some people this mythic notion retains its ancient power today. According to some recent Christian exegesis, the signalling of the End Times by a new sun fulfils not only Mayan but also biblical prophecy. Scholars believe that the rising of The Sun of Righteousness foretold in Malachi 4:2 refers to the coming of Jesus at the time of judgement, and with a little nifty scriptural footwork it turns out that one may interpret this verse as predicting the arrival of a terrible sun, bringing scorching and devastation that will burn the wicked like stubble, simultaneous with the arrival of a second sun bringing "healing in His wings" for the good and the godly.[15]

"According to the Bible," insists one commentator, "there *are going* to be two suns. What the Mayans don't know and what their prophecies don't tell you is one of the suns is going to bring destruction and devastation. The other is going to bring healing in His wings. One is going to burn up much of the earth, and those on it... Along with all the talk about hurricanes, tsunamis, earthquakes, comets, and more horrifying stuff than you can think of, the 'Mayan prophecies' seem to indicate there will be two suns in 2012."[16] Another article agrees that the verses in Malachi "have great prophetic significance" and that the Sun of Righteousness does indeed explain the two suns of the Mayan revelation.[17]

But not all mythological symbolism is religious, and not all of it is ancient either. Some of us will recall the setting twin suns of the desert world Tatooine, marking a watershed moment of tragedy in the destiny of Luke Skywalker, in George Lucas's 1977 epic space-opera *Star Wars* (Fig.2), whilst others may recall Pink Floyd's "Two Suns In The Sunset" with its "suspicions of the holocaust to come...could

Fig.2 The twin suns of Tatooine from *Star Wars*[18]

be the human race is run". The latter apparently echoes the Pacific Marshall Islanders' description of the March 1, 1954 Crossroads Bravo hydrogen bomb as a "second sun" rising in the west; coupling the power of the atom to the power of the metaphor.

As already mentioned, the imagery of double suns has been widespread on the internet for some years, especially in the context of 2012 predictions, and with the appearance in March 2011 of the Chinese video with which we began the topic seemed to have "gone viral" across many news platforms in Asia and beyond, encouraging hysterical speculation about the the imminent end of the world. Of course, most of the photos and films are clearly either reflections in double-glazing units and the like, lens flares, or interesting but commonplace atmospheric ice haloes such as "sundogs". No case gives evidence of the arrival of a massive cosmic body in the Earth's neighbourhood, whose presence would be disclosed in short order both by routine scientific and military surveillance of local space on various wavelengths and by its disruptive gravitational effects on orbiting bodies and so forth. But there is no denying that people can be captivated and affected by these beliefs. As one gentle American lady's video diary rather movingly recorded on 02 Nov 2010:

> I could not sleep last night thinking about that double-sun I filmed. Nibiru is coming by the look of it. Double suns are not normal. I filmed Nibiru today. Two suns. And now I know. We are in trouble, we are in such trouble... It's going to be just like *The Day After Tomorrow*. Don't waste another moment doing foolish stupid things like going to work, being a slave.[19]

Historical & Modern Observations of Multiple Suns

The Roman naturalist Pliny the Elder remarked that "once several suns were seen at midday at the Bosphorus, and these lasted from dawn till sunset. In former times three suns have often been seen at once… and our generation saw this during the principate of his late Majesty Claudius [41–54 AD]… Also three moons have appeared at once, for instance in the consulship of Gnaeus Domitius and Gaius Fannius."[20]

Pliny doubted that more than three suns had ever been seen, but in 1629 a great display of "five suns" was seen by citizens in the area of Rome, and the account given in Gassendi's *Phenomenon Rarum* of that year, based on detailed observations by Christoph Scheiner, was a significant watershed in the history of atmospheric optics. An even more complex display in 1630 generated a remarkable "seven suns"![21]

These and many similar observations are obviously ice halos, "mock suns" or parhelia. Such "suns" are usually (but not always) patches of fuzzy light positioned 22° or 46° from the true sun and produced by refraction through horizontally-oriented hexagonal ice crystals in the atmosphere. No doubt a great many mythological as well as historical references to double and triple so-called suns are explained by such halos, whose physics are quite well (if not completely) understood. Other observations where the setting or rising sun is split or distorted *vertically* are explicable as optical mirages, caused by temperature gradients that produce sharp changes in the refractive index of the atmosphere. But not all cases fall in these categories. Reports of properly focused true images of side-by-side multiple suns (and moons) do exist and are a different matter.

Nothing in atmospheric or meteorological optics predicts these phenomena; nevertheless it seems to be quite widely accepted amongst experts that they have occurred, even though the scanty evidence is to a very large degree anecdotal and untested. Is this, perhaps, because of a certain non-rational attachment to the idea of celestial wonders even amongst academic scientists? How *ought* we to approach these claims?

Probably the classic "respectable" account that most atmospheric scientists would cite is the one discussed by the Belgian astronomer Marcel Minnaert and first published in the journal *Weather* in

1966.[22] Minnaert was the author of many papers and books, including the oft-cited three-volume opus *Light and Colour in the Open Air* (1st ed. 1937), and was widely respected as an expert on atmospheric optics. Consequently his account of a remarkable double sun photographed by a passenger on the steamship *Fairstar* in the Sea of Timor, South Pacific, on July 15th 1965 has been influential and extremely persuasive (Fig.3).

Minnaert's account prompted the well-known physicist Philip Morrison, for example, to contrast the case with many reports of UFOs, citing it during a Symposium on UFOs sponsored by the American Association for the Advancement of Science in 1969[23] as a "spectacular example" of an atmospheric phenomenon that we do not yet understand, a "striking case" supported by "hard evidence" in the form of the photograph, and presented of course by an impeccable authority in a scientific journal. Morrison's complacency in regard to the story is understandable. But it should be said that the "link by link chain of evidence" upon which Morrison himself was wont to insist in other circumstances is broken in the case of the Minnaert photo.

Fig.3 Detail from a photo of a double sun reportedly taken from the ship *Fairstar* in the Sea of Timor, July 15 1965 (Minnaert, 1966; see note 22)

Morrison is impressed to be able to report that "twenty or thirty other passengers in the first-class salon all testified that they had seen this very same phenomenon", thus apparently ruling out a photographic artefact; however the paper by Minnaert[24] cited by Morrison as his source contains no such claim, rather it says only that the effect "was also seen by the few other passengers who happened to be on deck." This is confirmed in the original account by Minnaert published three years earlier, which states that only "a few" people were on deck, and that the witness pointed out the effect to "two other passengers, who then also noted the phenomenon". He concludes by reiterating that it was "noticed visually by three persons".[25] So there is actually no evidence at all that Morrison's "twenty or thirty" witnesses existed.

Moreover, Morrison's claim that other witnesses "all testified" is misleading, inasmuch as this suggests depositions or interviews or at least some independent account purporting to represent their impressions. But no such source appears to exist. The agreement of the two other anonymous observers exists only insofar as it was reported by the photographer, Mrs. N.S., herself, in her account given in some fashion to Minnaert, at some unknown time after the event.

Morrison says of his "twenty or thirty" other witnesses that "they got the woman, who was the best photographer among them, to walk out to the rail of the ship in clear air to take the photograph", a bit of circumstantial picture-painting of the sort which would be very convincing did we not know that most of these people were in fact imaginary. And Morrison appears to have invented the bit about how the witnesses determined Mrs N.S.'s relative photographic prowess; neither his cited source nor any other of Minnaert's published accounts contains any such colourful detail. But whatever the number and actions of the witnesses, Morrison found it significant that they had seen the same thing that later appeared on the photo, and in this he faithfully follows Minnaert, who remarked that "there were no window panes between them and the landscape"[26] proving that the image the three people saw was not a local reflection.

But note that Minnaert does not explicitly say that there was no window glass between the *camera* and the sun. Minnaert wrote in his original article that the *sighting* was made on deck with "no glass pane interposed", but there he says that Mrs N. S. then "*ran to her cabin*, grasped her camera, and made a colour photograph [emphasis added]". One understands why so many readers of Minnaert have missed the implication of this short sentence.[27] In discounting the specific possibility of photographic reflections, Minnaert merely says, "it seems impossible to explain the observation by any reflexion or by instrumental effects inside the camera, because it was first noticed visually by three persons." We easily fail to notice that he does not explicitly rule out the possible presence of a window or porthole glass in front of the camera.

And something was indeed "first noticed visually by three persons", according to the photographer, at least; but *what*, precisely, was noticed? When you get down to it, what we have is a story told to Minnaert by one person who took the photo, who evidently gave him to understand that two others on deck had seen something just like the photo. But we can't prove that. We can't even prove that these people would have claimed it to be so.

Conceivably if Minnaert had published an interview with Mrs N.S., or at least the raw text of whatever testimony was originally supplied by her, certain things would be clearer. But as it stands, one has to consider possibilities – including the possibility that the story she told Minnaert was an improvisation around the discovery of an accidental photo artefact. Perhaps she had photographed the sunset from her cabin, unwittingly capturing an image of the sun and its own twinned image produced either by reflections between the front and back surfaces of the thick porthole glass; by a similar reflection between the inner and outer panes of a sealed double-glazing unit; or from some other surface in the cabin? Perhaps only when the film was processed after the voyage did she discover the double sun, prompting a good after-dinner story which found its way to Minnaert.

Can we test this speculative scenario? If the photograph was taken through a small porthole the field of view (FOV) would imply a camera position close to the glass, obstructing possible reflection raypaths from behind the photographer.[28] Reflections between the glass and the front surface of the lens would not do, because the lens surface is quite steeply convex and this would produce only an out-of-focus reflection.[29] And as far as I can discover porthole glass, whilst often extremely thick, tends to be plane sheet glass, whose tolerance would be too small to explain a 3.5° displacement of the reflection from the primary image.[30] Marine historian Reuben Goossens advises[31] that no double-glazed ports or windows were fitted on the *TSS Fairstar*; but rows of large picture windows (each about 2ft or 60cm square to judge from photos) were indeed fitted to cabins and suites on the Boat Deck.

Plans of the accommodation on the *Fairstar's* passenger decks show that there were only 12 cabins or suites on the Boat Deck (a superstructure level immediately below the Officers' Deck which would presumably also have been the location of Morrison's "first class salon"), and *if* Mrs N.S. occupied one of these it would also explain why there were only "a few" passengers out on deck with her enjoying this "almost perfectly clear" sunset and a "very quiet" sea. No doubt things may have been busier on the promenade deck below. So a multiple reflection from a mirror or other reflective surface on a nearly-coplanar vertical wall behind the witness, to the window glass and thence back into the lens, may be a realistic possibility.

On the other hand, it turns out that for privacy these windows were constructed with extra thick, shatter-proof glass with a "one-way treatment that gave the exterior a smoky mirrored look".[32] Andrew Young points out that given this deliberately poor transmissivity, the slow speed of colour slide films available in 1965 would probably not have allowed capture of the degree of shadow detail visible in the published half-tone.[33] Furthermore, it would take no more than 10-20 seconds for Mrs N.S. to have gone from the cabin to the open deck,[34] so there is little reason for her to have taken her photo through an imperfect window. Finally, and perhaps decisively, photogrammetric study of photos[35] of the *Fairstar's* Boat Deck area indicates that the maximum unobstructed vertical angle between the top of the rail and the bottom of the awning, measured from the centre point of one of the cabin windows, is only about 20°. From a position further back in the cabin this angle would only narrow further. Based on Minnaert's measurements and calculations the total vertical angular height of the double-sun photo FOV is about 18°. So there is an immediate tension here, and indeed the amount of sea visible (~12°) seems to be greater than the maximum vertical angle of sea visible above the deck rail even from the very *top* of the window (~10 deg). So we have strong reasons to doubt that the photo was taken through this window glass.

But there is another possibility. To produce an in-focus image we need two nearly-aligned plane reflectors. Two possible surfaces are a lens filter – such as a UV or polarising filter, or even a clear filter sometimes used for lens protection – and the film emulsion itself, lying of course in the image plane. Light reflected from the film surface to the filter and back can create a secondary image in perfect focus.[36] The sun is so bright that even a few percent reflection efficiency is good enough, and in this this case a small misalignment of a degree or two becomes possible. (The same effect occurs with modern digital cameras when light is reflected by the surface of the image sensor. A good recent example provided by Wim van Utrecht is shown in Fig. 4.[37])

Of course this last hypothesis does not depend on the photographer's location at all, but the same crucial factor applies: there is no guarantee that the effect claimed to have been seen visually was the same as the effect captured on the photo. As well as detailed information about the camera and lenses and any possible filters, and the location of the photography, it would have been interesting to get independent descriptions from those other anonymous witnesses. Unfortunately

Fig.4 Sun with internal camera reflection caused by a polaroid filter, detail of photo taken by Wim van Utrecht at Antwerp, July 10 2011

Minnaert was inexperienced in this sort of investigation. As it stands, one has to say that if this was a UFO report one could make a hole in it big enough to admit the reasonable doubt of a sceptical scientist.

The only other academically-credited multiple-sun photograph known to the author is one taken by the French meteorologist R. Richard in 1953 (Fig. 5). Stanford Research Institute meteorologist William Viezee, in his chapter on "Optical Mirage" for the highly-influential 1969 Condon Report on UFOs,[38] lists the Richard photo as an example of atmospheric "light refraction". But he doesn't discuss it, so we don't know how he would have justified that conclusion. In fact it is most unlikely that he could have done so. No modern authority on atmospheric optics knows of even a conjectural mechanism that could produce mirage images of this type, number and disposition.

Nevertheless, as quoted by Minnaert, "...besides and above the sun appeared seven other images of the sun, undistorted and sharp. And this time the phenomenon was photographed, clearly and convincingly. The sun was perhaps 2 degrees above the horizon of the sea, the phenomenon was visible for three minutes at most; the companion suns were bluish, the real sun orange."[39]

Minnaert was plainly convinced by Richard's photo. In a 1968 article he said that because of it he had recanted his previous scepticism of like stories. Although he had originally thought them to be ocular anomalies in the observers' eyes, he said, "I was wrong. In 1953 a similar observation was published by Richard...seven images were seen, shortly before sunset. But this time the phenomenon was also photographed!"[40] Note the important word "also". Richard's account appears to have been widely accepted not simply on the basis of the photo, but because Richard, in a respectable professional journal, reported seeing the same display visually, apparently guaranteeing that the photo records a remarkable display in the free atmosphere.

But today Richard's extraordinary report of eight true images of the sun stands conspicuously alone as an isolated anomaly, without any prospect of an explanatory mechanism in the realm of atmospheric or meteorological optics, and it rests on the arguably slim foundation of one man's testimony. Is this enough?

Fig.5 Detail from photo published by French meteorologist R. Richard in 1953, showing a total of 8 images of the sun, claimed to have been visually observed.[41]

In the opinion of mirage expert Andy Young, Richard's picture is almost certainly a photographic artifact, ghosts caused by multiple reflections between misaligned elements in the optical train. The blue colour of the ghosts would be typical of multiple reflections between coated lens elements in a camera of 1950s vintage, before the days of modern anti-reflection

Fig.6 Alleged double sun photographed in China, Jan 16, 2011

coatings, when most lenses were coated with simple 1/4-wave layers of magnesium fluoride, and the remaining reflection from these surfaces had a characteristically bluish or purplish colour.[42]

I am unaware of any recent examples of comparable photographs with a pedigree as respectable as that of the Richard picture. Of course, during the build-up to 2012, tales of the imminent apocalyptic appearance in the heavens of Nibiru, like a second sun, have prompted numerous blog articles and YouTube videos about the fearful implications of twin suns. Many photos and videos of double and triple suns have been produced around the world in Europe, the Americas and Asia. A spate of "sightings" in China at the beginning of this year included the picture shown in Fig. 7, one of a series taken on January 16, 2011.[43] But in the absence of careful and well-documented investigation one lacks a reason to suppose that this is not a filter reflection or the like, similar to the example shown in Fig. 5.

In the same month it was said that three suns appeared in the sky in the province of Jilin, northern China: "This phenomenon is quite natural but rare. The people of the Chinese province of Jilin believed they were seeing things when they observed the phenomenon… Caused by refraction of sunlight in the atmosphere, the phenomenon of 'sun phantom' occurs only rarely. All the more reason to see these images of the three suns of China."[44] But the idea – tossed out complacently – that such an effect can be produced by atmospheric refraction is outlandish, and although "the people of Jilin" are enlisted as witnesses to the three "suns" in Fig. 7 we have no names or details to support the claim. The photo could well be something as simple as a reflection of light fixtures in a window, or a fabrication.

Of Mirages, Mirrors & Mysteries...

Are there any completely reliable cases of genuine multiple sun images in the free atmosphere? And if so, is there any plausible mechanism in meteorology or atmospheric optics to explain them? As already mentioned, mock suns or parhelia caused by ice-haloes occur at calculable angular radii fixed by the crystal geometry[45] and, especially when appearing at smaller radii close to the sun, are not true images but rather are bright patches embedded in vertical segments of diffuse bright arcs. Parhelia at radii smaller than 9° might be possible with rare crystal forms, but focused facsimile images of the solar disc do not seem to be predicted by any understood ice crystal reflection geometry.

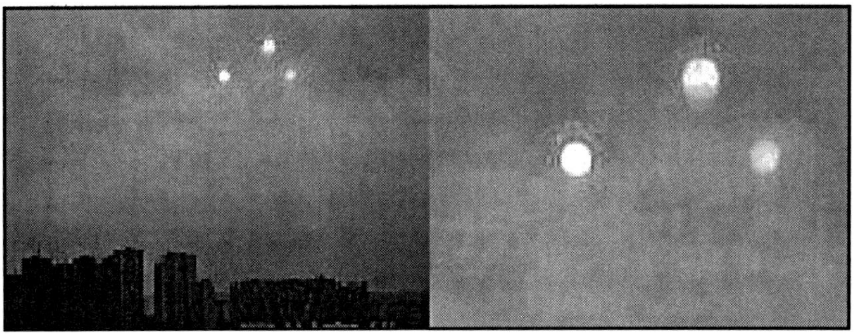

Fig.7 Photo of "three suns" allegedly taken in Jilin province, northern China, January 2011

Aside from the *TSS Fairstar* photo, the late scientific anomalist William Corliss[46] lists two other anomalous "close, one-sided mock suns". Whilst there's little to be said about a Welsh account of a pale white image "a few degrees" displaced from the "dark red" sun, which seems to be a scrap of anonymous hearsay, the other one is more interesting, but is not an effect in the same class as the *Fairstar* photo. The image, about 10° to the left of the true sun, is described as looking like the sun behind cloud dense enough to diffuse it, defined enough for taking a bearing but not defined enough for a reliable sextant altitude. That suggests to me not a true image but a patch of light with vertical blurring, an ellipse or streak with major axis vertical – so possibly a parhelion associated with a 9° halo arc.

Another oft-heard proposal is "lateral mirage", but there are uncertainties clouding all known accounts of putative lateral mirage, and too often casual assumptions are made about the possibility of laterally refracted images without appreciation of the unrealistic physical conditions implied.

Corliss quotes several anecdotal historical examples of lateral mirage of which the following is typical:

> A curious case of lateral mirage was observed at Geneva on the 17th September 1818 at 10 o'clock, PM, by MM. Jurine and Soret. A bark near Bellerive, at the distance of about 4000 toises[47] from Geneva, was seen approaching to Geneva by the *left* bank of the lake; and at the same time, an image of the sails was observed above the water, which, instead of following the direction of the bark, separated from it, and appeared to approach Geneva by the *right* bank of the lake – the image moving from east to west, while the bark moved from north to south. When the image separated from the bark, it was of the same dimensions as the bark; but it diminished as it receded from it, so as to be reduced to one half when the image ceased.[48]

But I think there is room for doubt that this is a reliable observation of any kind of atmospheric-optical phenomenon. Could it not have been a simple optical illusion caused by two similar boats travelling initially in the line of sight, one obscuring the other, which then separated and travelled in different directions?

Two other observations are listed by Corliss as lateral mirages. One case (GEM 3, X2, p.146; Snowdonia, Wales, Oct. 1927) is evidently a shadow of a mountain projected on sunlit foreground mist, and another (GEM 3, X4, p.146; an undated and unsourced reference to an undescribed photograph of a nine-image lateral mirage) is avowedly "associated with the nature of the heat transport from a vertical surface", i.e. it was caused by the heated layer of air next to a hot wall and is not truly a lateral mirage in the sense usually implied by this term (Andy Young proposes the term "mural mirage" to distinguish this effect from a lateral mirage in the free atmosphere[49]).

Corliss offers only one clear case of an apparent "lateral mirage" of the sun in the free atmosphere, an observation made from a ship in the North Atlantic on June 14, 1956, remarking himself that "it appears to be unique". But it is only a visual report; no photograph

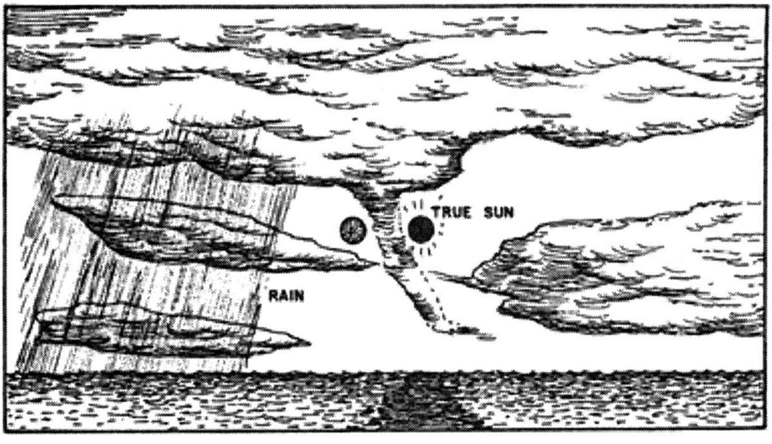

Fig.8 June 14 1956, North Atlantic. According to William Corliss, "a double sun probably created by a lateral mirage" (see text)

was taken, although a drawing (Fig. 9) shows the positions of the true sun and the faux sun in relation to the horizon and some unusual-looking weather. The entry in Corliss' book reads as follows:

> 2145 G.M.T. "Shortly before sunset, with the sun at an altitude of 2°35', bearing 298°, twin suns were observed side by side, quite clearly separated. The image was to the right of the true sun, there being no distortion of either. This phenomenon persisted for 2 min, after which the image gradually elongated in the direction of the true sun, eventually merging with it within 1/2 min..." Note. This is an extremely interesting observation of a lateral mirage and appears to be a unique one. For lateral mirage it is necessary for the air to be stratified into vertical masses of different densities. Ordinary abnormal refraction, which may produce an image vertically above the object, is produced by more or less horizontal distribution of layers of air of different densities....[50]

The phrase "lateral mirage" is really no more than a verbal pigeon-hole. The elongation and merging of the secondary image appears to rule out an ice halo (if it was not an illusion due to some rare small parhelic spoke developing just as the mock sun faded) and does sound suggestive of a mirage effect. But Corliss himself concisely indicates why the theory is physically incredible.

Mirage depends on stable gradients of temperature, which form between horizontally stratified layers, and the steepest gradients produce vertical image displacements in the region of half a degree of arc (one solar diameter) or less. What could possibly account for the much steeper *lateral* temperature gradients in the order of tens of °C/100m, sustained for minutes in an unstable condition in the free atmosphere, that would be needed to displace a perfectly-focused solar image laterally by several degrees of arc?[51]

One might wish to speculate that the odd "funnel cloud"-like structure shown in the drawing is itself a completely unknown phenomenon with some truly astonishing thermal properties. But could such a natural wonder really be accepted on the basis of a single drawing (which as a matter of fact contradicts the quoted witness description, showing the "mirage" to the left, not to the right of the sun[52])? One such anecdotal account cannot have much scientific weight.

It seems more plausible that the "rain" shown on the left might really have been falling ice crystals responsible for some rare close halo. Andy Young is unconvinced, concluding that "the gradual blending of the images sounds exactly like inter-reflections between two pieces of slightly uneven glass as the viewing geometry changed to bring a less-tilted area of glass into line with the Sun... Reflections between slightly curved surfaces sound to me like the correct explanation."[53] Perhaps reflections between the objective lens of a telescope or binocular and adjacent window glass?

But what about a true image of the solar disc, as in the *Fairstar* photo? Philip Morrison commented that a huge flat sheet of reflective plastic suspended over the sea within half a degree of the vertical would yield a "proper bright reflected image" of the right kind.[54] Could it be that a sheet of billions of hexagonal crystals provides an effective vertical mirror? The orientation of the falling crystal platelets would tend to become horizontal, eliminating the reflecting area of the crystal faces but making available six vertically oriented edges. Could they present enough collective area near the critical angle? Neglecting the third dimension, at any instant 1/6 of randomly rotated hexagons would have one edge within 30° or less of the critical angle, implying that about 1.7% would be less than 3° from the critical angle at any instant. So one might think that at any time about 1% of edges could be within a degree or so of being elements of an approximate plane mirror, and even 1% of sunlight is quite bright.

But this doesn't work to produce a sharp image of the solar disc – or rather, there could in principle be a somewhat sharp image of the solar disc formed by the tiny proportion of crystals oriented within a small fraction of the 0.5° angular width of the sun, but it would be as it were only virtually present, completely swamped by the much larger number of incoherent non-image-forming reflections. Without a mechanism to orient the freely rotating crystals in azimuth there is no way of selecting out the image-forming reflections from all the rest – and worse still, even the 1% of sunlight optimistically estimated above assumes 100% reflection efficiency, but reflection from a single ice-air interface is only a few per cent efficient,[55] so that even if the crystals could be aligned the image would be barely visible.

So, do close lateral double suns occur? It seems they are more myth than meteorology, resting on notably shakier evidential ground than some types of reports of Unidentified Flying Objects. For tractable evidence we are left with Minnaert's article. But is the Timor Sea report a reliable observation? Even this is not satisfactorily established: No original report from the photographer is available; no testimony is available from other claimed witnesses to verify what was seen visually; no investigation was undertaken to establish the chain of evidence; and insufficient technical details of the camera, film and circumstances are presented to rule out the possibility of a spurious reflection.

We can't claim to have a strong explanation, but we can argue reasonable doubt based on the sort of objection we would usually raise against a UFO report. One can be too sceptical, but as far as I know this unique photo is the *only* piece of non-anecdotal evidence for laterally-doubled suns, and there aren't even many decent anecdotes either. I think the photo has been treated with exaggerated respect because of who Minnaert was, and it has single-handedly influenced the consensus, but the context which Minnaert gives us to interpret the photo is really only undocumented anecdote and many questions remain unanswerable.[56]

What is the bottom line? Has anyone ever seen a focused true image of a laterally doubled sun in the free atmosphere? Is a handful of ambiguous stories from decades past really good evidence? I don't see it. Most of the sightings of laterally multiplied suns in history seem to be more commonplace parhelia, fuzzy and/or located at large angular distances from the true sun. Lateral mirages seem to be impossible, and Corliss' few proffered examples are unimpressive, being, with one exception, obvious mistakes, cloud shadows, or a mirage caused by a hot wall. Perhaps we can't neatly explain away the *Fairstar* report, but personally I feel uncomfortable that the evidence for so remarkable a phenomenon boils down to one intriguing but inconclusive photo.

In conclusion, the prophets of Mayan doom can probably look forward untroubled to many more conventional sunrises and sunsets after 2012. Oh, and that March 2nd 2011 Taiwanese video that triggered so much excitement? Researcher Manuel Borraz Aymerich recently discovered[57] that it is evidently a hoax, made from a still photo (of uncertain provenence) that had been posted on an internet blog the previous month.[58]

Martin Shough is a Research Associate for the National Aviation Reporting Center on Anomalous Phenomena (at the invitation of Dr Richard Haines, ex-NASA Human Factors head and NARCAP Chief Scientist) and is author or co-author of a number of papers and other publications. His main interest has been radar events. He has worked with several international collaborations to study cases in different parts of the world going back to 1946, and is the originator of a major ongoing effort to compile an historical catalogue of such events. He was trained in photographic and print science at London College of Printing and was a landscape artist and gallery-owner in the Highlands of Scotland for many years. He has also been a semi-professional folk musician. His website is www.martinshough.com, and he can be reached via email via parcellular@btinternet.com.

Jean-Julien Champagne, *Le Vaisseau du Grand Oeuvre* ("Vessel of the Great Work")

Elusive Fulcanelli and the Hermetic Magistery

Decoding the truth behind one of history's great esoteric figures

by *Blair MacKenzie Blake*

For several years the rumors persisted. Vague allusions of a genuine 20th century alchemist who was on the brink of perfecting the fabled Philosopher's stone – a mysterious substance that supposedly enables one to transmute baser metals into gold, as well as the production of minute, precious, quantities of an elixir for prolonging life. The time was the early 1900s and the occult milieu, Paris. Cryptic mentions of a contemporary adept who was being compared to the renowned alchemists of the past in all their legendary embroidery circulated through esoteric book shops, artist salons, and boulevard cafes where the hushed conversations had originated from a small circle of enthusiasts of the Hermetic tradition. Among this select group, the loudest voice was an impoverished, though highly gifted artist named Jean-Julien Champagne. Eccentric, intelligent and whimsical, the man with the expressive blue eyes and drooping moustache stood out from his company, not only because of his untidy appearance and outmoded attire, but mostly due to his habit of speaking in riddles. Yet, despite these peculiarities, he gave the impression of possessing considerable knowledge, especially when it came to the opacities of alchemical literature. Over glasses of Pernod, he continued to drop hints of great secrets behind the veils of matter – secrets that were granted to only a privileged few throughout the ages...secrets now in the hands of the anonymous Master who was about to accomplish the Great Work in his private makeshift laboratory.

While no doubt many were skeptical about this modern-day adept and his successful experiments, the appearance of a remarkable book in the autumn of 1926 caused quite a sensation in the Parisian occult subculture. Suddenly the rumors gained substance. Published in a deluxe edition of only 300 copies, the work was entitled *Le Mystere des Cathedrales* ("The Mystery of the Cathedrals"), with a subtitle that read: "An Esoteric Interpretation of the Hermetic Symbols of the Great Work", signed under the pseudonym, "Fulcanelli", and dedicated to the "Brothers of Heliopolis." Destined to become a classic on the subject, the book's main premise is that the major Gothic cathedrals in Europe contain encoded instructions for the transformation of the nature of human existence. Unsuspected by the masses for centuries, the medieval decorations constitute a stone textbook that quite openly displays precise and detailed technical information of various alchemical procedures. (For example, the shifting color manifestations* of certain stained-glass windows might indicate the subtle changes that the substance inside the glass-alembic undergoes during its multiple reactions). Taking the reader on a guided tour of the magnificent structures, the author offers

* Indeed, the vowels in "Fulcanelli" denote the correct color sequence.

his initiated interpretation of the aesthetic ornamentation, being as explicit as he dares when touching upon features of key significance, while repeatedly stressing that there are certain bounds that he is obliged by oath not to overstep.

With its erudite observations of Gothic architecture, the book had the unique distinction of re-establishing a long-forgotten recondite mode of communication. This was the phonetic cabala (not to be confused with the traditional Hebrew mystical system known as the Qabalah).

The Color of Initiation

For according to the book's learned author, Gothic art (art gothique) was a corruption of the word *argotique*, the slang/argot also known as the *langue verte* or green tongue (with argot defined as "a language peculiar to all individuals who wish to communicate their thoughts without being understood by outsiders.") Based on Greek etymology, it was this particular vernacular that was the key to deciphering the scientific revelations preserved in these secret textbooks of sculptured stone. Those who spoke this slang were the (symbolic) descendants of the Argonauts – fellow seekers on the mythical quest for the Golden Fleece (an alchemical text, or sign of the perfected Work?). Understandably, this strange word-play might seem to be merely wild speculation were it not for the author's prodigious knowledge. For how was one to explain the astute perceptions and masterly exposition? In conveying the rich complexity of the alchemical endeavor without all the smoke-stained pageantry of the medieval treatises, the Master hiding behind the alias 'Fulcanelli' was perceived as one who was intimately familiar with the elaborate Hermetic processes. Here, at last, was a genuine Philosopher of Fire – one who had labored in utmost secrecy until finally being rewarded with the treasure of treasures!

Entrusted with publishing the manuscript of *Le Mystere des Cathedrales* was Fulcanelli's young pupil, Eugene Canseliet. As for the 36 illustrations of the cathedrals' Hermetic imagery, this task was given to J.J. Champagne, the talented painter who frequented the gathering places of esoteric groups while appearing to have stepped out of an earlier century. In the book's preface (written by the disciple, Canseliet), readers were informed that the Master was "no longer with us", that "when the final hour struck" he had discreetly left this world – a self-imposed exile, thus keeping with the true Hermetic tradition. Without biographical details, the subject of Fulcanelli's true identity became a favorite conversation piece among those passionate about alchemy. And with exciting new scientific discoveries at the time of the book's publication, there was a bit of an alchemical resurgence among the literati in the French capital (the once fashionable pursuit of artificially manufacturing gold having fallen into disrepute at the end of the 18th century, mostly due to the influence of the French chemist Lavoisier). Hence, the small print run quickly sold out, with copies clutched in the hands of those attracted to the odor of sulphur and collectors of rare esoterica. Not long after, however, the man who chose to remain incognito was all but forgotten.

Jean Julien Champagne

Cultural Phenomenon

But things would change dramatically with the publication in 1960 of the international bestseller *Le Matin des Magiciens* ("The Morning of the Magicians") by Louis Pauwels and Jacques Bergier. Reaching a much wider audience once translated into English, the groundbreaking study of mysterious phenomena that modern science couldn't adequately explain included intriguing new details pertaining to the Fulcanelli affair that greatly added to the enigma, and was largely responsible for the Master Alchemist's now legendary status.

One of these curious events involved an alleged personal encounter in 1937 by co-author Jacques Bergier with a mysterious personage whom he believed to be none other than Fulcanelli. In a test laboratory of the Paris gas board where he was employed, one afternoon a stranger entered unannounced. With an authoritative voice he warned the future nuclear physicist about the terrible dangers of the liberation of atomic energy and nuclear explosions – something, he asserted, that alchemists had been aware of for centuries. Providing further details in order to substantiate his claims, the stranger insisted that scientists were currently about to re-discover that "geometrical arrangements of highly purified substances" could release atomic forces with dire consequences. When Bergier asked the man how he obtained this information, the reply was that the alchemists understood ways of manipulating energy-fields that acted upon the observer, putting them in a privileged position in relation to the universe. In this elevated state one has access to realities that are normally concealed from human perception. With the stranger's business concluded, abruptly the scene switches to 1945, with Bergier describing how he was interrogated by a Major working with an American intelligence agency that was attempting to track down anyone with sufficient knowledge of nuclear physics. In particular, they were looking for the whereabouts of Fulcanelli. While first hand testimony like this continued to fuel the mystique, to the minds of some, the following episode would seem to have firmly placed the Master in the realm of his illustrious predecessors.

(Photo: Blair MacKenzie Blake)

An Airplane Ticket to the 16th Century

Although several versions of the extraordinary "Spanish encounter" story have been published, other than conflicting dates and a few other minor discrepancies, most of the details in the various accounts are fairly consistent. It was a close friend of Canseliet, Fulcanelli's only known disciple, who betrayed his trust by revealing publicly what was supposedly told to him in strict confidence: In 1954, Canseliet received a plane ticket to Madrid from a wealthy old Castilian family who had invited him to spend a week with them near Seville. From the airport, their chauffeur proceeded to drive him to a stately mansion enclosed by high walls. Having arrived, he was surprised to realize that the driver's appearance was more like that of a coachman from yesteryear, garbed as he was in old-fashioned livery. He also noticed that the chateau had no electricity, its sumptuous furnishings illuminated by flickering candlelight. Odder still, his hosts greeted him in the extravagant clothing of the 16th century, which he assumed were the costumes for a masquerade party. In their velvets and brocades, these people regularly spoke in antique French and, as he came to learn, had a thorough knowledge of ancient alchemy.

But things only got stranger. As the hours went by, the surroundings took on a vivid, dreamlike quality. Planes crossed the sky without making the slightest noise, and cars passed outside in total silence. From the windows of his room, he watched as children similarly dressed in the peculiar apparel of the 16th century frolicked about in delightful gardens. It was as if he had stepped through a *mirror fantastique* into a terrestrial paradise.

And then one day as some ladies approached, he was stunned to realize that the one who turned and smiled at him had features that he instantly recognized. There was no mistaking it – it was the face of Fulcanelli! (Additionally the Master appeared to be younger than he was prior to his vanishing act some 30 years ago.) From that moment on he had the distinct impression that he had been invited to a secret retreat of distinguished alchemists – a colony of illuminated adepts who had shed their human slough and become glorious beings as the result of swallowing aurific tinctures. Yet, what was he to make of the fact that Fulcanelli now appeared as a woman in this parallel existence? Did he/she represent the Hermetic androgynous state? Was the pre-arranged rendezvous in the atmosphere of old-Spain an initiatory phenomenon (hypnotic suggestion?) arranged by the Master to graphically symbolize to his faithful pupil the perfection of matter at the completion of the alchemical opus?

How can we reconcile this strange incident? Was it merely a figment of the studious disciple's imagination? The delusional ramblings of one repeatedly exposed to toxic metallic brews? Or could it be explained by a treasured secret involving our occult anatomy (i.e. tantric psycho-sexual essences)?

A King Cannot Possess More of it Than a Beggar

By now, even those without any previous knowledge of the subject should begin to suspect that there is more to alchemy than the conventional notion of converting lead into gold via magico-mystical or hyper-chemical methods. And while the medieval portrait of a cloaked figure hunched over bubbling apparatuses in lamp-fire still persists, most historians now accept the idea that the alchemists used metallurgical terminology to disguise their true pursuit – the transformation of themselves. With the sacred patience and dedication required to gain objective insights into the structure of matter, speculative alchemists believe that the operator is mystically (and, perhaps, biologically) transfigured by the experience. And it was this noble undertaking – searching for a remedy for the perceived tragic distancing between man and God

– that attracted some of the greatest minds on the planet. As for the coveted Powder of Projection that facilitates the transmutation of metals, this was but a subsidiary aspect of the divine chemistry – an experiment performed at the conclusion of the Work to assure the quality of the Philosopher's stone they produced. Similarly, the unfolding processes taking place inside the murky crucible merely reflected the profound changes that occurred within the hidden recesses of the alchemist's own consciousness. Simply put, it was an observable (chemical) enactment of an essentially invisible (spiritual) occurrence.

During the Middle Ages, with the alchemists' prized stone in the imagination of the general populace, dabblers of the forbidden Art began conducting experiments using the exotic paraphernalia depicted along with the unintelligible jargon of moldering tomes. In their lust for (vulgar) gold, the unexpected by-products of these puffers' (a derogatory term due to their sooty appearance) frivolous operations were responsible for alchemy being recognized as the forerunner of modern chemistry. But along with these self-deceivers were clever imposters whose sole motivation was a financial extraction from their gullible victims.

With their promises of endless riches (after using sleight of hand techniques to remove the desired precious ore from a lump of coal), it was these wandering rogues that fostered intense suspicion on the sincere alchemists. Dubious reputation or not, with their lofty spiritual pretensions without the inclusion of church doctrine, most had already drawn the unwanted attention of religious authorities. With their use of allegorical codes it was evident to the alchemists as well that the clergy would prefer that these ideas about 'metals redeemed from baseness' remained the relic of a buried philosophy. That alchemy preserved fragments of a science of an advanced civilization of remote antiquity – as Fulcanelli believed – this was unthinkable...

Purposely Invented to Mislead

To prevent this knowledge from falling into the wrong hands, the alchemists devised an ingenious system of simultaneously revealing and concealing their most profound secrets. As a result, alchemical treatises have been described as "a fantastic species of literature."

Once separated of its gross impurities, the textual imagery contained a second language in which a different layer of meaning could be perceived. Along with densely coded text, most volumes were also copiously illustrated with a bewildering array of symbols, emblems, and splendorous imagery. Often-lurid ornamentation included fanciful menageries, predatory feedings, chemical marriages, regal copulations, spectral entombments and glorious rebirths. Always on their guard not to divulge too much, the nebulous language and bizarre woodcuts weren't the only hurdle one had to overcome. As master-works of subterfuge, when the alchemist appeared to be the most straightforward, his true meaning was likely concealed by the most convincing camouflage. Also confusing to the student was a multiplicity of imaginative synonyms used to describe the exact same thing. To further thwart the undeserving, the progressive stages of the Work (with their transitory colors) were rarely, if ever, listed in their correct sequence. Along with this deliberately misleading tactic, the cunning adepts were wholly silent on the crucial initial step, merely asserting that this most precious of things was despised by fools, whereas the wise could find 'our' stone in a dunghill.

Yet, despite the aura of complexity, the alchemists maintained that the stone could be fashioned with little difficulty. Once something was acquired, the methods employed were unfathomably simple. Furthermore, any obfuscation could be overcome by humble supplications, as was shown by depictions in ancient books of the alchemist praying at the athanor. However, without divine assistance the Work could not be completed. Alchemical treatises are not meant to be read in a logical manner – not like following a recipe in a cookbook. Instead, using one's intuitive faculties, the aspirant contemplates the text (pseudo-obscurities included!), hoping for a breakthrough – a divinely inspired revelation, whereupon he becomes attuned with the sagacious author's mentality. As to the nature of this mysterious intervention, we are left only to speculate. Perhaps at some point during the operations, the alchemist developes some extra-sensory organ – a hitherto unknown superior mode of perception that enables him to detect faint impressions. Which brings us back to Fulcanelli, who many believe had tapped into some force that gave him an acute awareness of things. This, they concluded, was affirmed by his astute analysis of the Hermetic symbolism enshrined in Gothic edifices.

Depending on how much one masks and reveals, alchemists are said to be either grudging or generous. Having provided a linguistic decipherment so that key operative techniques were not irretrievably lost, many are convinced that the 'cathedrals' book attributed to Fulcanelli isn't filled with the same smoky obscurities as are the tortuously abstract and deliberately misleading ancient treatises. However, even with the author's assurance that "we may have faith in his sincerity", others contend that – in detailing the alchemical praxis from "Calcination" to "Multiplication" – the text is so intentionally jumbled up that certain sentences that begin in one chapter end in another! In truth, there can be no doubt that Fulcanelli often dons the Philosopher's cloak (which exerts an even more powerful attraction). But, with an uncanny ability to animate the medieval decorators' petrified arcanum, and having awakened the curiosity of those desirous of unraveling Hermetic enigmas, to this day, scores of researchers have attempted to determine the civil status card identity of this modern adept considered to be in league with Artephius, Flamel, Valentine, Philalethes and Cyliani.

Unmasking Fulcanelli

The list of likely candidates for the veiled Master isn't that long, with most researchers focusing on the small circle of Parisian Hermeticists that the painter J.J. Champagne was known to associate with. This tightly knit group, which formed the secretive *Freres d' Heliopolis*, included Fulcanelli's pupil, Eugene Canseliet, occult bookstore owner Pierre Dujols, esotericist-writer Jules Boucher, and a chemist who flirted with left-hand magick named Gaston Sauvage. Although all were 'burning with the same fire', most investigators have come to the conclusion that the most plausible choice for Fulcanelli was Champagne. The reasons are many. As we have seen, Champagne behaved as if he lived in a by-gone era and often engaged in language games while holding court in his Bohemian haunts. Besides his flamboyant personality, he was known to be wickedly mischievous. A man with a contradictory nature, he was passionate and sincere, yet a braggart and prankster. At times he even confided to others that he was Fulcanelli. To go along with this, researchers have shown that samples of his ornate handwriting match perfectly to that supposed to be from Fulcanelli. There were also witnesses at the time, such as the publisher of '*Mystere*', who thought that Champagne and his alter-ego were one and the same. In fact, the disciple Canseliet was said to have shown great respect to his older friend, often addressing him as "my Master."

However, the most convincing evidence comes from tantalizing clues inserted into the pages of *Le Mystere des Cathedrales* itself. In the 1930s, a Parisian occultist named Robert Ambelain, who was impressed by the alchemist's treatise, conducted a thorough investigation into the matter and discovered, among other things, that the nom de plume Fulcanelli is an anagram of "L 'ech final", meaning "the final shield." This almost certainly refers to the heraldic crest shield that Champagne devised and added to the final page of the book. When Ambelain learned that Champagne's real first name was Hubert, the game was all but given away, for the dog-Latin motto on the shield: UBER CAMPA AGNA is the phonetic approximation of… HUBERT CHAMPAGNE.

Still, not everyone was convinced. Until his death in 1982, Canseliet insisted that his good friend was only the book's illustrator. Fulcanelli, he hinted, was a wealthy and distinguished individual, possibly of an aristocratic up-bringing. He was only being faithful to his oath in not revealing his true identity. Others were equally dismissive of Ambelain's attempts at disambiguation. What about the brilliant thesis and eloquent prose? The man who brought vividly to life the bas-reliefs of Notre-Dame couldn't possibly be a shabby, boastful, leg-puller who died miserably after developing gangrene. Prior to the time of his death in 1932 Champagne was nearly destitute – a bedridden alcoholic who indulged in absinthe and inhaled galbanum to go into trance states. He simply didn't have the knowledge and resources to accomplish the Hermetic oeuvre. Besides, both Canseliet and Champagne lived in adjoining attic rooms, separated only by a common wash area. Therefore, how could Canseliet not be aware of wondrous experiments carried out under polarized light in his wretched surroundings?

Also disputing Ambelain's allegations, more recently, the historian Patrick Riviere suggested that Fulcanelli was a prominent physicist and member of the French Academy of Sciences named Jules Violle. Riviere, too, analyzed the ornamental crest at the conclusion of the book, in particular the bottom third of the heraldic device ('coincidently' known as the "champagne") where the tail of a sea-horse forms the letter "J." Using a phonetic cabala-style process, he teases out of the final illustration a second initial, this being a "V" (Jules Violle). As an expert on solar radiation and the melting points of rare earth metals, the pseudonym Fulcanelli (meaning "the Fire of the Sun") would appear to serve Violle well and, in the eyes of Riviere, all of this made him a "Thermo-Master", a title whose relevance we are about to see, although not without sinister implications…

Notre Dame de Paris (Photo: Sarah Gregory)

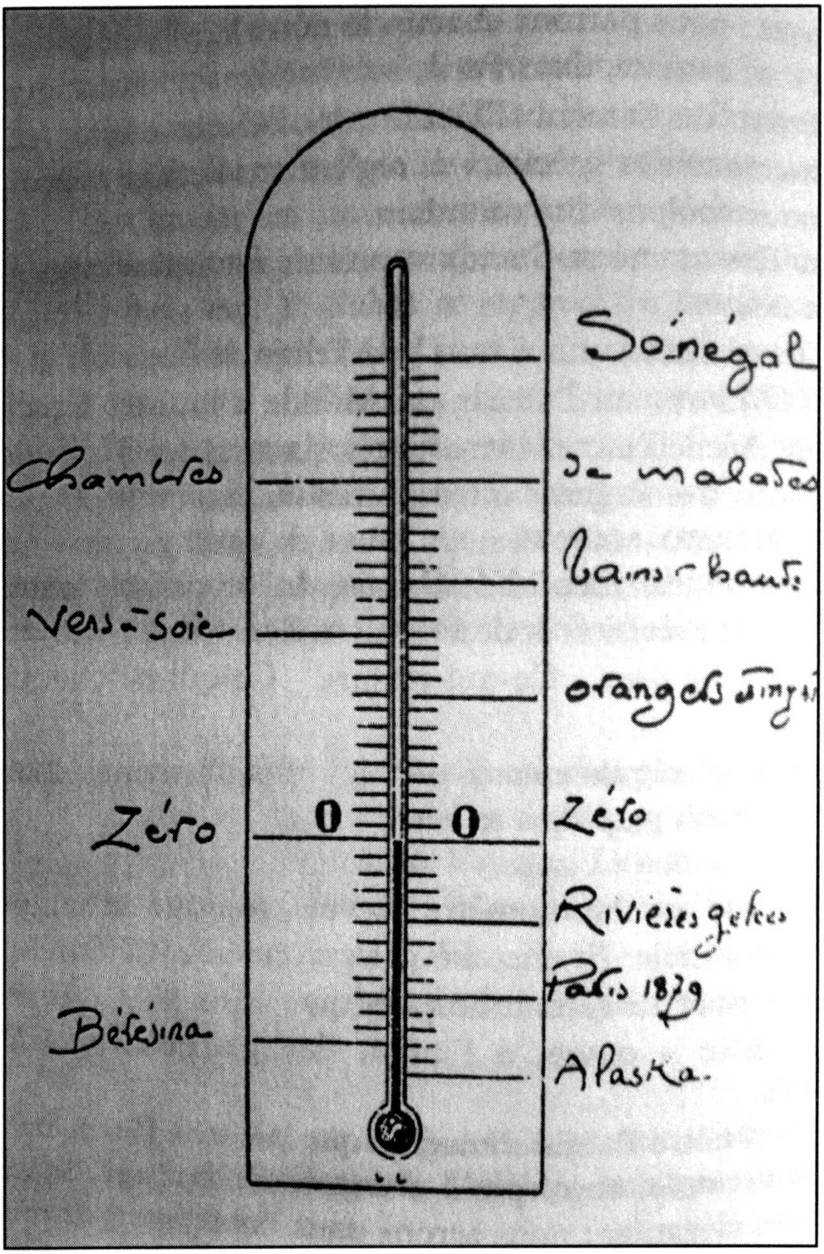

Curious thermometer image found within *Voyages en Kaleidoscope*
(photo: Blair MacKenzie Blake)

Voyages en Kaleidoscope

Further compounding our mystery is a marvelous hodge-podge of a little book entitled *Voyages en Kaleidoscope* that was published in France in 1919. Written in the style of the avant-garde Dadaist movement by a wealthy socialite named Irene-Hillel Erlanger, what at first appears to be a romance novel of sorts is in actuality a thinly disguised alchemical tract. The plot of the book centers around a brilliant inventor named Mr. Joel Joze, whose latest brainchild is a fantastic kaleidoscope that enables one to penetrate the hidden meaning of all things, as well as to lucidly experience something as another does via a "transcendental physical chemistry." The shifting phantasmagoria of the surreal prose offers many distractions from these decidedly Hermetic ideas, but the author's description of the inventor's loyal servant as "The Salt of the Earth" definitely must not be overlooked. Nor should the book's only illustration – a curious thermometer, which is believed to indicate in a very open manner the carefully guarded temperature scale required for the Great Work. During a celebratory soiree for the book's publication, the author contracted food poisoning, ostensibly from tainted oysters. Days latter she died under questionable circumstances.

Adding to these suspicions, on the eve of its release, all copies of the book were confiscated by persons unknown and later destroyed, with only a few surviving in bookstalls along the banks of the Seine. Open to question also, is that the book was dedicated to the chemist (and reputed alchemist) Louise Barbe, who had died after ingesting (or unwittingly been given?) a lethal dose of potable gold. But who would want these women dead? Were they being silenced by someone? Were the contents of the book suppressed because of the plot's alchemical underpinnings? Or was it because the storyline came too close to unmasking someone's true identity? Those who think this is merely an unrelated coincidence should keep in mind that not only did the book's author move in Parisian high circles, she also regularly attended the same establishments patronized by J. J. Champagne and his coterie. Furthermore, it is said that the painter with the Gallic mustache ascribed great importance to "Voyages." Could the reason for this be the critical heating procedures displayed by the puzzling thermometer*, or did it have something to do with a passage where the faithful servant of Mr. Joze states: "The life of a man surprising as my Master cannot remain unknown."

Before proceeding, there is another connection perhaps worth mentioning. Louise Barbe, to whom *Voyages en Kaleidoscope* was dedicated, was purported to have been the model for an evocative painting by J. J. Champagne entitled, "The Vessel of the Great Work" (see the title image on the first page of this essay). Full of alchemical symbolism, the painting shows a voluptuous naked priestess standing inside a large, prismatic, glass matrass. The myriad tiny blazing flames adorning her body are suggestive of the Secret Fire of the Art, which some have equated with the semi-dormant current of powerful energy known to the practitioners of erotic mysticism as kundalini. In portraying the alchemist's secret partner (*soror mystica*), she becomes the human vessel from which are obtained certain essences or secretions of the endocrine glands that are used to produce rejuvenating elixirs. Though it might be tempting to explain Canseliet's account of Fulcanelli aging backwards and changing gender with these hormonal-rich substances, the imagery of the painting involving our occult anatomy could have an even more esoteric interpretation than tantric parallels with alchemy.

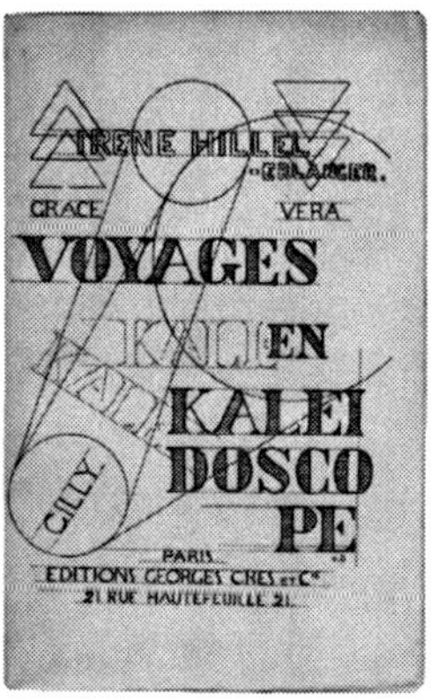

* Oddly enough, one of the thermometer's numerical values is "silkworms', which brings to mind another possible Fulcanelli candidate – the Count Hilaire de Chardonnet (1839-1924), a French chemist and inventor of RAYON.

The True Genius Behind the Myth

It was in a Parisian café in 1913 that the painter Champagne first met the philosopher, Hermeticist and future godfather of "New Egyptology", R.A. Schwaller de Lubicz (1887–1961), whose exhaustive studies of sacred architecture called for a complete re-appraisal of ancient knowledge. In his book *Al-Kemi: A Memoir,* author Andre VandenBroeck recounts in de Lubicz's own words how he and Champagne agreed, under the strictest of terms, to collaborate on a secret undertaking that concerned replicating the famous red and blue stained-glass of Chartres. With the methods employed to create the radiant hues having long defied scientific analysis, it would appear that Champagne might have found the solution. While working in a bookshop, he discovered – inside a rare copy of Isaac Newton's writings on alchemy – six-pages of hand-written notes that indicated an alchemical manipulation expressed in terms of color. Having stolen the mysterious text, he showed it to de Lubicz, who suggested that they apply the techniques mentioned.

Around the same time that they were concentrating on the laboratory procedures involving the volatile spirit of metals and glass tinted without chemical pigmentation, de Lubicz loaned Champagne his own notes on the Hermetic symbolism encoded in Gothic cathedrals. It was this research, augmented by his intellectual friends, which Champagne later published without de Lubicz's knowledge. Thus, according to de Lubicz, *Le Mystere des Cathedrals* was entirely based on his work.* In what amounted to an elaborate hoax, the anonymous Master was but a symbolic figurehead with a mystical shimmer for the "Brothers of Heliopolis" founded by Champagne, whose life revolved around perpetuating the Fulcanelli myth. (With

* In 1929 Fulcanelli published a second book entitled *Les Demeures Philosophales* ("The Dwellings of the Philosophers") that is essentially an expansion on the themes contained in the first work. A purposed third book, *Finis Gloria Mundi*, never appeared.

his tendency of compartmentalizing his different relationships, even Canseliet may have been duped at first, although, it should be noted, he claimed to have performed a successful alchemical transmutation in 1922 using a small quantity of the Powder of Projection that he received from Fulcanelli.) And yet, despite this plagiarism, de Lubicz continued to support Champagne financially until his death, the unpleasant nature of which he believed to be a consequence of violating his Hermetic pledge.

What Takes Nature Thousands of Years...

Such were the details as related to VandenBroeck during a brief period of discipleship with de Lubicz in 1959. For the most part, the story seems conceivable, although some might question why he reacted as he did after such treachery. The answer, it would appear, is that the color theory involved in the experiments carried out by Champagne offered additional clues concerning an alchemical manipulation of far greater importance. The spiritual imprint captured in glass inspired de Lubicz to contemplate the problem of the fixed Salt of the Philosophers, which ultimately led to an anthropocosmic reality that was, millennia before the design of the cathedrals by medieval Freemasons, preserved in the temples of Pharaonic Egypt. For the word "alchemy" is derived from "Khem" (with the added article: Al-), meaning the "black earth", an allusion to the rich alluvial soil of the Nile valley. Central to the alchemical process was an all-inclusive, indestructible, prime substance believed to be a certain mineral salt 'inscribed' with patterns of energy that remains after the death and organic decomposition of every vegetable, animal and human being over countless centuries. This physical residue is circulated in nature (via the food chain) for a later incarnation unless it is prevented from doing so by a special burial (embalming) procedure. Were this golden seed to be extracted from the earth's crust and exposed to the action of the Secret Fire (dew?), might the alchemist have the ability to greatly accelerate and/or change specific characteristics of the biological evolutionary sequence? If so, where did this science of energy transformation originate?

"He Wanted to Tell Everything"

Unless vandals have struck again, today the tombstone of J.J. Champagne is ornamented with a large scallop shell – the Hermetic emblem of an initiatory journey that corresponds with the medieval pilgrimage to the shrine of St. James of Compostela in Spain (similar to the allegorical itinerary made by other celebrated alchemists). Because the shell itself resembles the setting sun, in its pre-Christian origins this was a death journey, with the traveler's route terminating at 'Land's End' (*Finisterrae*) and into the glittering field of stars. While to some the abyss of death represents the lost civilization of Atlantis, to others it indicates the alchemist's starting point...

Let us now return one last time to the Gothic cathedral, and a curious legend associated with the sculpture of a crow (alchemical symbol for the stage of putrefaction) that once exerted such a powerful attraction before being decapitated by the ravages of the centuries. Supposedly, this feature was the only clue to the secret location of the Philosopher's Stone, whose mysterious hiding place under one of the pillars in the huge nave was "precisely determined by the angle of the vision of the crow." Referring specifically to this symbolic bird, Victor Hugo is quoted by Fulcanelli as saying that the designer of the porch of Notre Dame "was doubtless damned for having added such an infernal frontispiece to the holy poem eternally sung by the rest of the building." This puzzling remark might be a rather cryptic way of drawing our attention to the frontispiece of *Le Mystere des Cathedrales* (devised by Champagne), which features a crow perched on a human skull, with that great riddle, the Sphinx of Giza, poised

Frontispiece of *Le Mystere des Cathedrales*

under a twinkling sky behind a traditional alchemical laboratory. Is it the angle of vision of *this* crow that indicates where a sacred horde is concealed? Or is this just another hopeless enigma?

VISITETIS INTERIORA TERRAE RECTIFICANDO INVENIETIS OCCULTUM LAPIDEM VERAM MEDICINAM

Blair MacKenzie Blake has been studying, practicing, and writing about the western esoteric tradition for over twenty years. He is the author of two books: *Ijynx* and *The Wickedest Books in the World: Confessions of an Aleister Crowley Bibliophile*. In his 'other life', he is the writer/content manager for www.toolband.com and www.dannycarey.com.

The God with the Upraised Arm

An astronomical archetype of the ancient Near East?

by *Greg Taylor*

In the depictions of mythological scenes on Near Eastern archaeological monuments and artefacts, a number of 'archetypal images' are apparent. One of the most intriguing of these is the 'God with the Upraised-Arm', which can be found in scenes from Egypt, right through the fertile-crescent to Anatolia. In Egypt it is apparent from the time of unification onwards, seen in identical depictions which capture the god-pharaoh in the act of smiting his enemies. The Narmer Palette (Fig. 1) is often seen as a historical depiction of the unification of Upper and Lower Egypt.[1] The image of King Narmer, wearing the white crown of the south and smiting an enemy commonly held to be a northerner, is cited as evidence that he was the unifier of the two lands.[2] This became a standard picture of the king throughout the

Fig.1: The Narmer Palette

history of Egypt (see Fig. 2), whether the king holds a mace, a spear or even a bowstring in his right hand.

The respected scholar of ancient civilizations, Henri Frankfort, saw this as not only a scene showing a decisive historical battle, but also as a representation of the king as the divine ruler. He asserts that the real meaning of the scene is that the king's victory represents the "reduction of chaos to order",[3] an important pre-occupation with the ancient Egyptians;[4] chaos assumed many forms: death, drought, invading enemies – and these were all seen as manifestations of the god Seth.[5] It was the pharaoh's job, as the earthly incarnation of the god Horus, to overpower Seth/chaos and maintain the established order. This is obvious from ancient Egyptian texts. For example, in the *Cosmology of Abydos* we find the following passage describing the triumph of Horus over Seth:

> Dignity has been set in place, honesty has been established through his laws, evil has departed, wickedness is gone, the land is at peace under its lord.[6]

If the Narmer Palette scene is thus considered a symbolic representation of Horus defeating Seth, we would expect to see

Fig.2: Depictions of King Den and King Sekhemkhet

similar representations explicitly showing these gods battling. There is ample evidence of this and, importantly, certain elements such as the 'upraised arm' of the god seem to hold great significance.

At the Temple of Edfu there is an abundance of imagery concerning the contendings of Horus and Seth. On approaching the temple one is immediately met by huge images on the pylons of the king in 'smiting pose' in the presence of his archetypal forebear, Horus. Inside the temple can be found the dramatic text *The Triumph of Horus*, with illustrated scenes which were enacted by the Egyptians in an annual drama. Dated to approximately 110 BCE, the story has ancient antecedents, originally appearing in feasts and texts from the earliest dynasties almost three thousand years past.[7] The drama concerns the harpooning of Seth by Horus (ten times, a symbolic detail which might perhaps shares a common origin with the ten decapitated bodies on the Narmer Palette), after which Horus is crowned the King of Upper and Lower Egypt. Again, Horus is depicted with his arm raised (Fig. 3), this time harpooning Seth (represented by a hippopotamus).

Fig.3: *Triumph of Horus*: Horus Harpooning Seth (*Source*: Fairman 1974)

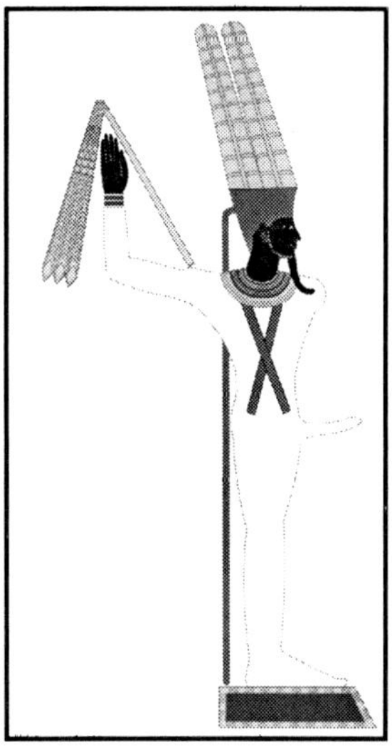

Fig.4: Min

That this pose is not simply incidental is confirmed by the explicit naming of Horus in the text as "Him-with-the-upraised-arm".[8] This was originally the epithet of Min (a rather obvious association, see Fig. 4), the early Egyptian god of rain and fertility (the latter again a rather obvious association, ahem!). He is often pictured with an upraised arm holding what is thought to be a thunderbolt. Horus and Min became increasingly identified as one and the same during the Middle Kingdom, although Min was already associated with the Pharaoh at least as early as the 4th Dynasty. On the verso of the Stela of Sobek-iry is found the Hymn to Min, which includes the verse "I worship Min, I extol arm-raising Horus".[9] The overall impression is that the upraised arm of Min-Horus was considered to be a characteristic pose of vital importance.

The Chief of Heaven

Another crucial point to emerge from the *Triumph of Horus* is that Horus was the "Great God, Lord of the Sky",[10] a quote which is followed by the passage "we grant strength to thine arm". There are numerous other references implying that Horus is to be looked for in the sky; for example "the gods of the sky are in terror of Horus".[11] Perhaps significantly, Min in pre-Dynastic times was also a sky-god called the "Chief of Heaven".[12] This raises the question of whether the archetypal image of Horus and Min has its origin in the sky. A look at the astronomical ceilings of Senmut and Seti I would appear to confirm this. On Senmut's ceiling

Fig.5: Astronomical ceiling of Seti I (*Source*: Parker 1974)

there is an almost identical depiction of Horus as at Edfu, with the arm upraised in the act of harpooning Seth (represented as the constellation Meskhetiu).[13] There is also an unidentified individual in the same pose amongst the group of constellations at the lower part of the image, this time harpooning a crocodile (another incarnation of Seth). He appears almost identically on the Seti I ceiling (Fig. 5). Thus the 'God with the Upraised Arm' may be considered a constellation recognisable by the ancient Egyptians. The obvious question therefore, is which one?

The outstanding candidate to fit the description is the constellation of Orion (Fig. 6), at the very least on sheer resemblance. This constellation was well known to the Egyptians, mentioned in the *Pyramid Texts* in connection with the stellar destiny of the "resurrected pharaoh". For example, in Utterance 442 we find "Lo, Osiris has come as Orion".[14] That Osiris is seen as Orion is not considered a problem to the thesis currently under discussion; Egyptian gods had multiple and overlapping associations – Orion was also thought to be incarnate in the Moon and the Nile, and ancient Egyptian cosmologies often contain seemingly contradictory concepts.[15]

Turning our attention to Horus, we find evidence in Plutarch's *Isis and Osiris* of a connection with Orion: "the soul of Isis is called Sothis

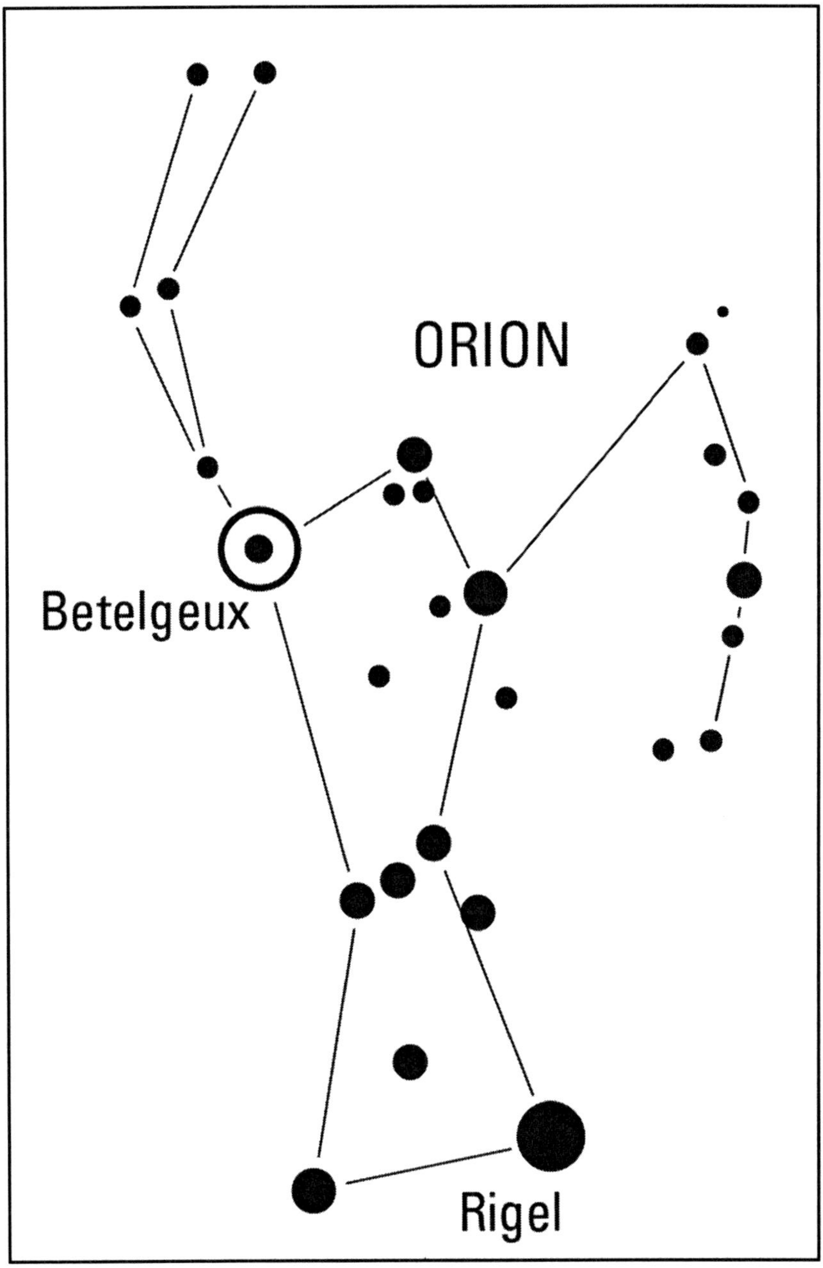

Fig.6: Constellation of Orion

(Sirius), the soul of Horus is called Orion, and the soul of Typhon (Seth) the Bear".[16] Plutarch may be thought of by scholars as being unreliable in regards to the recording of Egyptian culture, however, considering the correct attribution of Isis and Seth to their respective constellations the conflation of Horus and Orion should in this case be taken seriously. More circumstantial is evidence to be found in the story recorded on the Metternich Stela, in which the young Horus is stung and killed by a scorpion – a well-known mythological motif suggesting the setting of Orion as the constellation Scorpius rises.[17] It should be taken into account as well that Horus was said to have been placed upon the "seat of his father Osiris", perhaps an indication that they were both identified with Orion.

One of the arguments against this identification could well be that the constellations on this section of the 'astronomical ceilings' are all supposed to be north of the ecliptic.[18] However, it is pertinent to note that this attribution by Egyptian astronomy experts Parker and Neugebauer is qualified by Parker with the words "*we are reasonably sure* they are all north of the ecliptic" [my emphasis], and Neugebauer names them as the northern constellations directly after mentioning that "artistic principles determined the arrangement of astronomical ceiling decorations".[19] Also, in describing the northern constellations on the Denderah Zodiac, Parker mentions that these are "presumably all north of the ecliptic but none is depicted in the usual group of northern constellations".[20] Interestingly Plutarch mentions that the Egyptians hold the lion in honour because the Nile overflows when the sun comes into conjunction with Leo, which lies on the ecliptic.[21] This suggests that the 'Lion' constellation on the astronomical ceilings may in fact be Leo (contrary to current thought). Lastly, to illustrate the difficulties in placing constellations such as Meskhetiu in the northern sky, consider the following passage from a tomb at Luxor, describing the movements of the ship of Re: "Once the constellation of Masheti (Meskhetiu) has been passed, they reach shelter in the centre of the sky on the side south of Sah-Orion, and they turn towards the western horizon".[22] From this account of the east-west passage of the sun, the ancient Egyptians' conception of the heavens appears to be more complex than usually thought. Another argument against the Horus-Orion link may be that the figure with the upraised arm is sometimes reversed; however, the same is true of the northern constellation of the hippopotamus on the Denderah circular zodiac, so this may well be dismissed as simply an issue of artistic representation. However, accepting a link between Horus and Orion has the strong point of explaining the attributes of the god, especially once Orion's role as a seasonal marker is understood.

The Resurrection of Orion

Using stars and constellations as seasonal markers was commonplace in the ancient world. The heliacal rising of Sirius in July was considered by the Romans to be the reason for the sultry weather.[23] To the Egyptians this same event signalled the beginning of the Nile flood and thus the New Year. The heliacal rising of a star or constellation was seen as its resurrection after being 'dead' for a period of time. This is due to the apparent motion of the stars and constellations throughout the year (a result of the motion of the Earth around the sun). When the sun 'moved' into the vicinity of a certain star or constellation (ie. the star/constellation was in the stellar background on the opposite side of the Sun from the Earth) it would only be seen late in the west just after the setting of the sun, and after a time would eventually 'disappear' (once the sun was in direct conjunction with it). Once the sun moved away from the vicinity of the star/constellation, it would then appear in the morning sky in the east just before dawn: this was its heliacal rising. Sirius and Orion both 'died' for approximately 70 days, which could well be the origin of the embalming time for Egyptian mummies.[24]

In the time of the ancient Egyptians, Orion was 'dead' from around the spring equinox through to mid-summer. Interestingly, Frankfort notes that in Egypt the usual prevailing wind is from the north, which gives relief from the heat of the sun and makes life much more comfortable, but in late spring (the time of Orion's 'death') the hot dry winds bringing "sandstorms and a brittle heat out of Africa to the south" became more prominent.[25] It was also from this period until Sirius' heliacal rising that the Nile was at its lowest ebb. Plutarch explicitly states that Seth was considered the power of drought and the south wind, while Horus was the north wind, the "seasonal tempering of the surrounding air".[26] He asserts that the story of their battles is actually an allegory for the seasonal change: as Horus 'dies' in spring, Seth gains the upper hand, until the reappearance of the rightful king. Thus Orion, connected with Horus, seems likely to have been used as a seasonal marker indicating the return of 'orderly' weather. As E.C. Krupp says, the "apparent connection between celestial and terrestrial phenomena greatly affected the Egyptian view of the world".[27] This is just as evident when we turn our gaze to other parts of the Near East.

The God as an Astronomical Archetype

The 'God with the Upraised Arm' was present in many cultures and across a wide timeframe in the Near East. The gods Teshub, Adad, Baal (Fig. 7) and the unnamed Hittite weather god (Fig. 8) all had similar appearances and mythological contexts and could be considered incarnations of this one god.[28] A common motif in the depiction of all of these is the upraised arm wielding a mace or lightning. Also sometimes present is a vertical object in the left hand such as a spear or lightning, which has a parallel in the depictions of the Egyptian pharaohs in their smiting pose. The god is also often presented as riding on two mountain gods, or some sort of animal,

Fig.7: Depictions of (from left) Teshub, Adad and Baal

Fig.8: Hittite Weather God

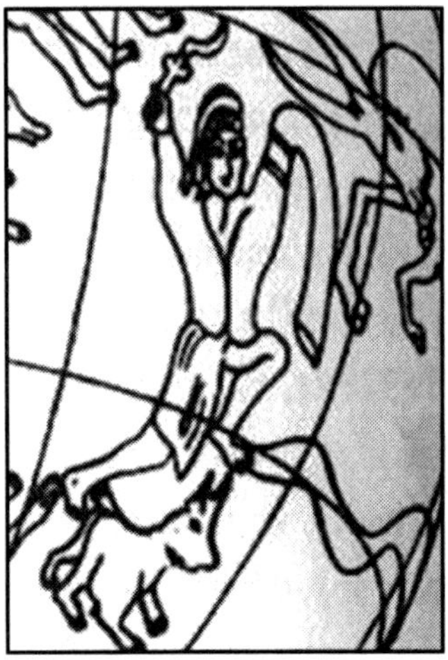

Fig.9: Islamic Orion
(*Source*: Santillana & Von Dechend)

another parallel with Horus standing upon the hippopotamus (see Fig. 3) and with Narmer standing upon two 'conquered enemies'(Fig. 1).

All of these characteristics are indicative of the constellation Orion, which is also often depicted with these same elements – see, for example, Fig. 9 which is an Islamic depiction of Orion taken from a celestial globe. The visual similarity is striking, but does the 'meaning' behind the image match up as well? Treating the Ugaritic god Baal as representative of this group of gods may prove illuminating, as a number of common elements again suggest an association with the constellation Orion.

The myths concerning Baal have two major themes, which are very similar to the mythic themes surrounding Horus. The first is Baal's battle with Yamm, which personifies the battle of order against chaos. The other is Baal's death at the hand of Mot, and subsequent resurrection. This myth clearly suggests the yearly cycle, and also that Baal may well be a constellation. In a direct parallel to the Horus-Seth confrontation, Baal finds out that he is to be swallowed by Mot, the god of death and drought. His descent suggests that he is a sky-god: he is to be "numbered with those who descend into the earth" and sets his face "to go to the mountains where [the sun sets]".[29] Also, after his death Athtar (who is identified with the planet Venus) tries to take Baal's throne, but he cannot reach it.[30] In his absence "Shapash (the Sun) the luminary of the gods glowed hot, the heavens languished under the hand of Mot (drought)…the days passed into months",[31] a clear indication of the heat of summer. Baal's return heralds the return of the rain, for he was believed to be manifest in the storms of late autumn and winter.[32] While acknowledging that cultivation was of the utmost importance to these early civilisations, it is difficult to subscribe to the common opinion that this is simply a "vegetation myth".[33] This is likely a *part* of it, but the myth's meaning surely encompasses more than this. For the result of the weather gods' disappearance is not restricted to the suffering of vegetation; *every* aspect of life is affected.[34] This indicates an allegory for seasonal change. And the seasonal marker *par excellence* of the Mediterranean was Orion. His heliacal rising indicated summer, and the time of threshing; his evening appearance the approach of winter and its attendant storms.[35] Even taking into account the precession of the equinoxes, this attribute of Orion would have been reasonably constant for the time period concerning ancient civilisations in the Near East.

The similarity in depictions of this god across the Near East argues for its importance. As others have noted previously, in ancient civilizations "certain types of scene are repeated time and time again...the wealth of meaning which must have lain behind the monuments...was so alive to those who produced them that they did not require any explanatory notes".[36] Also the common mythological motifs: Baal goes into the earth, the Hittite weather god is deemed to have withdrawn into a hole; Horus's victory marks the return of the cooling north wind, Marduk's vanquishing of Tiamat results in the "bringing of rain and coolness".[37] The acceptance of this 'God with the Upraised Arm' as Orion, and as seasonal marker, fits the pictorial and contextual evidence well. Needless to say however, restricting any definition of these gods to one particular manifestation – such as astronomy – would be unwise. The significance of the ancient gods was manifold to their respective cultures, the many aspects of Osiris being good evidence of this. But the archetypal model upon which the 'God with the Upraised Arm' was based is quite probably the constellation Orion, in both depiction and 'nature'. Describing these mythological concepts as being agricultural in nature only covers part of the territory, as agriculture depends upon the celestial cycles. The importance of these cycles to ancient people cannot be underestimated. It is a proven fact that they recognised significant 'markers' within this cycle, and it is only natural that one of most important of these should be the constellation of Orion. To paraphrase (and thus update) Sir James Frazer's conclusions in his *The Golden Bough,*[38] in the course of our enquiry it has, I trust, been made clear that there is another natural phenomenon to which the conception of death and resurrection is as applicable as to the agricultural cycle. This phenomenon is the yearly death and resurrection of the constellation of Orion, as represented in the mythic themes concerning the various incarnations of the 'God with the Upraised Arm'.

Greg Taylor is the owner and editor of the online alternative news portal, *The Daily Grail* (www.dailygrail.com), and is also the editor of *Darklore*. He is widely read in topics that challenge the orthodox worldview, from alternative history to the mysteries of human consciousness. Greg currently resides in Brisbane, Australia. His first book, *The Guide to Dan Brown's The Lost Symbol*, is a guidebook to the esoteric history and locations featured in the best-selling sequel to *The Da Vinci Code*.

Anthropology of the WEIRD

Ethnographic Fieldwork and Anomalous Experience

by *Jack Hunter*

Immersing oneself in another culture is always going to be a strange experience, and most anthropologists will be expecting to encounter different ways of thinking about the world when they first embark on their fieldwork. What they do not necessarily expect, however, is to start *experiencing* the world around them differently; to begin seeing and feeling things that, from the perspective of western science, simply cannot be possible. We might class such experiences, therefore, as "anomalous" because they do not sit comfortably with our rational scientific view of the world, but that is not to say such experiences are considered anomalous by the ethnographer's host culture. Indeed while such experiences may not be particularly common or widespread amongst the population of the host culture, they may yet have a place, and significant meaning, within that culture's broader world-view. In other cultures, therefore, experiences such as telepathic communication between two individuals, predicting the future in dreams, seeing the dead reanimate, witnessing an apparition, communicating with spirits through entranced mediums, or being afflicted by witchcraft (amongst others) may be considered entirely possible. Many highly respected anthropologists, in conducting ethnographic fieldwork amongst other cultures, have gone several steps beyond appreciating different modes of thinking about the world and have crossed the threshold into alternate ways of experiencing it. E.B. Tylor, E.E. Evans-Pritchard, Bruce T. Grindal and Edith Turner all crossed this threshold during their fieldwork, and all interpreted and presented their experiences in different ways. Through examining the ways in which these ethnographers documented their experiences, and how their personal world-views accommodated such unusual phenomena, it is possible to gain an insight into both changing academic attitudes towards the anomalous and the mysterious nature of the paranormal itself.

Raps, Trances and Victorian Anthropology

E.B. Tylor (1832-1917) is widely regarded as the founding father of the anthropological discipline, and is also held up as the epitome of the so-called "armchair anthropologist." Tylor preferred to carry out his research in the comfort of his library rather than in the field amongst the people he wrote about. It is a little known fact, however, that he did conduct a form of ethnographic fieldwork in 1872 with some of the most prominent mediums of the Spiritualist movement, which had spread rapidly across America and Europe since its advent in New York State in 1848. Tylor was intrigued, as indeed were many of the Victorian intellectual community,[1] by the radical claims of the Spiritualists to be able to demonstrate the continued existence of human personality after death. Belief in spiritual beings was to become the central theme of Tylor's highly respected anthropological theory for the origin of religion, and it has been suggested that his ideas developed in parallel with his researches into the Spiritualist movement.[2] Tylor saw Spiritualism as a modern remnant, what he termed a 'survival,' of primitive animist beliefs and as such was keen to gain firsthand personal experience of the movement: to observe animism in action. Naturally Tylor entered into his fieldwork as a sceptic convinced that Spiritualist mediums possessed at best a "deluded belief" in the efficacy of their performances or, at worst, a malicious desire to con unsuspecting individuals with deliberate acts of fraud. Tylor's personal field notes from the time, however, reveal a much more ambiguous state of affairs. Indeed, although Tylor did detect evidence of deliberate fraud in the performances of some of the mediums he observed, with others (most notably the famous mediums Daniel Dunglas Home, the Reverend Stainton Moses and Kate Fox), Tylor had some rather unusual experiences which challenged his initial suppositions. After a seance with Home Tylor wrote that he had "failed to make out how either raps, table-levitation, or accordian-playing were produced," with Stainton Moses he described how "[h]is trance seemed real," and concluded that his experience with Kate Fox was "very curious, and her feats are puzzling to me," noting that her phenomena "deserve further looking into." Tylor's experiences with these mediums forced him to admit, in his own words, "a prima facie case on evidence" for the abilities of certain mediums and to state that he could not deny the possibility "that there may be a psychic force causing raps, movements, levitations, etc.".[3] Regardless of his

Daniel Dunglas Home Levitating

experiences with the Spiritualists, and his inability to account for them in any normal terms, Tylor did not see it fit, or even at all necessary, to publish these observations in his public writings on animism. Tylor's experiences, it could be argued, seemed to imply that such experiences were not by any stretch of the imagination limited to the so-called "primitives," but could in-fact be had by anyone, including members of the Victorian intelligentsia. In the face of ridicule from the scientific community, as later happened in the case of the chemist Sir William Crookes when he published his findings in support of D.D. Home's mediumship in 1874, Tylor opted to keep his anomalous experiences to himself.

Anomalous Lights Among the Azande

By the beginning of the twentieth century anthropological methods had made several advances since Tylor's day. Armchair anthropology was out of fashion, and good ethnographic research, after developments put in place by Dr. Bronislaw Malinowski (1884-1942), required the ethnographer to engage with the society under study in as intimate a way as possible. This is what is now called "participant observation"; the central pillar of contemporary ethnographic theory and practice. In 1926 Edward Evans-Pritchard (1902-1973) was employed by the colonial British government to learn more about the beliefs and life-ways of the Azande in Sudan. In order to do this Evans-Pritchard lived amongst the Azande, semi-permanently, for four consecutive years and participated, to the best of his abilities, in the everyday life of the village he lived in. Through this process of intimate interaction with the Azande people Evans-Pritchard came to an appreciation of fundamental differences in the cosmological and metaphysical systems of the colonial English and the Azande, particularly concerning the way in which the Azande attributed causality to occurrences.[4] Evans-

Pritchard discovered that witchcraft, in the Azande world-view, was an ever present force used to explain unfortunate and unusual occurrences. Furthermore, the anthropologist learned that the Azande world-view was by no means an irrational one, in fact he concluded, quite radically at the time, that Azande beliefs were logical and that belief in witchcraft was not incompatible with a rational appreciation of nature. Evans-Pritchard's anomalous experience occurred within this cultural context late one night while writing up field-notes in his hut. He writes:

> About midnight, before retiring, I took a spear and went for my usual nocturnal stroll. I was walking in the garden at the back of the hut, amongst banana trees, when I noticed a bright light passing at the back of my servant's hut towards the homestead of a man called Tupoi. As this seemed worth investigation I followed its passage until a grass screen obscured the view. I ran quickly through my hut to the other side in order to see where the light was going to, but did not regain sight of it. I knew that only one man, a member of my household, had a lamp that might have given off so bright a light, but next morning he told me that he had neither been out late at night nor had he used his lamp. There did not lack ready informants to tell me that what I had seen was witchcraft. Shortly afterwards, on the same morning, an old relative of Tupoi and an inmate of his household died. This fully explained the light I had seen. I never discovered the real origin, which was probably a handful of grass lit by someone on his way to defecate, but the coincidence of the direction along which the light moved and the subsequent death accorded well with Zande ideas.[5]

To the Azande, then, the phenomenon witnessed by the anthropologist that night was clearly of supernatural origin; it was witchcraft-substance, a mysterious substance believed to reside inside the body of witches, externalized and sent on a murderous errand. However, despite the conviction of his informants that what he had seen was disembodied witchcraft, Evans-Pritchard suggests that it was "probably a handful of grass lit by someone on his way to defecate." This "explaining away" of the experience entirely ignored the Azande interpretation of the phenomenon, though Evans-Pritchard clearly understood the significance of such experiences within the Zande world-view. It is interesting to note at this point that in 1944 Evans-Pritchard became a convert to Roman Catholicism, and it has been suggested that his fieldwork experiences with African religious systems motivated this dramatic shift in perspective.[6,7] It could be argued, therefore, that Evans-Pritchard's conversion to the Catholic faith was a means to reconcile his personal world-view with his experiences in the field. Such a transformation, combined with a willingness to publish his experience publicly, represents a distinct departure from E.B. Tylor's complete suppression of his own anomalous fieldwork experiences seventy years earlier.

The Dancing Dead in Sisala Death Divination

Bruce T. Grindal's anomalous, or in his own terms "altered, or supernatural" experience occurred amongst the Sisala people of Ghana in October 1967.[8] Following the ominously close deaths of two members of the same village it was deduced that the resultant funeral would be a "hot" event "involving ritual danger, or *bomo*". Grindal's ethnographic account of this incident included several days leading up to the funeral in which the author's daily routine was significantly disrupted, so that by the time of the funeral, and the "death divination" that accompanied it, he was physically and mentally exhausted. His description of the event is so rich in detail that it seems only fair to present it in its entirety, rather than attempt to summarize the experience and reduce its complexity:

As I watched them I became intensely aware of their back-and-forth motion. I began to see the *goka* and the corpse tied together in the undulating rhythms of the singing, the beating of the iron hoes, and the movement of feet and bodies. Then I saw the corpse jolt and occasionally pulsate, in a counterpoint to the motions of the *goka*. At first I thought that my mind was playing tricks with my eyes, so I cannot say when the experience first occurred; but it began with moments of anticipation and terror, as though I knew something unthinkable was about to happen. The anticipation left me breathless, gasping for air. In the pit of my stomach I felt a jolting and tightening sensation, which corresponded to moments of heightened visual awareness. What I saw in those moments was outside the realm of normal perception. From both the corpse and *goka* came flashes of light so fleeting that I cannot say exactly where they originated. The hand of the *goka* would beat down the iron hoe, the spit would fly from his mouth, and suddenly the flashes of light flew like sparks from a fire. Then I felt my body become rigid. My jaws tightened and at the base of my skull I felt a jolt as though my head had been snapped off my spinal column. A terrible and beautiful sight burst upon me. Stretching from the amazingly delicate fingers and mouths of the *goka*, strands of fibrous light played upon the head, fingers, and toes of the dead man. The corpse, shaken by spasms, then rose to its feet, spinning and dancing in a frenzy. As I watched, convulsions in the pit of my stomach tied not only my eyes but also my whole being into this vortex of power. It seemed that the very floor and walls of the compound had come to life, radiating light and power, drawing the dancers in one direction and then another. Then a most wonderful thing happened. The talking drums on the roof of the dead man's house began to glow with a light so strong that it drew the dancers to the rooftop. The corpse picked up the drumsticks and began to play.[9]

Such an intense experience as this could hardly have been ignored, and Grindal's determination to document and publish it in such vivid detail, and in accordance with the Sisala's own interpretation of the events, is clearly evidential of a shift in anthropological acceptance of anomalous occurrences. In concluding his discussion of this unusual experience Grindal confirmed that it definitely happened as described, and that others present at the time saw the same things that he did. Grindal used this experience as a gateway towards understanding Sisala culture, through sharing this experience he had essentially become one with the people he was studying. Nevertheless, and perhaps unsurprisingly, this experience was quite enough for Grindal who noted in his write-up that he was happy with it being a once in a lifetime experience. He felt no further compulsion to go in search of similar experiences, preferring to look back on it philosophically from the comfort of his office.

Drawing Out the Ihamba Spirit

Edith Turner's unusual fieldwork experience with the Ndembu in Zambia is perhaps the most widely discussed ethnographic encounter with the paranormal. Turner was a participant in the *Ihamba* healing ceremony, a long and intense ritual during which the ritual doctor (Singleton) attempted to remove the malignant *Ihamba* spirit from an afflicted patient (Meru). At the culmination of this particular ceremony Turner saw with her own eyes an unusual, almost ectoplasmic, mass being extracted from the patient's back:

> And just then, through my tears, the central figure swayed deeply: all leaned forward, this was indeed going to be it. I realised along with them that the barriers were breaking -- just as I let go in tears. Something that wanted to be born was now going to be born. Then a certain palpable social integument broke and something

> calved along with me. I felt the spiritual motion, a tangible feeling of breakthrough going through the whole group. Then Meru fell -- the spirit event first and the action afterward...Quite an interval of struggle elapsed while I clapped like one possessed, crouching beside Bill amid a lot of urgent talk, while Singleton pressed Meru's back, guiding and leading out the tooth -- Meru's face in a grin of tranced passion, her back quivering rapidly. Suddenly Meru raised her arm, stretched it in liberation, and I saw with my own eyes a giant thing emerging out of the flesh of her back. This thing was a large gray blob about six inches across, a deep gray opaque thing emerging as a sphere. I was amazed -- delighted. I still laugh with glee at the realisation of having seen it, the ihamba, and so big! We were all just one in triumph. The gray thing was actually out there, visible, and you could see Singleton's hands working and scrabbling on the back- and then the thing was there no more. Singleton had it in his pouch, pressing it in with his other hand as well. The receiving can was ready; he transferred whatever it was into the can and capped the castor oil leaf and bark lid over it. It was done.[10]

For Edith Turner this experience was of such a significant magnitude that it called the traditional methodologies and theoretical positions of anthropology into question. She realised that for decades anthropologists had been completely ignoring the claims of their informants to the existence of spirits, she writes: "again and again anthropologists witness spirit rituals, and again and again some indigenous exegete tries to explain that spirits are present...and the anthropologist proceeds to interpret them differently".[11] Turner's solution to this problem was to cast aside the strictures of "positivists' denial," as she termed it, and to ultimately learn to "see what the Natives see." This approach goes beyond anthropology's traditional position of maintaining an "objective" distance between the ethnographer and the society they study, and plunges headfirst into a completely new way of interpreting and experiencing the world. Moreover, Turner's personal perspective on spirit beliefs was radically altered by this experience, prompting her to move in the direction of considering spirits as ontologically real entities.

Towards an Anthropology of the Weird

What, if any, conclusions can be drawn from this collection of anecdotal reports?

One of the most significant insights, I believe, is that these types of experience can be had by anyone so long as they participate in the relevant cultures and ritual situations. This, I feel, is a fundamental aspect of the paranormal in general: it requires our participation in the moment, whether spontaneously or within a ritualized context, in order to be experienced. E.B. Tylor left the comfort of his study to conduct fieldwork in Spiritualist seances and in so doing experienced phenomena for which he could find no explanation; Evans-Pritchard was fully immersed in Azande culture and belief when he encountered disembodied witchcraft in the African bush; Bruce Grindal's encounter with the numinous occurred in the midst of a traditional Sisala death divination after several days worth of disrupted daily routine, and Edith Turner's "breakthrough moment" erupted when she finally let go of her emotions and fully participated in the *Ihamba* ceremony. These illuminating insights into the nature of the paranormal are precisely the reason that I believe ethnographic methodologies should be used to supplement parapsychology's laboratory based experiments. The ethnographic approach lends itself to a greater appreciation of the wider context in which paranormal phenomena occur: it demonstrates the significant role of culture both in terms of the way in which such phenomena manifest and the way they are interpreted by those who experience them. The element of participation allows the researcher to experience firsthand the phenomena they are investigating and reveals the significance of alternate states of consciousness and emotional engagement in experiences of the paranormal. These anecdotes also demonstrate a gradual shift in the way that anthropologists have dealt with anomalous experiences in the field. The move towards a greater reflexivity on behalf of the ethnographer has led to an emphasis on the anthropology of experience, which in turn has prompted certain anthropologists to consider the ontology of the anomalous phenomena they witness in the field. Further ethnographic research in this direction may reveal yet more fascinating insights into the nature and experience of the paranormal.

Jack Hunter is a PhD student in Social Anthropology at the University of Bristol, UK. His research looks at contemporary trance mediumship in Bristol, and focuses on themes of personhood, personality, altered states of consciousness and anomalous experience. He is the founder and editor of the peer-reviewed journal "Paranthropology: Journal of Anthropological Approaches to the Paranormal" (www.paranthropology.co.uk). In 2010 he received the Eileen J. Garrett scholarship from the Parapsychology Foundation, and in 2011 received the Schmeidler award from the Parapsychological Association.

Endnotes

Ian 'Cat' Vincent - The Slenderman (p. 9)

Acknowledgements:

My deepest thanks to all the creators and commentators in the Slenderverse, and especially to my colleagues Damien, Mikey and John W. for their input.

Notes:

In Part 2, I will be looking deeper into the mythological aspect of Slenderman's evolution – especially in relation to its basis as a tulpa – and how, both within the storylines and from outside, attempts have been made to combat it. I will also examine the parallels with Slenderman's manifestation to other expressions of fictional paths to occult validity, especially in the work of Alan Moore and Grant Morrison.

A page of links to the various aspects of the Slenderman mythos can be found at my website http://www.catvincent.com/.

Robert M. Schoch - Death Star (p. 59)

Bibliography:

Berge, Elizabeth. "Solar Issues Send Up Flares." Facultative Matters, Gen Re Research, April 2011, pp. 1-4. Available from http://www.genre.com/sharedfile/pdf/FacMatters201104-en.pdf Accessed 11 July 2011.

Brooks, Michael. "Space storm alert: 90 seconds from catastrophe." Article dated 23 March 2009. *New Scientist* (Preview available at http://www.newscientist.com/article/mg20127001.300-space-storm-alert-90-seconds-from-catastrophe.

html Accessed 11 July 2011). Copy available from http://www.cc.gatech.edu/classes/AY2009/cs4001c_spring/documents/Space_storm_alert__90_seconds_from_catastrophe-_New_Scientist.pdf Accessed 11 July 2011.

Carrington, R. C. "Description of a Singular Appearance seen in the Sun on September 1, 1859." *Monthly Notices of the Royal Astronomical Society,* vol. 20, p. 13-15 (1859). Available from http://articles.adsabs.harvard.edu/full/seri/MNRAS/0020//0000013.000.html Accessed 11 July 2011.

Cliver, E. W. "The 1859 space weather event: Then and now." *Advances in Space Research,* vol. 38, pp. 119-129 (2006).

Don, Sallie, and Amos Aikman. "Brits to shut grid for solar flare." Article dated June 20, 2011. Available from http://www.theaustralian.com.au/news/nation/brits-to-shut-grid-for-solar-flare/story-e6frg6nf-1226078128738 Accessed 11 July 2011.

Green, James L., and Scott Boardsen. "Duration and extent of the great auroral storm of 1859." *Advances in Space Research*, vol. 38, pp. 130-135 (2006).

Haug, Espen Gaarder. "When Will God Destroy Our Money?" (Paper dated 18 April 2010). Available from http://papers.ssrn.com/sol3/papers.cfm?abstract_id=1591768 Accessed 3 July 2011.

Hodgson, R. "On a curious Appearance seen in the Sun." *Monthly Notices of the Royal Astronomical Society,* vol. 20, pp. 15-16 (1859). Available from http://articles.adsabs.harvard.edu/full/seri/MNRAS/0020//0000015.000.html Accessed 11 July 2011.

International Business Times. "Solar Storms Could Cause Power Outages, Scrambled GPS, Communications Failure." Article dated 8 August 2011. Available from http://www.ibtimes.com/articles/194172/20110808/solar-storm-flare-electricity-risk-grid-caution-danger-magnetosphere-earth-electricity-space-geomagn.htm Accessed 8 August 2011.

Jaggard, Victoria. "As Sun Storms Ramp Up, Electric Grid Braces for Impact." Article dated 3 August 2011. Available from http://news.nationalgeographic.com/news/energy/2011/08/110803-solar-flare-storm-electricity-grid-risk/ Accessed 8 August 2011.

Kusch, Heinrich, and Ingrid Kusch. *Tore zur Unterwelt: Das Geheimnis der unterirdischen Gänge aus uralter Zeit.* Graz: V. F. Sammler, 2009 (Second edition, 2011).

LaViolette, Paul A. "Evidence for a Solar Flare Cause of the Pleistocene Mass Extinction." *Radiocarbon*, vol. 53, no. 2: 303 – 323 (1 June 2011). Manuscript (version consulted for this article) available from http://starburstfound.org/downloads/superwave/SPE.html and http://www.starburstfound.org/downloads/superwave/SPE.pdf Accessed 6 June 2011.

Lovett, Richard A. "What If the Biggest Solar Storm on Record Happened Today? Repeat of 1859 Carrington Event would devastate modern world, experts say." Article dated 2 March 2011. Available from http://news.nationalgeographic.com/news/2011/03/110302-solar-flares-sun-storms-earth-danger-carrington-event-science/ Accessed 8 August 2011.

Marusek, James A. "The Sun is Undergoing a State Change." Note by Marusek: "The first version of this article has been published, in Spanish language, in Athanor magazine, under the title 'El Sol y el cambio climático' ('The Sun and the climate change') (March-April 2010) (http://www.athanor.es)." Available from http://www.breadandbutterscience.com/StateChange.pdf Accessed 4 July 2011.

McCracken, K. G., G. A. M. Dreschhoff, E. J. Zeller, D. F. Smart, and M. A. Shea. "Solar cosmic ray events for the period 1561-1994. 1. Identification in polar ice, 1561-1950." *Journal of Geophysical Research*, vol. 106, no. A10, pp. 21,585-21,598 (1 October 2001); K. G. McCracken, G. A. M. Dreschhoff, D. F. Smart, and M. A. Shea, "Solar cosmic ray events for the period 1561-1994. 2. The Gleissberg periodicity." *Journal of Geophysical Research*, vol. 106, no. A10, pp. 21,599-21,609 (1 October 2001).

NRC [National Research Council of the National Academies (United States)], Committee on the Societal and Economic Impacts of Severe Space Weather Events: A Workshop. *Severe Space Weather Events – Understanding Societal and Economic Impacts, A Workshop Report.* Washington, D.C.: The National Academies Press, 2008. [Members of the Committee on the Societal and Economic Impacts of Severe Space Weather Events: Daniel N. Baker, Roberta Balstad, J. Michael Bodeau, Eugene Cameron, Joseph F. Fennell, Genene M. Fischer, Kevin F. Forbes, Paul M. Kintner, Louis G. Leffler, William S. Lewis, Joseph B. Reagan, Arthur A Small III, Thomas A. Stansell, and Leonard Strachan, Jr. Staff of the Committee on the Societal and Economic Impacts of Severe Space Weather Events: Sandra J. Graham, Theresa M. Fisher, Victoria Swisher, and Catherine A. Gruber.] Available from http://www.nap.edu/catalog.php?record_id=12507 and http://lasp.colorado.edu/education/journalists/solar_dynamics_ws/papers/lowres%20Severe%20Space%20Weather%20FINAL.pdf Accessed 4 July 2011.

Odenwald, Sten. "The Day the Sun Brought Darkness." Article dated 13 March 2009. Available from http://www.nasa.gov/topics/earth/features/sun_darkness.html Accessed 9 August 2011.

Odenwald, Sten F., and James L. Green. "Bracing for a Solar Superstorm." *Scientific American*, August 2008. Available from http://www.sciamdigital.com/index.cfm?fa=Products.ViewIssuePreview&ARTICLEID_CHAR=08DBE2D9-3048-8A5E-10E2CC1AAD5D93C1 Accessed 4 July 2011. Text of article available at http://www.eons.com/groups/topic/1041457-Bracing-for-a-Solar-Superstorm Accessed 4 July 2011.

Smart, D. F., M. A. Shea, and K. G. McCracken. "The Carrington event: Possible solar proton intensity-time profile." *Advances in Space Research*, vol. 38, pp. 215-225 (2006).

Solanki, S. K., I. G. Usoskin, B. Kromer, M. Schüssler, and J. Beer. "Unusual activity of the Sun during recent decades compared to the previous 11,000 years." *Nature*, vol. 431, pp. 1084-1087 (28 October 2004). Available from http://www.nature.com/nature/journal/v431/n7012/abs/nature02995.html Accessed 21 August 2011.

Southwest Research Institute. "What's Down with the Sun? Major Drop in Solar Activity Predicted." Press release, 14 June 2011. Available from http://www.boulder.swri.edu/~deforest/SPD-sunspot-release/SPD_solar_cycle_release.txt Accessed 20 June 2011. (See also popular articles summarizing this topic: Anonymous. "Solar event that may have caused last ice age happening again?" Article dated 14 June 2011. Available from http://losangeles.ibtimes.com/articles/162919/20110614/solar-flare-ice-age-global-warming-sun.htm Accessed 5 July 2011. Anonymous. "Scientists change tack on Sun cycle." Article dated 16 June 2011. Available from http://www.theaustralian.com.au/news/health-science/scientists-change-tack-on-sun-cycle/story-e6frg8y6-1226076023422 Accessed 5 July 2011.)

Space Daily. "Did A Massive Solar Proton Event Fry The Earth[?]" Article dated 6 June 2011. Available from http://www.spacedaily.com/reports/Did_A_Massive_Solar_Proton_Event_Fry_The_Earth_999.html Accessed 6 June 2011.

Space Ref. "Major Drop in Solar Activity Predicted." Article dated June 14, 2011. Available from http://www.spaceref.com/news/viewpr.html?pid=33826&utm_content=api&utm_medium=srs.gs-twitter&utm_source=direct-srs.gs Accessed 20 June 2011.

Stewart, Balfour. "On the Great Magnetic Disturbance which extended from August 28 to September 7, 1859, as recorded by Photography at the Kew Observatory." *Philosophical Transactions of the Royal Society of London*, vol. 151, pp. 423-430 (1861).

Stoller, Matt. "How America Could Collapse." Article dated 27 July 2011. Available from http://www.thenation.com/article/162317/how-america-could-collapse Accessed 7 July 2011.

Usoskin, I. G., S. K. Solanki, and G. A. Kovaltsov "Grand minima and maxima of solar activity: new observational constraints." *Astronomy & Astrophysics*, vol. 471, pp. 301–309 (2007).

Notes

1. Cliver, 2006.
2. Carrington, 1859, p. 14; also quoted in Stewart, 1861, p. 427.
3. Carrington, 1859, p. 14.

4. Hodgson, 1859.
5. Odenwald and Green, 2008.
6. Smart et al., 2006.
7. Green and Boardsen, 2006, p. 130.
8. Quoted from NRC, 2008, p. 6.
9. Odenwald and Green, 2008.
10. Stoller, 2011.
11. Brooks, 2009; the NAS report that *New Scientist* is referring to is cited in the Bibliography above under NRC, 2008.
12. See also International Business Times, 2011; Lovett, 2011; NRC, 2008.
13. Jaggard, 2011.
14. Berge, 2011.
15. Odenwald, 2009.
16. Jaggard, 2011.
17. Odenwald, 2009.
18. Odenwald, 2009.
19. See NRC, 2008.
20. Haug, 2010, p. 2.
21. McCracken et al., 2001.
22. Solanki et al., 2004, and Usoskin et al., 2007; the amount of beryllium-10 and carbon-14 in the atmosphere correlates with solar activity.
23. LaViolette, 2011.
24. *Space Daily*, 2011.
25. LaViolette, 2011, p. 1.
26. LaViolette, 2011, p. 17, footnote.
27. *Space Daily*, 2011.
28. Kusch and Kusch, 2011.
29. Solanki et al., 2004, p. 1084.
30. Marusek, 2010.
31. Space Ref, 2011; Southwest Research Institute, 2011.
32. Kintner quoted in Brooks, 2009.
33. These smaller earthquakes could still be substantial from a human perspective; for example, it takes about thirty-two magnitude 6 earthquakes to equal the energy released by one magnitude 7 earthquake.
34. Don and Aikman, 2011.
35. Don and Aikman, 2011.

Lynn Picknett and Clive Prince - When Science Lost its Soul (p. 77)

Notes:

1. Robert Lomas, *The Invisible College: The Royal Society, Freemasonry and the Birth of Modern Science*, Headline, 2002, p. 66.
2. All the relevant correspondence of Boyle, Hartlib and Worthington can be found in Margery Purver's *The Royal Society: Concept and Creation* (Routledge & Kegan Paul, 1967) from which the following quotes are taken.
3. Macaria seems to have been a name Hartlib picked up from Thomas More's *Utopia*. Hartlib wrote his own utopian tale in a short pamphlet of 1641, *A Description of the Famous Kingdome of Macaria.*
4. See R.K. Bluhm, 'Henry Oldenburg, FRS (c.1615-1677)', *Notes and Record of the Royal Society of London*, vol. 15, July 1960
5. Quoted in *ibid.*, pp. 185-6.
6. Quoted in *ibid.*, p. 185.

Neil Arnold - There's Something Strange in the Sewers (p. 97)

Notes:

1. 'Sewer Monster Scares Children In Florida Town', *The Sumter Daily Item*, S.C., Thursday 24th February 1983, Page 29
2. 'Teen May Be Cause Of Sewer Monster Scare', *Ocala Star Banner,* 25th February 1983, Page 16
3. *Monster! The A-Z Of Zooform Phenomena* – Neil Arnold (CFZ Press 2007)
4. 'Sewer Monsters Stinks Up Neighbourhood', *Lakeland Ledger*, 13th May 1982, Page 24
5. *Mystery Animals Of The British Isles: London* – Neil Arnold (CFZ Press 2011)
6. 'Urban Legends Of The Underbelly', http://londonist.com/2007/11/the_saturday_st_26.php, 24th November 2007
7. *Living Wonders* - John Michell & Robert J.M. Rickard (Thames & Hudson 1982), page 153
8. 'Alligator appears in New York City, may have crawled from sewer', *Herald Sun*, 23rd August 2010
9. 'New York Sewer Expert Dispels Crocodile Myth', *Sarasota Herald-Tribune,* 21st May 1982, page 25

10. 'Alligator clogs sewer in Fort Myers Street', *The Miami News*, 21st October 1921, page 9

11. 'Alligator found in Uptown sewer', *New York Times*, 10th February 1935

12. 'Alligator swimming from Brooklyn shore is captured by mystified barge captain', *New York Times*, 1st June 1937

13. 'Alligator in subway, calmly walks towards terrified crowd – policemen capture it', *New York Times*, 7th June 1937

14. 'Well boys, what now?', *The Windsor Star*, 8th June 1963, page 37

15. 'Warden lassoes gator in sewer', *The Free-Lance Star*, 8th September 1977, page 11

16. 'Alligator killed after attack', *Ocala Star Banner*, 29th June 1978, page 16

17. 'Alligator lives in sewer', *Altus Times*, 10th March 1982, page four

18. 'Alligator in sewer line a surprise', *Daily Times*, 3rd May 1984, page 21

19. 'Croc rocks residents', *The Morning Call*, 5th August 1987,

20. 'Alligator living high life in sewer', *Spokesman Review*, 21st July 1994, page 2

21. 'City tail – alligator is found in New York City park lake', *Star News*, 28th July 1995, page 2

22. 'Miles of sewer lines, and he knows them well', *New York Times*, 16th February 2011

23. 'Crocodile causes panic', *Times Daily*, 7th November 1987, page 98

24. 'Crocodile in sewer', *Victoria Advocate*, 20th April 1998, page 10

25. 'Crocodile adopts sewer for a home', *Milwaukee Journal*, 23rd June 1912, page 1

26. 'No, it's not a hoax! Video of alien life form found in sewer…', *Daily Mail*, 2nd July 2009

27. 'Real life turtles live in N.Y. sewers', *The Times-News*, 5th April 1990, page 31

28. 'Bog turtle jeopardizes NJ sewer', *Milwaukee Journal*, 19th April 1979, page 82

29. 'Hunting a lion in a sewer', *New York Times*, 20th October 1889

30. 'Baby hippo found dead in sewer', *Bangkok Post*, 13th January 2011

31. 'Cow is rescued after twelve hours in storm sewer', *Chicago Tribune*, 13th November 1941

32. 'Rogue heifer rescued from sewer drainpipe', *Victoria Advocate*, 17th October 1992

33. 'Sewer workers saved from vicious lizard', *Press of Atlantic City*, 17th September 1992

34. 'Old bone find near Kamiah to be tested', *Spokesman Review*, 24th April 1957, page 32

35. '10ft snake popped out of lavatories at block of flats', *Times Online*, 18th October 2005

36. 'Found in sewers: a snake, toy soldiers, and a cow', *STV.TV*, 22nd March 2010

37. 'Pet python grips town with shivers', *Free-Lance Star*, 12th June 1984, page 2

38. 'Boys says a snake came out from sewer and bit his hand', *New York Times*,

8th August 1963
39. 'Anaconda roams city's sewers', *Ocala Star-Banner*, 9th August 1965, page 7
40. 'Snake's alive! What a surprise', *Los Angeles Times*, 18th November 1975
41. 'Sewer snake to be stuffed', *Lawrence Journal-World*, 15th February 1981, page 1
42. 'Paranormal beings reported at the sewage station', *Hastings Observer*, 14th February 2008
43. 'Merseyside sewer monster hunt, after mysterious beast seen on CCTV', *Liverpool Echo*, 31st March 2011
44. 'Apparition on Christmas Eve. Bondi sewer ghost', *Sydney Morning Herald*, 28th December 1933, page 4
45. Creative Commons Attribute Share Alike 3.0 Licence, original creator Neurovelho.
46. 'Carmen Winstead was pushed down a sewer', http://urbanlegends.about.com/od/ghoststories/a/carmen_winstead.htm
47. http://www.weirdasianews.com/2007/12/22/10-year-chinese-haunting-finally-debunked/
48. 'Unholy Smoke!', *Fortean Times Magazine*, Issue 267, September 2010

Nigel Watson - Alien Messages and Impressions (p. 139)

Notes:

Norman Harrison's real name and address are on file. More details about Norman's experiences are covered in:

- "Stranger In The City" by Nigel Watson, *MUFOB* New Series 14, Spring 1979 and online at: http://magonia.haaan.com/2009/stranger/
- *Portraits of Alien Encounters* by Nigel Watson, VALIS Books, 1990.

John Reppion - The Calderstones of Liverpool (p. 157)

Acknowledgements:

With thanks to Julia McLaughlin Cook at the Merseyside Archaeological Society, and Roger Hull at the Liverpool Record Office. Also, as always, love and thanks to Leah for all her help and support.

References:

1. http://www.liverpoolparks.org/red/docs/parks/calderstones_park/index.html

2. http://www.bbc.co.uk/liverpool/content/articles/2007/11/14/nob_autumnwatch_favourite_tree_feature.shtml

3. http://www.liverpooltennis.co.uk/

4. *The Calderstones – A Prehistoric Tomb in Liverpool* (Merseyside Archaeological Society, 1984)

5. R. W. Cowell: *The Prehistory of Merseyside* (Merseyside Archaeological Society, 1988)

6. *Journal of the Merseyside Archaeological Society* Vol. 13 (2010)

7. Ron Cowell: *The Calderstones – A Prehistoric Tomb in Liverpool* [2nd, revised edition] (Merseyside Archaeological Society, 2008)

8. Ron Cowell: *The Calderstones – A Prehistoric Tomb in Liverpool* [2nd, revised edition] (Merseyside Archaeological Society, 2008)

9. http://www.allertonoak.com/merseySights/SouthLiverpoolCP.html

10. W.A Herdman: *A Contribution to the History of the Calderstones, near Liverpool* (1896)

11. Ron Cowell: *The Calderstones – A Prehistoric Tomb in Liverpool* [2nd, revised edition] (Merseyside Archaeological Society, 2008)

12. Dave Roberts: *Discussion of the Prehistoric Origins of Calderstones Park* (Journal of the Merseyside Archaeological Society Vol. 13 2010)

13. http://www.megalithicwalks.co.uk/liverpool.htm

14. John Stuart (ed): James Y. Simpson – *Archaeological Essays, Vol. 1* (Project Gutenberg, 2008)

15. http://en.wikipedia.org/wiki/Cup_and_ring_mark

16. R. W. Cowell: *The Prehistory of Merseyside* (Merseyside Archaeological Society, 1988)

17. http://www.megalithics.com/wales/

18. http://www.pasthorizonspr.com/index.php/archives/03/2011/the-llwydiarth-esgob-stone

19. Ron Cowell: *The Calderstones – A Prehistoric Tomb in Liverpool* [2nd, revised edition] (Merseyside Archaeological Society, 2008)

20. George Nash & Adam Stanford: *Recording Images Old and New on the Calderstones in Liverpool* (*Journal of the Merseyside Archaeological Society* Vol. 13 2010)

21. http://www.knowth.com/megalithic-art.htm

22. http://en.wikipedia.org/wiki/Cup_and_ring_mark#United_Kingdom

23. George Nash & Adam Stanford: *Recording Images Old and New on the Calderstones in Liverpool* (*Journal of the Merseyside Archaeological Society* Vol. 13 2010)

24. George Nash & Adam Stanford: *Recording Images Old and New on the Calderstones in Liverpool* (*Journal of the Merseyside Archaeological Society* Vol. 13 2010)

25. Ron Cowell: *The Calderstones – A Prehistoric Tomb in Liverpool* [2nd, revised edition] (Merseyside Archaeological Society, 2008)

26. http://myweb.tiscali.co.uk/celynog/liverpool.htm

27. Ron Cowell: *The Calderstones – A Prehistoric Tomb in Liverpool* [2nd, revised edition] (Merseyside Archaeological Society, 2008)

28. George Nash & Adam Stanford: *Recording Images Old and New on the Calderstones in Liverpool* (*Journal of the Merseyside Archaeological Society* Vol. 13 2010)

29. http://www.megalithic.co.uk/article.php?sid=6340485

30. http://www.megalithic.co.uk/search.php?country=11&sitetype=48

31. *British Archaeology Journal* #54 (August, 2000)

32. http://en.wikipedia.org/wiki/Druidry

33. http://news.nationalgeographic.com/news/2009/03/090320-druids-sacrifice-cannibalism.html

34. http://news.nationalgeographic.com/news/2009/03/090320-druids-sacrifice-cannibalism.html

35. http://www.megalithic.co.uk/article.php?sid=2146411507

36. http://www.megalithic.co.uk/article.php?sid=2146411507

37. William Stukeley M. D.: *Stonehenge, A Temple Restor'd to the British Druids* (1740)

38. http://en.wikipedia.org/wiki/William_Stukeley

39. http://en.wikipedia.org/wiki/Ancient_Order_of_Druids#Hut09

40. George Nash: *Art in this World and Art in the Underworld: An Appraisal of the Later Prehistoric Menhir of Robin Hood's Stone, Allerton, Liverpool* (*Journal of the Merseyside Archaeological Society* Vol. 13 2010)

41. Ron Cowell: *The Calderstones – A Prehistoric Tomb in Liverpool* [2nd, revised edition] (Merseyside Archaeological Society, 2008)

42. http://www.bookerline.com/history.htm

43. George Nash: *Art in this World and Art in the Underworld: An Appraisal of the Later Prehistoric Menhir of Robin Hood's Stone, Allerton, Liverpool* (*Journal of the Merseyside Archaeological Society* Vol. 13 2010)

44. George Nash: *Art in this World and Art in the Underworld: An Appraisal of the Later Prehistoric Menhir of Robin Hood's Stone, Allerton, Liverpool* (*Journal of the Merseyside Archaeological Society* Vol. 13 2010)

45. Ron Cowell: *The Calderstones – A Prehistoric Tomb in Liverpool* [2nd, revised edition] (Merseyside Archaeological Society, 2008)

46. http://liverpool.gov.uk/leisure-parks-and-events/parks-and-greenspaces/calderstones-park/

Martin Shough - Double Trouble (p. 181)

Acknowledgements:

Special thanks are due to mirage expert Andrew Young (see the website http://mintaka.sdsu.edu/GF/bibliog/toc.html)and Belgian researcher Wim van Utrecht (http://www.caelestia.be/) for technical advice, discussion, corrections and the provision of images and original documents. Thanks also to marine historian Reuben Goossens (www.ssmaritime.com).

Notes:

1. http://www.youtube.com/watch?v=a8fWUPlqwlQ&feature=related
2. http://cdweb2012.blogspot.com/2008/07/blog-2-planet-x-nibiru-facts-2012.html
3.http://www.akiat.net/legends-about-the-earth-heavenly-bodies-and-natural-phenomena.html
4. Curiously, a new theory (2011) says that the anomalous lunar farside highlands were dumped there by the ancient impact of a second moon, see: http://www.physorg.com/news/2011-08-big-splat-moon-mountainous-side.html
5. See: Kyalundzyuga, V.T. The Two Suns (Udegey Folk Tales). Khabarovsk, 1974, cited in: http://www.arcticmuseum.com/en/?q=l117
6. Hodson, T.C., *The Meitheis - A Study of the Tribe of the Brahmaputra Valley* (1906), Read Books, 2006.
7. Hastings, J. & J.A.Selbie, *Encyclopedia of Religion and Ethics*, Pt.15, 2003, p.48 (Google books)
8. *Ibid.*, quoting Skeat, W.W,. & C.O.Blagden, *Pagan races of the Malay Peninsula*, London 1906.
9. http://en.wikipedia.org/wiki/Malacca
10. Huo Jianying, 'Fly Me to the Moon – and Back', *China Daily* htp://www.chinatoday.com.cn/English/e2008/e200801/p72.htm
11. http://en.wikipedia.org/wiki/Mithraic_mysteries; 'Mithras and the Hypercosmic Sun' in John R.Hinnells, ed. *Studies in Mithraism*, Rome 1994 pp. 257-64; http://www.well.com/user/davidu/appendix2.html
12. Tong Yun, 'A Rare, Spectacular Astronomical Sight' http://zhengjian.org/zj/articles/2002/12/23/19731.html
13. http://www.nostradamus.org/
14. Spence, L. *Myths & Legends of the North American Indians,* Rudolph Steiner Publications 1975. The katcina myths are complex but the "blue star" prophecy

has been borrowed by many 2012 catastrophists, and was quickly identified with the oddly-behaving Comet Holmes in 2007: http://2012rising.com/article/was-comet-holmes-the-hopi-blue-star

15. http://www.enduringword.com/commentaries/3904.htm

16. http://www.the2012warning.com/category/two-suns; http://beforeitsnews.com/story/372/422/Two_Suns_in_the_Bible.html

17. http://EzineArticles.com/3410047

18. http://en.wikipedia.org/wiki/Star_Wars

19. http://www.youtube.com/watch?v=bzWM4wvIku8

20. Pliny, *Natural History,* Harvard University Press, Cambridge, Massachusetts, 1958

21. Tape, Walter, et al., 'The Legendary Rome Halo Displays', *Applied Optics*, Vol. 47, No. 34 / 1 December 2008

22. Minnaert, M.G.J., 'An Exceptional Phenomenon of Atmospheric Optics: A One-Sided Mocksun at 3 30'', *Weather*, 21, 250 (1966). Thanks to Wim van Utrecht and the Belgian Royal Observatory for locating this article.

23. Morrison, P., 'The Nature of Scientific Evidence', in: Sagan, C. & T. Page (eds), *UFOs - A Scientific Debate*, Cornell University Press, 1972, p.287.

24. Minnaert, M.G.J., 'Unusual or Neglected Optical Phenomena in the Landscape', *Journal of the Optical Society of America*, 58 (1968), 3: 297

25. Minnaert, M.G.J., 'An Exceptional Phenomenon of Atmospheric Optics: A One-sided Mocksun at 3º 30',' *Weather*, 21: 250 (1966)

26. Minnaert, *JOSA*; *op. cit.*

27. One small contributing factor may be a misquotation of Minnaert in the very widely-read Sourcebook Project collection of William Corliss. Corliss' version says only that Mrs N.S. "ran to her cabin, and made a colour photograph", omitting the circumstantial detail of her there "grasping her camera", a phrase which tends if anything to concretise the impression given by Minnaert that she took the photo there and then in her cabin. See: Corliss, W., *Rare Halos, Mirages, Anomalous Rainbows and Related Electromagnetic Phenomena*, The Sourcebook Project, Glen Arm, U.S., 1984, Section GEH 13, p.79.

28. Email from Wim van Utrecht 01.08.2011

29. Email from Andy Young 24.07.2011

30. Amateur telescope makers often use old porthole glass for mirror blanks. Mirrors are ground from plane glass.

31. Email from Reuben Goossens, 03.08.2011

32. Ibid.

33. Email from Andy Young, 03.08.2011. But note that a process halftone c. 1966 is subject to a certain amount of manual intervention during screening, development, retouching and etching. The original slide is unavailable.

34. Email from Reuben Goossens, 04.08.2011

35. Email from Reuben Goossens, 03.08.2011

36. Email from Andy Young, 24.07.2011

37. Email to the author 11.07.2011

38. Viezee, W., 'Optical Mirage',in: Condon (ed), *Scientific Study of Unidentified Flying Objects*, Vision Press 1970 p. 603

39. Minnaert, Marcel, *De natuurkunde van 't vrije veld*, 1968 (5th edition), Thieme & Cie, Zutphen. (Trans. W. Van Utrecht.)

40. Minnaert, M.G.J., 'Unusual or Neglected Optical Phenomena in the Landscape', *Journal of the Optical Society of America*, 58 (1968), 3: 297

41. Richard, R., 'Phenomene Optique Remarquable,' *La Météorologie*, 4, 32, pp. 301-302, October/December 1953

42. Emails to the author from Andrew Young, Feb 02 2008; May 04 2009

43. http://wang888.skynetblogs.be/archive/2011/01/18/chine-deux-soleils-dans-le-ciel-du-jiangxi.html

44. http://www.lepouvoirmondial.com/archive/2011/01/12/3-soleils-apparaissent-en-chine-un-signe-cosmique-annonciate.html

45. See: Tape, W. & G.P.Konnen, 'A General Setting for Halo Theory', *Applied Optics*, Vol.38, No. 9/20 March 1999; Rikonen, M. et.al., 'Halo Observations Provide Evidence of Airborne Cubic Ice in the Earth's Atmosphere', *Applied Optics*, Vol.39, No. 33/20 Nov 2000

46. Corliss, W., *Rare Halos, Mirages, Anomalous Rainbows and Related Electromagnetic Phenomena*, The Sourcebook Project, Glen Arm, U.S., 1984; Section GEM3 Lateral Mirages, X1, p.146. See also the sections: GEH13 Close, One-Sided Mock Suns; GEL4 Abnormal Refraction Phenomena as Astronomical Objects Approach the Horizon.

47. Metrical unit originating in pre-revolutionary France. 1 Toise was exactly 6 *pieds* (6 feet or about 1.949m) in France until 1812. The bark was therefore at a distance of about 4.5 miles. See: http://en.wikipedia.org/wiki/Toise

48. *Journ. de Physique*, March 1820, xc, p.217; 'A Case of Lateral Mirage', *Edinburgh Philosophical Journal*, eds. Sir David Brewster, Robert Jameson, Royal Society of Edinburgh, Wernerian Natural History Society, Edinburgh, Printed for Archibald Constable, Vol.3, p.400, 1820

49. Email from Andy Young 05.08.2011

50. Corliss, W., *Rare Halos, Mirages, Anomalous Rainbows and Related Electromagnetic Phenomena*, The Sourcebook Project, Glen Arm, U.S., 1984; Section GEM3 Lateral Mirages, X1, p.147

51. To put some numbers on this, maximum lateral displacements in free-air refraction in nature have been experimentally measured at around 10 seconds of arc, or typically three orders of magnitude smaller than the total refractive displacement (Email from Andrew Young, 05.08.11). The surface of a strong inversion may be slightly tilted across a weather front, or more locally tilted by wind- or gravity-waves, or by a land breeze front near the shore, causing asymmetrical sunset distortions; but the skewing is never more than a few minutes of arc, a small fraction of the solar diameter.

52. But this appears to be Corliss' own error, since the true sun is not identified on the original drawing in *The Marine Observer*; email from Wim Van Utrecht, 12.08.2011

53. Email from Andrew Young 08.05.2009

54. Morrison, P., 'The Nature of Scientific Evidence', in: Sagan, C. & T. Page (eds), *UFOs - A Scientific Debate,* Cornell University Press, 1972, p.287.

55. Email from Andy Young 18.07.2011

56. Minnaert's articles and book contain some discrepancies in his plate measurement of the 'mocksun' angle, as well as inaccurate references to his own papers, so his record is not quite impeccable. Future research including study of Minnaert's private papers at the University of Utrecht and elsewhere may yet provide answers to some outstanding questions in this fascinating case. Certain notes and sketches were recently recovered by Frits Van der Veldt from the Noord-Hollands Archief in Haarlem at the behest of Wim Van Utrecht. A further research article may be published by Wim at www.caelestia.be.

57. Email from Manuel Borraz Aymerich to Wim van Utrecht, Aug 04 2011

58. http://www.phsea.com.tw/phseaforum/posts/list/43842.page;jsessionid=46860 30E111BD242B11085527EC746AC.phsea

Greg Taylor - The God with the Upraised Arm (p. 227)

Bibliography

Aldred, Cyril, 1965. *Egypt to the End of the Old Kingdom.* Thames and Hudson, London.

Allen, Richard Hinckley, 1963. *Star Names: Their Lore and Meaning.* Dover Publications, New York.

Arnold, April 1999 'Min', Ancient Egypt: The Mythology, http://www.ixpres.com/netjert/min.htm.

Colless, Brian, 1994. *Hieroglyph and Cuneiform: Ancient religious writings.*
Deighton, Hilary J. 1982. "The 'Weather-God' in Hittite Anatolia: An Examination of the Archaeological and Textual Sources." *Biblical Archaeology Review,* Oxford.
Fairman, H. W. (ed.), 1974. *The Triumph of Horus: An Ancient Egyptian Sacred Drama*. B. T. Batsford Ltd, London.
Frankfort, H. and H. A., Wilson, John A., Jacobsen, Thorkild, Irwin, William A., 1946. *The Intellectual Adventure of Early Man.* The University of Chicago Press, Chicago.
Frankfort, H., 1948. *Kingship and the Gods.* University of Chicago Press, Chicago
Frazer, Sir James George, 1922. *The Golden Bough: A Study in Magic and Religion* (Abridged edition). Macmillan Press Ltd., London.
Gray, John. 1969. *Near Eastern Mythology.* Hamlyn Publishing Group Ltd., Sydney.
Grimal, Nicolas, 1988. *A History of Ancient Egypt,* trans. Ian Shaw, Blackwell, Oxford.
Guirand, Felix, 1996. *The Larousse Encyclopedia of Mythology,* trans Richard Aldrington and Delano Ames, Chancellor Press, London.
Krupp, E. C. 1979. *In Search of Ancient Astronomies.* Chatto and Windus, London.
Krupp, E. C. 1991. *Beyond the Blue Horizon: Myths and Legends of the Sun, Moon, Stars and Planets.* Harper Collins, New York.
Krupp, E. C. 1997. *Skywatchers, Shamans and Kings: Astronomy and the Archaeology of Power.* John Wiley & Sons Inc., New York.
Lichtheim, Miriam. 1973. *Ancient Egyptian Literature, Volume I: The Old and Middle Kingdom.* University of California Press, Los Angeles.
Neugebauer, O. 1957. *The Exact Sciences in Antiquity.* Brown University Press, Providence, Rhode Island.
Parker, Richard A., "Ancient Egyptian Astronomy", in *The Place of Astronomy in the Ancient World,* ed. F. R. Hodson, Oxford University Press, London.
Plutarch, 1927. *Plutarch's Moralia,* trans. Frank Cole Babbit, William Heinemann Ltd., London.
Ringren, Helmer, 1973. *Religions of the Ancient Near East,* trans. John Sturdy, S.P.C.K, London.
Sidgwick, J. B., 1951. *Introducing Astronomy,* Faber & Faber Ltd., London.

Santillana, Georgio and Von Dechend, Hertha, 1969. *Hamlet's Mill: An essay investigating the origins of human knowledge and its transmission through myth.* David R. Godine, New Hampshire.

Zinner, Ernst, 1957. *The Stars Above Us.* George Allen & Unwin, London.

Notes:

1: Aldred 1965, p 64
2: Grimal 1992, p. 37
3: Frankfort 1948, pp. 7-9
4: Aldred 1965, p 64)
5: Frankfort 1948, p. 183
6: Colless 1994, p. 23
7:Fairman 1974, p. 34
8:Fairman 1974, pp. 106, 117
9: Lichtheim 1973, p. 204
10: Fairman 1974, p. 90
11: Fairman 1974, p. 102
12: Arnold 1999
13: Parker 1974
14: Lichtheim 1973, p. 45
15: Frankfort et al. 1946, p. 47
16: Plutarch 1927, p. 53
17: Krupp 1991, p. 137
18: Parker 1974, p.60
19: Neugebauer 1957, p.89
20: Parker 1974, p. 63
21: 1927, p. 93
22: Zinner 1957, p. 28
23: Krupp 1991, p. 222
24: Neugebauer 1957, p. 87
25: Frankfort et al. 1946, p. 35
26: Plutarch 1927, pp. 93-99
27: Krupp 1979, p. 189
28: Krupp 1997, p. 147
29: Colless 1994, pp. 166-167

30: Gray 1969, p. 75
31: Colless 1994, p. 169
32:Gray 1969, p. 81
33: Ringren 1973, p. 134
34: Deighton 1982, p. 71
35: Allen 1963, p.306
36: Deighton 1982, p. 29
37: Colless 1994, p. 102
38: Frazer 1922, p. 506

Jack Hunter - Anthropology of the Weird (p. 243)

References:

1. Blum, D. 2007. *Ghost Hunters: The Victorians and the Hunt for Proof of Life After Death.* (London: Arrow Books).
2. Stocking, G.W. 1971. Animism in Theory and Practice in E.B. Tylor's Unpublished 'Notes on Spiritualism.' *Man* 6 (1):88-104.
3. Ibid.
4. Evans-Pritchard, E.E. 1976. *Witchcraft Oracles and Magic Among the Azande.* (Oxford: Clarendon Press Press).
5. Ibid.
6. Lienhardt, G. (1974). E-P: A Personal View: Sir Edward Evans-Pritchard, 1902-1973. *Man* 9 (2): 299-304.
7. Barnes, J. (1987). Edward Evan Evans-Pritchard, 1902-1973. *Proceedings of the British Academy* LXXIII, 447-490.
8. Grindal, B.T. 1983. Into the Heart of Sisala Experience: Witnessing Death Divination. *Journal of Anthropological Research* 39 (1):60-80.
9. Ibid.
10. Turner, E. 1998. *Experiencing Ritual.* (Philadelphia: University of Pennsylvania Press).
11. Turner, E. 1993. "The Reality of Spirits: A Tabooed or Permitted Field of Study?". *Anthropology of Consciousness* 4 (1): 9-12.

CPSIA information can be obtained at www.ICGtesting.com
Printed in the USA
BVOW04s1717220114

342707BV00001B/34/P

9 780980 711189